BLUE RIBBON DESSERTS

Cook's Country

BLUE RIBBON DESSERTS

Rediscover More Than 120 Heirloom Treasures
and Regional Favorites

FROM THE EDITORS AT AMERICA'S TEST KITCHEN

PHOTOGRAPHY

Keller + Keller, Carl Tremblay,
and Daniel J. van Ackere

America's Test Kitchen
17 Station Street
Brookline, MA 02445

Library of Congress Cataloging-in-Publication Data
The Editors at America's Test Kitchen

Cook's Country Blue Ribbon Desserts
Rediscover More Than 120 Heirloom Treasures
and Regional Favorites

1st Edition
ISBN-13: 978-1-933615-79-0
ISBN-10: 1-933615-79-6
(hardcover): U.S. $29.95
I. Cooking. I. Title
2011

Manufactured in Thailand by Sirivatana

10 9 8 7 6 5 4 3 2 1

Distributed by America's Test Kitchen,
17 Station Street, Brookline, MA 02445

Editorial Director: Jack Bishop
Executive Editor: Elizabeth Carduff
Executive Food Editor: Julia Collin Davison
Senior Editor: Lori Galvin
Associate Editor: Kate Hartke
Editorial Assistant: Alyssa King
Design Director: Amy Klee
Art Director: Greg Galvan
Associate Art Director: Matthew Warnick
Designer: Tiffani Beckwith
Photography: Keller + Keller, Carl Tremblay,
and Daniel J. van Ackere
Food Styling: Mary Jane Sawyer, Marie Piraino
Illustrations: © Greg Stevenson/www.i2iart.com
Production Director: Guy Rochford
Senior Production Manager: Jessica Lindheimer Quirk
Senior Project Manager: Alice Carpenter
Traffic and Production Coordinator: Kate Hux
Workflow and Asset Manager: Andrew Mannone
Production and Imaging Specialists: Judy Blomquist,
Heather Dube, and Lauren Pettapiece
Copyeditor: Barbara Wood
Proofreader: Debra Hudak
Indexer: Elizabeth Parson

The Staff of *Cook's Country* Magazine:
Executive Editor, Magazines: John Willoughby
Executive Editor: Peggy Grodinsky
Managing Editor: Scott Kathan
Senior Editors: Lisa McManus, Cali Rich, and Diane Unger
Test Kitchen Director: Erin McMurrer
Associate Editor: Lynn Clark
Test Cooks: Sarah Gabriel, Kelly Price
Assistant Editor: Taizeth Sierra
Assistant Test Cook: Carolynn Purpura
Test Kitchen Manager: Gina Nistico
Copy Editors: Nell Beram, Amy Graves
Executive Food Editor, TV, Radio & Media: Bridget Lancaster

Pictured on the front cover: Chocolate Blackout Cake (page 84)
Pictured opposite the title page: Southern Caramel Cake
(page 106)

CONTENTS

WELCOME TO AMERICA'S TEST KITCHEN

This book has been tested, written, and edited by the folks at America's Test Kitchen, a very real 2,500-square-foot kitchen located just outside of Boston. It is the home of Cook's Country magazine and Cook's Illustrated magazine and is the Monday-through-Friday destination for more than three dozen test cooks, editors, food scientists, tasters, and cookware specialists. Our mission is to test recipes over and over again until we understand how and why they work and until we arrive at the "best" version.

We start the process of testing a recipe with a complete lack of conviction, which means that we accept no claim, no theory, no technique, and no recipe at face value. We simply assemble as many variations as possible, test a half dozen of the most promising, and taste the results blind. We then construct our own hybrid recipe and continue to test it, varying ingredients, techniques, and cooking times until we reach a consensus. The result, we hope, is the best version of a particular recipe, but we realize that only you can be the final judge of our success (or failure). As we like to say in the test kitchen, "We make the mistakes, so you don't have to."

All of this would not be possible without a belief that good cooking, much like good music, is indeed based on a foundation of objective technique. Some people like spicy foods and others don't, but there is a right way to sauté, there is a best way to cook a pot roast, and there are measurable scientific principles involved in producing perfectly beaten, stable egg whites. This is our ultimate goal: to investigate the fundamental principles of cooking so that you become a better cook. It is as simple as that.

You can watch us work (in our actual test kitchen) by tuning in to Cook's Country from America's Test Kitchen (www.cookscountrytv.com) or America's Test Kitchen (www.americastestkitchentv.com) on public television, or by subscribing to Cook's Country magazine (www.cookscountry.com) or Cook's Illustrated magazine (www.cooksillustrated.com). We welcome you into our kitchen, where you can stand by our side as we test our way to the "best" recipes in America.

PREFACE

The term "blue ribbon" came from a 16th-century group of knights, Les Chevaliers du Saint Esprit, whose costume included the wearing of a blue ribbon. Since they were partial to fine dining, the blue ribbon was soon associated with the highest form of culinary art, hence the Cordon Bleu cooking school that was established in Paris in the 1890s.

I recently attended the 139th Tunbridge Fair in Vermont that is more agricultural exposition than a collection of midway rides and fast food. There was a chicken barn, ox pulls, pig races (the announcer must have worked at NASCAR; he knew how to pull in a large crowd), sheepdog trials, and Floral Hall, which houses displays of giant watermelons (this year's winner weighed over 700 pounds) as well as canned goods and pies. The large collection of pies is sampled by just one judge who then awards blue ribbons to the winners. This may seem an envious task, but since this is what we do day in and day out in America's Test Kitchen, I can assure you that tasting hundreds, even thousands,

of desserts to produce this volume was hard work. Whether it is the ninth version of Wellesley Fudge Cake or only the second tasting of Pecan Kringle, our job is to opine on taste and texture in an effort to produce the best version of a dessert that we can. It is your job—the fun part—to simply make the recipe, serve it, and enjoy it. As I often say, we do the work so you don't have to.

So what is a "blue ribbon dessert"? These are the desserts, both heirloom and regional, that define the American dessert table, a collection of recipes that includes updated 19th-century classics as well as more modern creations that have earned their place in the pantheon of great American desserts. Chapters include pies, fruit desserts, old-fashioned puddings, great American cakes, coffee cakes and morning sweets, cupcakes, bake sale cookies, brownies, bars, and, finally, an entire chapter entitled "Holiday Cookie Swap."

And so many recipes in this book are either hard to find or in desperate need of updating for the modern kitchen. Old-timey offerings include Jefferson Davis Pie (similar to pecan pie), Southern Caramel Cake, Tick Tock Orange Sticky Rolls, our own homemade version of Hostess Chocolate Cream Cupcakes, an easy Icebox Strawberry Pie, Black-and-White Cookies, Candy Cane Pinwheels, plus updated, foolproof versions of classic recipes, but often with a twist, such as Fresh Blueberry Pie, Raspberry Chiffon Pie (my favorite recipe in this collection), Crustless Apple Pie, a to-die-for Banana Pudding, Icebox Lemon Cheesecake, Thick and Chewy Triple-Chocolate Cookies, Lemon Squares, All-Season Peach Squares, and Seven-Layer Bars.

A few months ago, I stopped by the Magnolia Bakery on 6th Avenue in New York to film a short introduction to one of our public television shows. I interviewed customers about what they liked best. Some preferred the icing, some the cake, but there was joy in those cupcakes (the Red Velvet is my personal favorite; our version is in this book), the kind of pleasure that only a good

dessert can bring. Pure pleasure is letting oneself go for a moment, to embrace the timeless passion of a sweet bite, a moment that connects to both our future and our past. This is what we offer in *Blue Ribbon Desserts*—not just a collection of recipes that work, but small pleasures that transport one to another shore. It is to a happier, simpler place that *Blue Ribbon Desserts* brings us, and all it takes is a handful of ingredients, a hot oven, and a few minutes of our time. We think the price of this ticket is trifling compared to the journey, the one started by the first bite of a Chocolate Turtle Cookie, a lick of a Black-Bottom Cupcake, or a forkful of French Silk Chocolate Pie.

Christopher Kimball
Founder and Editor
Cook's Country and *Cook's Illustrated*
Host, *Cook's Country from America's Test Kitchen* and *America's Test Kitchen*

ICEBOX OREO CHEESECAKE

Getting Started

TIPS FOR SUCCESSFUL BAKING

Here in the test kitchen, we've made our share of baking blunders. Of course, our testing process is designed so we can learn from these mistakes. At home, however, a mistake is a mistake, and few cooks take pleasure in turning out an unattractive pie, flat cookies, or a lopsided layer cake. So whether you are a practiced baker or just want to be able to make a birthday cake everyone will love, there are some baking basics that are worth repeating. Follow the suggestions below and on the pages that follow when you are making any of the recipes in this book, and we bet your baking skills and confidence will improve markedly.

1. Preheat your oven: It takes at least 15 minutes for a standard oven to reach the desired temperature, which is why this step is almost always first in recipe directions. Also, make sure the oven racks are set to the correct positions. A pie crust that browns properly on the lower rack will emerge pale and unappealing if you bake it on the middle rack.

2. Pay attention to temperature: An oven that runs hot or cold will ruin cookies, cakes, and everything else you bake. An oven thermometer is an affordable tool that guarantees peace of mind. Also, the temperature of your ingredients matters. Butter that is too cold or too warm can result in a flat, dense cake. Use an instant-read thermometer to check the temperature of your ingredients.

3. Choose the right measuring cups: For the most accurate measurements, milk, water, and the like must be measured in liquid measures (glass or plastic cups with pour spouts and handles), and flour, sugar, and other dry ingredients must be measured in dry measures (handled cups with straight edges so ingredients can be leveled off). For more about measuring, see page 3.

4. Use good, fresh ingredients: Baking powder can lose its punch after six months. Butter can pick up off-flavors after a few weeks in the fridge. And a gritty, low-quality chocolate can ruin baked goods. Always use high-quality ingredients and make sure they're fresh.

5. Use the right equipment: Whether you're making a fancy layer cake or a humble snack cake, if you use the wrong size pan, your baked goods will turn out flat and dense (if the pan is too large) or pale and underdone (if the pan is too small). Always use the specific equipment called for.

6. Don't make substitutions: Recipes are often complex chemical formulas with a precise balance of acids and leaveners and if you change one ingredient, the formula may no longer work. We do offer some substitutions in this book, but working with the ingredients called for is best. Be sure to read the recipe through before you begin baking and make sure that you have all the ingredients and equipment on hand.

7. Watch the mixing bowl or oven, not the clock: Most baking recipes, including those in this book, are filled with times for mixing and baking. The times are merely guidelines, so pay attention to visual cues. In many cases, a toothpick may emerge from brownies "with a few moist crumbs" before the end of the stated baking time.

8. Time your kitchen work properly: In other words, get organized! Many baking recipes contain multiple components that must come together in a specific order and time frame. Also, some recipes require chilling prior to assembly or serving, so make sure you've read the recipe through in advance and allotted enough time for every step.

MEASURING 101

Variations in measurement can have a significant effect on baked goods. Here's how we measure flour and other ingredients to ensure we're starting with the correct amount every time.

MEASURING FLOUR

The way you measure flour can make a big difference in your recipe. Spooning it into a measuring cup and then leveling it off can result in 20 percent less flour than you need. And too little flour can turn out baked goods that are flat, wet, or lacking in structure, while too much flour can result in tough, dry baked goods. We prefer to measure flour using the dip-and-sweep method.

Dip the measuring cup into the container of flour and scoop away the excess with a straight-edged object like the back of a butter knife.

MEASURING SUGAR

Granulated sugar can be measured the same way we measure flour, using the dip-and-sweep method. But brown sugar, which is moist and clumpy, requires a different treatment in order to completely pack the measuring cup and obtain an accurate measurement.

Use your fingers or the bottom of another measuring cup to pack brown sugar into a dry measure.

MEASURING STICKY INGREDIENTS

An adjustable measuring cup (a clear tube with markings and a plunger insert) makes it easy to cleanly extract sticky ingredients, like honey and molasses, and stiff ingredients, such as shortening and peanut butter. But if you don't have one, here are two ways to ensure an easy, clean release.

A. For sticky ingredients, spray the measuring cup with vegetable oil spray first. When emptied, the ingredient will slip right out.

B. For stiffer ingredients, line the measuring cup with plastic wrap first. Then simply lift out the plastic liner and the contents will come with it.

MEASURING LIQUIDS

Liquids must be measured in a wet measure, which allows you to see where the bottom of the concave arc is sitting so you can get an accurate read.

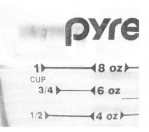

For liquid ingredients, set a liquid measuring cup on a level surface and bend down to read it at eye level. Read the measurement from the bottom of the concave arc at the liquid's surface.

BUTTER 101

We use unsalted butter—never salted butter—in baked goods. Not only does it provide a sweet, delicate flavor, but it also gives us more control over the salt content, so we don't end up with a salty frosting or cake. Margarine, although similar to butter in appearance and usage, should never be substituted for butter in a baking recipe.

BUTTER TEMPERATURES (AND WHY THEY MATTER)

The temperature of butter can dramatically affect the texture of many baked goods. There are three different stages of butter that we call for in baking: softened, chilled, and melted and cooled.

SOFTENED BUTTER (65 to 67 degrees), which creams easily, is often required for cakes and cookies.

Softened butter should give slightly when pressed but still hold its shape.

CHILLED BUTTER (about 35 degrees) is butter that has been cut into pieces and well chilled in the refrigerator or freezer so that it doesn't melt during mixing or rolling. Chilled butter makes rolling out pastry dough easier and the steam that the chilled butter produces during baking creates pockets in the dough that make the pastry flaky.

MELTED AND COOLED BUTTER should be liquefied and lukewarm (85 to 90 degrees). Melted butter is used to make some cookies and bars chewy. If the butter is too warm, it can cook the batter (or the eggs in it). Note that butter should be melted until just liquefied, but no longer; further heating will cause the milk solids to separate from the fat.

CREAMING BUTTER

Many cookie and cake recipes require that you beat butter and sugar together until light and fluffy, a process known as creaming. This makes the butter malleable, which allows the other ingredients to be easily mixed together and air to be incorporated, giving the baked goods lift. Here's how to know when your butter and sugar are properly creamed (the butter must be softened when you begin).

When under-creamed, the butter and sugar mixture will be yellow and dense. The resulting cookies will have a coarse, irregular texture.

When over-creamed (this can happen in just a minute or two), the butter and sugar mixture will appear greasy and dense; cookies will be flat and crisp.

When properly creamed, the butter and sugar mixture will be light and fluffy, resulting in cookies with perfect texture, spread, and chew.

EGGS 101

Eggs come in a range of sizes. In our recipes, we always call for large eggs, as a consistent size (and volume) of egg is especially important when baking (note that the color of your eggs doesn't affect baked goods). Here are three essential egg-related techniques that appear frequently in baking.

GETTING A CLEAN BREAK

It's best to crack an egg cleanly so there's no shell in your batter and so it's easy to separate the eggs.

For a clean break, crack the side of the egg against the flat surface of the counter, rather than the edge of the counter or mixing bowl.

SEPARATING EGGS

Many recipes require that you separate eggs and either whip the whites (for lift) or include extra yolks (for additional richness) or whites (for moisture or structure). Here are two easy ways to do this (if they're cold, they'll separate more easily).

A. Using the broken shell halves, gently transfer the egg yolk from one shell to the other, allowing the white to drip into a bowl below.

B. Alternatively, cup your hand over a bowl, then transfer the egg into your palm and slowly unclench your fingers to allow the white to slide through, leaving the yolk intact.

WHIPPING EGG WHITES

Egg whites should be whipped in a clean stainless steel bowl (washed in hot, soapy water and dried with paper towels). Whip the whites on low or medium-low speed until foamy, about 1 minute. Increase the mixer speed (adding cream of tartar and sugar if required) and whip to the desired consistency (soft peaks or stiff peaks). Here's how to tell when you've reached the right consistency.

Soft peaks will droop slightly downward from the tip of the whisk or beater.

Stiff peaks will stand tall.

Overbeaten egg whites will look curdled and separated.

RASPBERRY CHIFFON PIE

CHAPTER ONE

Blue Ribbon Pies

Classic Pie Dough

Great pie starts with a great crust—one that's crisp, flaky, and buttery. If the crust is tough and dry or completely devoid of flavor, dessert will be a letdown. Because pie crust is essentially a combination of flour, water, and fat, we knew that the path to a perfect crust meant we had to focus our testing on nailing down the ideal proportions of these ingredients (and any other flavorings, such as salt) and the best way to combine them to keep the crust tender and flaky.

We began with the most controversial ingredient in pie crust: the fat. While many cooks swear by an all-butter crust (which we'll admit is very flavorful), we find that crusts made with a combination of butter and shortening are more flaky and fine-textured, yet also offer great flavor. After experimenting with the amounts of fat and flour, we finally settled on a ratio of 2 parts flour to 1 part fat, which produced a crust that was easy to work with and, when baked, more tender and flavorful than any other. It's imperative that the butter and shortening be cold when you begin making pie dough; cold ingredients mean that more steam will be produced when the crust

---

HAND MIXING PIE DOUGH

A food processor makes quick work of mixing pie dough, but if you don't have one, you can mix the dough by hand with equally successful results.

Freeze the butter in its stick form until very firm. Whisk together the flour, sugar, and salt in a large bowl. Add the chilled shortening and press it into the flour using a fork. Grate the frozen butter on the large holes of a box grater into the flour mixture, then cut the mixture together, using two butter or dinner knives, until the mixture resembles coarse crumbs. Add the water as directed.

---

is baking, and the steam creates pockets in the dough that help make it flaky.

Next, we tackled the proportions of salt and sugar. After testing amounts ranging from ¼ teaspoon to as much as 2 tablespoons of each, we settled on 1 teaspoon of salt and 2 tablespoons of sugar for a double-crust pie, amounts that enhance the flavor of the dough without shouting out their presence.

For the liquid, we experimented with a variety of ingredients, such as buttermilk, milk, and cider vinegar, a common ingredient in many pastry recipes. No liquid additions improved our basic recipe, so we decided to stick with ice water, which didn't interfere with the flavor of our dough and helped to keep the butter and shortening cold.

Although pie dough can be made by hand (see below), we've found that a food processor is faster and easier and does the best job of cutting the fat into the flour. Proper mixing is of utmost importance. If the dough is undermixed, the crust will shrink when baked and become hard and crackly. If the dough is overprocessed, it will become crumbly, not flaky, when baked. To combine the ingredients, we started by pulsing the shortening with the flour until the mixture was sandy; we then pulsed in the butter until the mixture looked like coarse crumbs.

With the flour and fat combined, we could mix in the ice water. After transferring the flour mixture to a bowl, we sprinkled a few tablespoons of ice water over the top. We found that a rubber spatula was the best tool for mixing, and a folding motion was the best way to mix in the water. Using the flat side of the spatula allowed us to press the mixture until the dough stuck together. Incorporating the water in this manner meant that the least amount of water could be used (less water means a more tender dough) and reduced the likelihood of overworking the dough. (However, it doesn't pay to be too stingy with the water; if there isn't enough, the dough will be crumbly.)

Finally, we moved on to rolling out the dough. We found it essential that the dough be well chilled before rolling. We also had to keep an eye on the amount of flour we sprinkled on the work surface to roll out the dough. Flour added during rolling will be absorbed by the dough, and too much flour will cause the dough to toughen. If the dough seems too soft to roll, it's best to refrigerate it rather than add more flour.

With our double-crust pie dough down, we looked to scale down our recipe to create a single-crust pie dough. Cutting the ingredients in half seemed like the most obvious tack, but we found that certain ingredients—the shortening and butter—needed a bit more finessing, and so we reduced the amounts of these slightly more. Now we had the perfect foundation for a great single-crust or double-crust pie.

DOUBLE-CRUST PIE DOUGH

MAKES ENOUGH FOR ONE 9-INCH PIE

If you don't have a food processor, see "Hand Mixing Pie Dough" on page 8. See the photos at right for tips on rolling out pie dough.

2½	cups all-purpose flour
2	tablespoons sugar
1	teaspoon salt
½	cup vegetable shortening, cut into ½-inch pieces and chilled
12	tablespoons (1½ sticks) unsalted butter, cut into ¼-inch pieces and chilled
6–8	tablespoons ice water

1. Process the flour, sugar, and salt together in a food processor until combined. Scatter the shortening over the top and process until the mixture resembles coarse sand, about 10 seconds. Scatter the butter pieces over the top and pulse the butter into the flour until the mixture is pale yellow and resembles coarse crumbs, with butter bits no larger than small peas, about 10 pulses. Transfer the mixture to a medium bowl.

2. Sprinkle 6 tablespoons of the ice water over the mixture. Stir and press the dough together, using a stiff rubber spatula, until the dough sticks together. If the dough does not come together, stir in the remaining water, 1 tablespoon at a time, until it does.

ROLLING AND FITTING PIE DOUGH

1. Roll the dough outward from its center into a 12-inch circle. After every few rolls, give the dough a quarter turn to help keep the circle nice and round.

2. Toss additional flour underneath the dough as needed to keep the dough from sticking to the work surface.

3. Loosely roll the dough around the rolling pin, then gently unroll it over the pie plate.

4. Lift the dough and gently press it into the pie plate, letting the excess hang over the edge.

3. Divide the dough into 2 balls and flatten each into a 4-inch disk. Wrap each tightly in plastic wrap and refrigerate for about 1 hour. Before rolling out the dough, let it sit on the work surface to soften slightly, about 10 minutes. (The dough, wrapped tightly in plastic wrap, can be refrigerated for up to 2 days or frozen for up to 1 month. If frozen, let the dough thaw completely before rolling out.)

Variation
SINGLE-CRUST PIE DOUGH

MAKES ENOUGH FOR ONE 9-INCH PIE

If you don't have a food processor, see "Hand Mixing Pie Dough" on page 8.

1¼	cups all-purpose flour
1	tablespoon sugar
½	teaspoon salt
3	tablespoons vegetable shortening, cut into ½-inch pieces and chilled
5	tablespoons unsalted butter, cut into ¼-inch pieces and chilled
4–6	tablespoons ice water

1. Process the flour, sugar, and salt together in a food processor until combined. Scatter the shortening over the top and process until the mixture resembles coarse sand, about 10 seconds. Scatter the butter pieces over the top and pulse the butter into the flour until the mixture is pale yellow and resembles coarse crumbs, with butter bits no larger than small peas, about 10 pulses. Transfer the mixture to a medium bowl.

2. Sprinkle 4 tablespoons of the ice water over the mixture. Stir and press the dough together, using a stiff rubber spatula, until the dough sticks

together. If the dough does not come together, stir in the remaining water, 1 tablespoon at a time, until it does.

3. Turn the dough onto a sheet of plastic wrap and flatten into a 4-inch disk. Wrap the dough tightly in the plastic wrap and refrigerate for about 1 hour. Before rolling out the dough, let it sit on the work surface to soften slightly, about 10 minutes. (The dough, wrapped tightly in plastic wrap, can be refrigerated for up to 2 days or frozen for up to 1 month. If frozen, let the dough thaw completely before rolling out.)

4. Following the photos on page 9, roll the dough into a 12-inch circle and fit it into a pie plate. Trim, fold, and crimp the edge of the dough. Wrap the dough-lined pie plate loosely in plastic wrap and refrigerate for 40 minutes, then freeze for 20 minutes longer, before using. (The unbaked crust can be wrapped tightly in plastic wrap and frozen for up to 2 months.)

CRIMPING A SINGLE-CRUST PIE

FOR A FLUTED EDGE: Use the index finger of one hand and the thumb and index finger of the other to create fluted ridges.

FOR A RIDGED EDGE: Press the tines of a fork into the dough to flatten it against the rim of the pie plate.

No-Fear Pie Dough

Let's face it—mixing, rolling, and fitting pie dough can be frustrating (and messy) for many. Store-bought pie dough can work in a pinch on some occasions, but what about those times when only a homemade crust will do? Pat-in-the-pan crusts (where the dough is shaped right in the pan) are an option, but we've never met one that baked up flaky and full of buttery flavor. Thus, we made it our goal to develop a pat-in-the-pan crust whose flavor and texture rivaled those of traditional pie crust.

But after making more than 20 pat-in-the-pan crusts, we were discouraged. Without exception, our tests yielded dough that was either too sticky or too stiff to press into a pie plate thinly and evenly, and none baked up flaky enough to replace the store-bought standby. You can imagine our surprise when our 23rd test—a crust made with cream cheese—fooled several pie snobs in the kitchen.

Why was cream cheese so successful? It turns out that acidity promotes tenderness. But not any old acidic ingredient will work. Vinegar made a sour crust, and sour cream and buttermilk made the dough too sticky. Dense cream cheese made the dough easier to manipulate. We found this dough could handle a whopping 12 tablespoons of fat (significantly more than the 8 tablespoons in our single-crust dough), and it didn't require ice water. This dough also relies on an unusual mixing method. Softened butter and cream cheese are beaten together and then mixed with flour, sugar, and salt. The fat in the cream cheese coats the particles of flour and prevents toughness, a problem in many crusts. At last, we'd developed an easy pie crust that baked up flaky and tasted great.

MAKING PRESS-IN PIE DOUGH

1. Press the dough evenly over the bottom of the pie plate. With your fingertips, continue to work the dough evenly over the bottom and up the sides of the pie plate until evenly distributed.

2. Roll the reserved dough into three 8-inch-long ropes. Arrange the ropes around the perimeter of the pie plate, leaving small (about 1-inch) gaps between them. Squeeze the ropes into the crust to make a uniform edge.

EASY PRESS-IN SINGLE-CRUST PIE DOUGH

MAKES ENOUGH FOR ONE 9-INCH PIE

The cream cheese makes this dough easy to manipulate and press into the pan—no rolling required! Make sure you press the dough evenly into a glass pie plate; if you hold the dough-lined plate up to the light, you will be able to clearly see any thick or thin spots.

1¼	cups all-purpose flour
2	tablespoons sugar
¼	teaspoon salt
8	tablespoons (1 stick) unsalted butter, softened
2	ounces cream cheese, softened

1. Grease a 9-inch pie plate. Whisk the flour, sugar, and salt together in a medium bowl.

2. In a large bowl, beat the butter and cream cheese together with an electric mixer on medium-high speed until completely combined, about 2 minutes. Reduce the mixer speed to medium-low and beat in the flour mixture until it resembles coarse crumbs, about 20 seconds. Increase the mixer speed to medium-high and beat until the dough begins to form large clumps, about 30 seconds.

3. Transfer 3 tablespoons of the dough to a small bowl. Turn the remaining dough clumps out onto a lightly floured work surface, gather into a ball, and flatten into a 6-inch disk. Transfer the disk to the prepared pie plate.

4. Following the photos on page 11, press the dough evenly over the bottom of the pie plate using the heel of your hand. With your fingertips, continue to work the dough over the bottom of the plate and up the sides until evenly distributed.

5. On a lightly floured work surface, roll the reserved 3 tablespoons of dough into three 8-inch-long ropes. Arrange the ropes around the top of the pie plate, leaving small gaps between them. Squeeze the ropes into the crust to make a uniform edge. Crimp the edge of the dough. Cover loosely with plastic wrap and refrigerate for 40 minutes, then freeze for 20 minutes longer, before using. (The unbaked crust can be wrapped tightly in plastic wrap and frozen for up to 2 months.)

Deep-Dish Apple Pie

Apple pie is the epitome of classic American pies. And in keeping with the unspoken national motto of "bigger is better," we set out to make a sky-high deep-dish apple pie, not a plain old thin apple pie. We wanted a towering wedge of tender, juicy apples, fully framed by a buttery, flaky, lightly browned crust.

After foraging for recipes that met our specifications for deep-dish—a minimum of 5 pounds of apples as opposed to the meager 2 pounds in a standard pie—we realized why most recipe writers stick with pies of modest size: your standard apple pie may have a juicy filling, but most deep-dish pies are downright flooded, with the apples swimming in an ocean of liquid. As a result, the bottom crust becomes a pale, soggy mess. In addition, the apples tend to cook unevenly, with mushy, applesauce-y edges surrounding a crunchy, underdone center. Less serious—but no less annoying—is the gaping hole left between the apples (which shrink considerably) and the arching top crust.

After a week of rescue efforts, we had made little progress. Our failed attempts included slicing the apples into thick chunks to prevent overcooked edges, cutting large vents in the crust to promote steam release, and baking the pies at different temperatures. Chunky apples were unevenly cooked, and both larger vents and varied oven temperatures proved, well, fruitless. No matter what we tried, we were confronted with the same two problems: soupy filling and soggy crust. To sop up the copious amount of liquid exuded by 5 pounds of apples, we added a thickening agent. But so much thickener was required that it muddied the bright flavor of the apples.

Desperate times call for desperate measures. During our research, we had come across recipes that called for cooking the apples before assembling them in the pie, the idea being both to extract juice and to cook the apples more evenly. Although this logic seemed counterintuitive (how could cooking the apples twice cause them to become anything but insipid and mushy?), we went ahead with the experiment. We dumped a mound of apples (a combination of tart and sweet for balanced flavor)

into a Dutch oven and covered it to promote even cooking. After cooling and draining the apples (to prevent the butter in the crust from melting right away), we baked the pie, which was free of excess juice and had a nicely browned bottom crust. The apples were miraculously tender. And because the apples were shrinking before going into the pie rather than after, we had inadvertently solved the problem of the maddening gap! The top crust now remained united with the rest of the pie, and slicing was a breeze. At long last, we had the perfect slice sitting up nice and tall on the plate.

MAKING DEEP-DISH APPLE PIE

1. Cook the apples with the sugars, lemon zest, salt, and cinnamon in a covered Dutch oven to extract juice and ensure that the apples are evenly cooked.

2. Transfer the apples and juice to a rimmed baking sheet and let cool to room temperature so the heat from the apples doesn't melt the butter in the pie dough.

3. Drain the cooled apples in a large colander set over a large bowl to drain off as much juice as possible, reserving ¼ cup to mix with lemon juice and drizzle over the apple filling.

DEEP-DISH APPLE PIE

SERVES 8

A combination of sweet and tart apples works best in this pie. For sweet apples, we recommend Golden Delicious, Braeburn, Gala, and Jonagold. For tart apples, we prefer Granny Smith, Empire, and Cortland.

1	recipe Double-Crust Pie Dough (page 9)
2½	pounds firm tart apples (5 to 7 apples; see note above), peeled, cored, and sliced ¼ inch thick
2½	pounds firm sweet apples (5 to 7 apples; see note above), peeled, cored, and sliced ¼ inch thick
½	cup plus 1 tablespoon granulated sugar
¼	cup packed light brown sugar
½	teaspoon grated fresh lemon zest and 2 teaspoons fresh lemon juice
¼	teaspoon salt
⅛	teaspoon ground cinnamon
1	large egg white, lightly beaten

1. Following the photos on page 9, roll one disk of dough into a 12-inch circle on a lightly floured work surface, then fit it into a 9-inch pie plate, letting the excess dough hang over the edge; cover with plastic wrap and refrigerate for 30 minutes. Roll the other disk of dough into a 12-inch circle on a lightly floured work surface, then transfer to a parchment-lined baking sheet; cover with plastic wrap and refrigerate for 30 minutes.

2. Toss the apples, ½ cup of the granulated sugar, brown sugar, lemon zest, salt, and cinnamon together in a large bowl. Transfer the apples to a Dutch oven, cover, and cook over medium heat, stirring frequently, until the apples are tender when poked with a fork but still hold their shape, 15 to 20 minutes. Transfer the apples and their juice to a rimmed baking sheet and let cool to room temperature, about 30 minutes.

3. Adjust an oven rack to the lowest position, place an aluminum foil–lined rimmed baking sheet on the rack, and heat the oven to 425 degrees. Drain the cooled apples thoroughly in a colander set over a bowl, reserving ¼ cup of the juice. Stir the lemon juice into the reserved apple juice.

4. Spread the apples in the dough-lined pie plate, mounding them slightly in the middle, and drizzle with the lemon juice mixture. Following the photos at right, loosely roll the second piece of dough around the rolling pin and gently unroll it over the pie. Trim, fold, and crimp the edges, and cut 4 vent holes in the top. Brush the crust with the egg white and sprinkle with the remaining 1 tablespoon granulated sugar.

5. Place the pie on the heated baking sheet and bake until the crust is golden, about 25 minutes. Reduce the oven temperature to 375 degrees, rotate the baking sheet, and continue to bake until the juice is bubbling and the crust is deep golden brown, 25 to 30 minutes longer. Let the pie cool on a wire rack until the filling has set, about 2 hours; serve slightly warm or at room temperature.

Variations
CRANBERRY-APPLE PIE
We use all sweet apples here because the cranberries are quite tart.

Omit the tart apples and increase the amount of sweet apples to 3½ pounds. Cook 2 cups frozen or fresh cranberries, ¼ cup orange juice, ½ cup granulated sugar, ¼ teaspoon cinnamon, and ¼ teaspoon salt in a medium saucepan over medium-high heat, stirring often, until the berries have broken down and the juice has a jamlike

consistency, 10 to 12 minutes. Off the heat, stir in ¼ cup water and cool to room temperature. Spread the cooled cranberry mixture over the bottom of the dough-lined pie plate before adding the cooked apples in step 4.

CARAMEL-APPLE PIE
We like to use either Kraft Caramels or Brach's Milk Maid Caramels for this recipe, but any brand of soft caramels (not hard caramel candies) will do.

Sprinkle 30 soft caramels, halved, into the pie with the apples in step 4.

MAKING A DOUBLE-CRUST PIE

1. Loosely roll the chilled top crust around a rolling pin, then gently unroll it over the filling.

2. Using scissors, trim all but ½ inch of the dough overhanging the edge of the pie plate.

3. Press the top and bottom crusts together, then tuck the edges under.

4. Crimp the dough evenly around the edge of the pie, using your fingers, and cut vents in the crust.

Crustless Apple Pie

From crust to cooling, homemade apple pie can take several hours to prepare. While it's definitely worth it, sometimes we want an apple pie that's "as easy as pie." Enter the crustless apple pie (sometimes called Swedish apple pie), which is a hybrid of light cake and dense pie, with an apple-studded filling and a crisped top and bottom that resemble the crusts of a traditional pie.

Our research turned up several different styles of crustless apple pies, but we were most intrigued by the recipes in which a custardy batter of melted butter, flour, sugar, eggs, and cinnamon is mixed and then poured over thinly sliced apples before baking. We tried several recipes and the pies tasted pretty good, but they were disappointingly soggy, with no crisping of either the top or bottom crusts.

Looking to fix the crust first, we turned to an ingredient we often use to build structure and crispness: bread crumbs. We toasted fresh bread crumbs in butter until they were golden brown (a single slice of bread provided enough crumbs), buttered the pie plate, and coated the plate with a thin layer of crumbs. We then filled the plate with apples as usual and poured in our working batter. This provided a well-defined bottom crust, but the pie itself was too dense, with a soggy interior, slightly crunchy apples, and no crisp top crust.

To thicken the batter, we increased the amount of flour and added baking powder to give it some lift; also, 2 tablespoons of sour cream added a welcome tang. To solve the problem of the apples not cooking through in the time it took the batter to set up, we reduced the oven temperature to 325 degrees and cooked the pie longer to allow the apples to gently soften as the batter set. Now, after over an hour in the oven, our apples—a combination of tart Granny Smiths, which held their texture and shape in the oven, and sweet Braeburns—were

tender. Finally, for a contrast in texture, we sprinkled sugar over the pie before baking it; this pie came out nicely browned with some crisp bites.

Up to this point, we'd been making our pie in a deep-dish pie plate, but occasionally the batter would spill over the edge and make a mess in the oven. Also, the pie plate made it difficult to serve the pie without wrecking the thin bottom crust of bread crumbs. Switching to a deeper springform pan solved both issues. While we'll still break out the rolling pin for traditional apple pie on weekends and holidays, this easy apple pie definitely earns a spot in our weeknight dessert rotation.

CRUSTLESS APPLE PIE
SERVES 8

In step 3, be sure that the melted butter is still slightly warm when whisked into the dry ingredients. For sweet apples, we recommend Golden Delicious, Braeburn, Gala, and Jonagold.

8	tablespoons (1 stick) unsalted butter, melted and cooled, plus 2 tablespoons unsalted butter, softened
1	slice high-quality white sandwich bread, torn into quarters and pulsed in a food processor to crumbs
3	Granny Smith apples, peeled, cored, quartered, and cut crosswise into thin slices
2	firm sweet apples (see note above), peeled, cored, quartered, and cut crosswise into thin slices
1¼	cups sugar
1	cup plus 1 tablespoon all-purpose flour
1½	teaspoons ground cinnamon
½	teaspoon baking powder
½	teaspoon salt
¼	teaspoon ground nutmeg
2	large eggs, lightly beaten
2	tablespoons sour cream

MAKING CRUSTLESS APPLE PIE

1. Sprinkle half of the bread crumbs into the bottom of the prepared springform pan. Tip the pan on its side and evenly press the remaining crumbs halfway up the sides, turning the pan as you go.

2. Gently arrange the apples in the prepared pan to the edge, taking care not to press down too firmly on the apples. (You want the batter to seep between the apple slices.)

3. Slowly and evenly pour the batter over the apples. Then sprinkle the batter with sugar and bake.

1. Adjust an oven rack to the middle position and heat the oven to 325 degrees. Grease the bottom and sides of a 9-inch springform pan with 1 tablespoon of the softened butter. Melt the remaining 1 tablespoon softened butter in a large nonstick skillet over medium heat. Add the bread crumbs and toast, stirring occasionally, until golden brown, about 3 minutes. Transfer the toasted bread crumbs to a bowl and let cool.

2. Toss the apples with 2 tablespoons of the sugar and 1 tablespoon of the flour in a large bowl.

Following the photos, coat the bottom and sides of the prepared pan with the toasted bread crumbs, then gently arrange the apples in the pan.

3. Combine 1 cup more sugar, the remaining 1 cup flour, cinnamon, baking powder, salt, and nutmeg in a large bowl. Whisk in the eggs, sour cream, and 8 tablespoons melted butter until smooth. Pour the batter evenly over the apples. Sprinkle the remaining 2 tablespoons sugar evenly over the batter and bake until deep golden brown and crisp, 70 to 80 minutes, rotating the pan halfway through baking. Transfer to a wire rack and let cool completely, at least 1 hour. Remove the sides of the pan and serve.

Fresh Blueberry Pie

There's nothing like a slice of fresh blueberry pie to satisfy a summer afternoon's craving. Full of fresh, sweet, slightly tart berries and topped with a crisp, buttery crust, blueberry pie is undoubtedly a classic. But for something so simple in design, it's shocking how difficult it can be to turn out a great blueberry pie. Unlike apple pie, which requires little (if any) starch to thicken the fruit, the filling in blueberry pie needs special attention because the berries are so juicy, and when cut, the filling can slide out of the crust into a soupy puddle. Our goal was clear: we wanted a juicy, yet sliceable, pie with bright, fresh fruit flavor.

We started our search by filling our dough-lined pie dish with a fairly standard mixture of 6 cups of fresh blueberries, ¾ cup of sugar, and tapioca (which we ground so it would blend into the filling). The 6 tablespoons recommended on the back of the tapioca box produced a stiff, congealed mass, so we slowly cut back the amount. At 4 tablespoons, the filling was still too congealed for tasters' liking, but this amount proved to be the

tipping point; any less and the pie needed to be served with a spoon.

The problem, of course, was the juiciness of the berries. After some experimentation, we found that cooking just half of the berries was enough to adequately reduce the liquid. We then folded the remaining raw berries into the mixture, creating a satisfying combination of intensely flavored cooked fruit and bright-tasting fresh fruit that allowed us to cut down the amount of tapioca to 3 tablespoons. Encouraged by this success, we wondered if we could decrease the amount of tapioca even further.

As we watched the blueberries bubble away, we thought about blueberry jam, which has an even consistency that is neither gelatinous nor slippery. The secret to this texture is pectin, a carbohydrate found in fruit. Blueberries are low in natural pectin, so commercial pectin is usually added to make jam. The only downside to commercial pectin is that it needs a certain amount of sugar and acid in order to work. This would mean increasing the amount of sugar. No-sugar-needed pectin was an option, but this additive contains lots of natural acid, which compensates for the lack of extra sugar—and its sourness made our tasters wince. A colleague then offered a suggestion: since apples contain a lot of natural pectin, could an apple be added to the blueberries to help set the filling?

We folded one peeled and grated Granny Smith apple into a new batch of fresh and cooked berries that we had mixed with 2 tablespoons of ground tapioca. We baked the pie and waited. When we finally tried a slice, we knew we'd hit on a great solution. Combined with a modest amount of tapioca, the apple provided enough thickening power to set the pie, plus it enhanced the flavor of the berries without anyone guessing our secret ingredient. As a bonus, it left no evidence of its own texture.

Tweaking the crust was the last step. We found that baking the pie on a heated baking sheet on the bottom rack of the oven produced a crisp, golden bottom crust that didn't get soggy. As for the top crust, berry pies are often made with a decorative lattice topping that allows the steam from the berries to gently escape. But after making more than 50 lattice tops, we were determined to find a faster, easier approach. We decided to try making a crust we had seen in our research that had vents in the form of simple round cutouts. After rolling out the dough, we used a small biscuit cutter to cut out circles, then transferred the dough onto the pie. This method saved time and made an attractive top crust that properly vented the steam from the filling. At long last, we had a nicely thickened blueberry pie that was bursting with bright berry flavor.

FRESH BLUEBERRY PIE

SERVES 8

This recipe was developed using fresh blueberries, but unthawed frozen blueberries (our favorite brand is Wyman's) will work as well. In step 2, cook half the frozen berries over medium-high heat, without mashing, until reduced to 1¼ cups, 12 to 15 minutes. Grind the tapioca to a powder in a spice grinder or mini food processor. If using pearl tapioca, reduce the amount to 5 teaspoons.

1	recipe Double-Crust Pie Dough (page 9)
6	cups fresh blueberries (see note above)
1	Granny Smith apple, peeled and grated on large holes of box grater
¾	cup plus 1 tablespoon sugar
2	tablespoons Minute tapioca, ground (see note above)
2	teaspoons grated fresh lemon zest and 2 teaspoons fresh lemon juice
	Pinch salt
2	tablespoons unsalted butter, cut into ¼-inch pieces
1	large egg white, lightly beaten

1. Following the photos on page 9, roll one disk of dough into a 12-inch circle on a lightly floured work surface, then fit it into a 9-inch pie plate, letting the excess dough hang over the edge; cover with plastic wrap and refrigerate for 30 minutes. Roll the other disk of dough into a 12-inch circle on a lightly floured work surface, then transfer to a parchment-lined baking sheet; cover with plastic wrap and refrigerate for 30 minutes.

2. Adjust an oven rack to the lowest position, place an aluminum foil–lined rimmed baking sheet on the oven rack, and heat the oven to 400 degrees. Place 3 cups of the berries in a medium saucepan and set over medium heat. Using a potato masher, mash the berries several times to release their juice. Continue to cook, stirring frequently and mashing occasionally, until about half of the berries have broken down and the mixture is thickened and reduced to 1½ cups, about 8 minutes. Let cool slightly.

3. Place the grated apple in a clean kitchen towel and wring dry. Transfer the apple to a large bowl. Add the cooked berries, remaining 3 cups uncooked berries, ¾ cup of the sugar, tapioca, lemon zest and juice, and salt; toss to combine. Transfer the mixture to the dough-lined pie plate and scatter the butter pieces over the filling.

4. Using a 1¼-inch round biscuit cutter, cut a round from the center of the second round of dough. Cut another 6 rounds from the dough, 1½ inches from the edge of the center hole and equally spaced around it. Following the photos on page 15, roll the dough loosely around the rolling pin and gently unroll it over the pie. Trim, fold, and crimp the edges. Brush the crust with the egg white and sprinkle with the remaining 1 tablespoon sugar.

5. Place the pie on the heated baking sheet and bake for 30 minutes. Reduce the oven temperature to 350 degrees, rotate the baking sheet, and continue to bake until the juice is bubbling and the crust is deep golden brown, 30 to 40 minutes longer. Let the pie cool on a wire rack until the filling has set, about 4 hours; serve slightly warm or at room temperature.

MAKING A CUT-OUT CRUST

1. Use a 1¼-inch biscuit cutter (or spice jar lid) to cut holes in the dough.

2. The cut-out crust vents the steam from the berry filling and is an easy alternative to a fussy lattice.

SHOPPING WITH THE TEST KITCHEN

Store-Bought Pie Crusts: A flaky, buttery home-made pie crust is the ultimate crown for pie, but it's also a fair amount of work. How much would we sacrifice by using a store-bought crust instead? To find out, we tried several types and brands—both dry mixes (just add water) and ready-made crusts, either frozen or refrigerated. The dry mixes didn't save much work, and the frozen crusts, though timesavers, were difficult to remove from their packaging. More importantly, neither offered decent flavor or texture. The refrigerated option, Pillsbury Pie Crusts ($2.99 for two 9-inch crusts), had a somewhat bland flavor, but baked up to an impressive flakiness.

Mixed-Berry Streusel Pie

Fresh berries guarantee a pie with great flavor, but their juices can make for a sodden crust and streusel. We wanted to create a pie with intense berry flavor that would slice neatly and have a crisp crust and crunchy streusel topping. Most important, we wanted it to be as easy as possible to make.

Since we had developed a simple and flavorful press-in pie dough (see page 11), which relies on cream cheese to make the dough easy to handle, that's where we started. The texture was ideal, but we were disappointed when tasters said they wanted a more flavorful crust to accent the sweet berry filling. Next, we tried a basic graham cracker crust, which tasted great but was too sandy and loose to handle the moist berry filling. Thinking that flour and finely ground cracker crumbs aren't totally dissimilar, we made a hybrid dough by replacing some of the flour in our press-in pie dough with graham cracker crumbs. This dough had the best of both worlds: rich graham flavor and sufficient sturdiness.

A little lemon zest added brightness to our mixed-berry filling, but it was still too watery to slice neatly. Cooking the berries before adding them to the pie thickened the filling nicely, but it compromised their fresh flavor. Cooking just a portion of the berries gave us a thicker filling with nice depth of flavor, but we still couldn't coax tidy slices from the pie. We needed to thicken the berry juices somehow.

Thinking back to our blueberry pie (page 19), we wondered if a combination of ground tapioca and shredded apple (which contains natural pectin) would do the trick. We didn't want to make more work for ourselves if it wasn't necessary, so we began by including the tapioca alone. In a stroke of serendipity, we found that 3 tablespoons of tapioca worked magic—we could now cut perfect slices from the pie. Plus, we didn't even have to grind the tapioca into powder as we had done with our blueberry pie; the varying textures and sizes of the berries ensured that unground tapioca wasn't noticeable in the filling. All we had left to consider now was the streusel topping.

The raw pie dough already contained the butter and flour crumb mixture that forms the base of streusel, so we decided to kill two birds with one stone. We made a batch of our pie dough as usual and reserved enough to pat into the pan for our crust. We then fortified the remaining dough mixture with oats for texture and brown sugar for sweetness, filled the pie, and sprinkled the streusel on top. It baked up sweet, crunchy, and buttery. Finally, all the elements were in place for a perfect slice of berry pie.

MIXED-BERRY STREUSEL PIE

SERVES 8

Any combination of strawberries, blackberries, blueberries, and raspberries will work here, but we recommend using no more than 2 cups of strawberries, which tend to be watery. If your berries aren't sweet enough, you can add an extra ¼ cup of sugar to the filling in step 3.

CRUST AND STREUSEL

1½	cups all-purpose flour
9	whole graham crackers, broken into rough pieces
½	teaspoon salt
12	tablespoons (1½ sticks) unsalted butter, cut into ½-inch pieces and softened
2	ounces cream cheese, cut into ½-inch pieces
1	teaspoon vanilla extract
½	cup old-fashioned oats
½	cup packed light brown sugar

FILLING

- **6** cups mixed fresh berries (see note above)
- **¾** cup granulated sugar
- **½** teaspoon grated fresh lemon zest
- **3** tablespoons Minute tapioca

1. FOR THE CRUST AND STREUSEL: Grease a 9-inch pie plate. Process the flour, graham cracker pieces, and salt in a food processor until finely ground. Add the butter, cream cheese, and vanilla; pulse until a dough forms. Remove 2 cups of the dough from the food processor (leave the remaining dough in the food processor) and turn out onto a lightly floured work surface. Flatten the dough into a 6-inch disk and transfer to the prepared pie plate. Using the heel of your hand, press all the dough evenly over the bottom and up the sides of the pie plate until evenly distributed. Flute the edges following the photo on page 10. Cover the dough with plastic wrap and refrigerate until firm, at least 1 hour or up to 24 hours.

2. Add the oats and brown sugar to the food processor with the remaining dough; pulse until the mixture resembles coarse meal. Transfer to a bowl. Using your fingers, pinch the topping into peanut-size clumps; cover and refrigerate the streusel.

3. FOR THE FILLING: Adjust an oven rack to the lowest position and heat the oven to 350 degrees. Line a rimmed baking sheet with aluminum foil. Cook 2 cups of the berries in a saucepan over medium-high heat until juicy, about 3 minutes. Stir in the sugar and lemon zest and simmer until thickened, about 5 minutes. Let cool for 5 minutes, then gently toss the cooked berry mixture, remaining 4 cups berries, and tapioca together in a large bowl until combined.

THICKENING MIXED-BERRY FILLING

1. When the berry mixture is thick enough, it will be bubbling and a spoon or spatula will leave a trail when dragged through the mixture.

2. To further tighten the filling, toss the cooked berry mixture with the remaining fresh berries and tapioca.

4. Transfer the berry mixture to the chilled crust. Scatter the streusel evenly over the top. Place the pie on the prepared baking sheet; bake until the fruit is bubbling around the edges and the streusel is browned and crisp, 45 to 55 minutes, rotating the baking sheet halfway through baking. Let the pie cool on a wire rack for 30 minutes, then refrigerate until set, at least 2 hours or up to 24 hours.

Lemon Chess Pie

Unless you live in the South, you may not know about chess pie. This rich, intense, custardy pie dates back to the 1800s and is made from pantry ingredients that most cooks always had on hand, namely, lots of eggs (one recipe we found included 16 eggs), lots of sugar (that same recipe called for a pound), lots of butter, sometimes milk or cream, and, to thicken, either flour or cornmeal. In the pies that include cornmeal, this ingredient floats to the top, helping to create a delicate, crackly crust that adds to the pie's appeal. One common variation is lemon chess pie. The lemon flavor balances a home-spun, very sweet, but by no means ordinary pie.

We tested recipes old and new. None was perfect. They ranged from sour to over-the-top sweet. Some were airy like meringue, others were thick and jellied, but none were creamy and custardy as we expected. Although butter is a key ingredient, many pies used way too much, making the filling greasy. We wanted to perfect lemon chess pie so the filling was rich and custardy, with a bright citrus burst, but not overly dense and definitely not greasy.

Our first goal was to get the proportions right. Based on our initial tests, we combined 1¾ cups of sugar (considerably less than the norm), 4 tablespoons of butter, 4 eggs, 1 tablespoon each of flour and cornmeal, and 2 teaspoons of lemon juice. With 4 eggs, our pie wasn't quite firm enough. We went up by one (this was good) and then tried adding extra yolks for extra richness (this was bad and resulted in eggy overload). For the butter, we found that 4 tablespoons—the low end of the spectrum according to our research—made for a pie that was too lean. We were reluctant to go as high as the two sticks that some recipes recommended. Fortunately, a few more tests told us we didn't have to. One stick of butter was ample; now the butter made its mark pleasantly and added richness.

We ran tests using both flour and cornmeal to thicken the filling, but the filling turned too thick and gloppy, so we opted for just one thickener. We chose the cornmeal, because we liked the idea of a slightly crisp crust. In the next test, however, we were surprised to find that tasters complained the pie was now gritty. Luckily, the problem solved itself when we prepared the filling and waited for the pie shell to chill. As the combined filling ingredients sat, the cornmeal softened.

After testing various amounts of lemon juice and zest, we landed on 3 tablespoons of juice and 1 tablespoon of zest for a delicately tart flavor.

Milk or cream is sometimes added to make chess pie creamier, but tasters found they muted the lemon. We also tried orange zest, lemon and vanilla extracts, and nutmeg, but they all started to obscure the clean, lemony flavor of our pie.

To mix the filling, we started with the food processor. However, we found that the processor aerated the mixture, making the baked filling foamy. In the end, simply whisking the batter by hand worked best.

After pouring the filling into a fully baked crust, we baked the pie for 40 minutes. When it emerged from the oven, we decided to accentuate the slightly crunchy crust that forms on top by sprinkling the pie with sugar. It took several hours for the pie to set up, but when we tasted it at last, it was clear why chess pie has withstood the test of time.

THE AMERICAN TABLE
THE NAME GAME

Where did chess pie get its name? It has nothing to do with the game of chess. And its origins probably don't lie in the oft-repeated tale that a Southern gentleman who asked his wife what was for dessert was told "Jes' pie." More likely accounts, which culinary scholars debate, are that the name refers to "cheese pie" (in the 18th century, such pies had no cheese but did have a cheeselike texture); that it indicates the pie originated in Chester, England; or, finally, that "chess" refers to "chest," as in pie chest (also called a pie safe), where bakers cooled pies in the days before refrigerators. This much we know: a chess pie by any other name would taste as sweet.

LEMON CHESS PIE

SERVES 8

Regular yellow cornmeal (not stone-ground) works best here. Make the filling before baking the shell so the cornmeal has time to soften. Leftover pie should be refrigerated.

5	large eggs
1¾	cups plus 1 teaspoon sugar
1	tablespoon grated fresh lemon zest and 3 tablespoons fresh lemon juice
2	tablespoons cornmeal (see note above)
¼	teaspoon salt
8	tablespoons (1 stick) unsalted butter, melted and cooled
1	recipe Single-Crust Pie Dough (page 10), fitted into a 9-inch pie plate and chilled

1. Whisk the eggs in a large bowl until smooth. Slowly whisk in 1¾ cups of the sugar, lemon zest and juice, cornmeal, and salt until combined. Whisk in the butter and let the mixture rest for 1 hour.

2. Adjust an oven rack to the middle position and heat the oven to 375 degrees. Following the photos on page 30, line the chilled crust with a double layer of aluminum foil and fill with pie weights. Bake until the pie dough looks dry and is light in color, 25 to 30 minutes. Remove the pie shell from the oven, remove the weights and foil, and reduce the oven temperature to 325 degrees. (The crust must be warm when the filling is added.)

3. Whisk the filling to recombine. Scrape the filling into the warm pie shell and bake until the surface is light brown and the center jiggles slightly when the pie is gently shaken, 35 to 40 minutes. Sprinkle with the remaining 1 teaspoon sugar. Let the pie cool completely on a wire rack, about 4 hours, before serving.

Mile-High Lemon Meringue Pie

Lemon meringue pie has been a favorite American dessert since the 1800s, especially in the South, where lemon-based anything provides a refreshing respite from a hot and steamy day. We wanted our own lemon meringue pie, with a rich, sweet-tart filling, but we set out to up the ante—we wanted a mile-high meringue. Our extra-tall meringue had to be light, airy, and soft, the perfect crowning touch to the creamy filling below.

Making a modest meringue can be tricky enough. We quickly learned that double the amount of topping meant double the problems. Weeping (the leaching of liquid from the meringue) was a sad reality in every recipe we tried. Even when the whipped egg whites were mixed with cream of tartar, which helps to make them more stable, our meringue wept. Undercooking is the main problem. For regular lemon meringue pies, we've solved this problem in the past by spreading the meringue over a piping-hot filling and baking the pie in a hot oven. The hot filling cooks the bottom half of the meringue, while the heat from the oven takes care of the top half.

But when we used this normally reliable method with twice as much meringue, the topping disintegrated into a puddle as we sliced the first piece of pie. What went wrong? We realized that this method works only with a modest amount of meringue. The center of our super-size meringue wasn't cooking through. Baking the pie longer was not an option—the top of the meringue burned.

We then recalled Italian meringue, which is made by pouring boiling-hot sugar syrup into the egg whites as they are whipped. The hot syrup cooks the whites and helps transform them into a soft, smooth meringue that is stable enough to resist weeping.

MAKING EXTRA-FLUFFY MERINGUE

1. Cook the sugar and water until slightly thickened and syrupy.

2. Beat the egg whites with the cream of tartar and salt until they hold soft peaks.

3. With the mixer still running, carefully pour the hot sugar syrup directly into the beaten egg whites.

4. Add the vanilla and continue beating until the meringue has cooled and is thick and fluffy.

Best of all, this meringue is extra-fluffy and billowy. We needed eight egg whites to achieve mile-high results with a regular meringue, but four egg whites yielded plenty of Italian meringue. Doubling the amount of meringue without doubling the number of egg whites is a neat trick.

There's only one problem with an Italian meringue. Professional bakers use a candy thermometer to heat the sugar syrup to the correct temperature (between 238 and 245 degrees), but many home cooks don't have this tool. Could we make an Italian meringue without a thermometer? After

much trial and error, we found that boiling the sugar syrup for 4 minutes worked perfectly every time.

Since we no longer needed a hot filling to cook the meringue, we thought we might be able to let the filling set up in the shell in the fridge. Two hours later (this can even be done the day before), our filling emerged firm yet still silky. Tasters wanted the filling to be extra-lemony and very rich to balance all the meringue. It took a full cup of lemon juice, 2 tablespoons of zest, and 8 yolks—more than we had seen in any other recipe—to please everyone.

With lots of lemon, miles of meringue, and absolutely no weeping, this pie can be counted on to deliver smiles all around the table every time you make it—whether it's hot outside or not.

MILE-HIGH LEMON MERINGUE PIE

SERVES 8

You can use Single-Crust Pie Dough (page 10) or Easy Press-In Single-Crust Pie Dough (page 11) for this pie. If using a hand-held mixer, you will need a very large, deep bowl and should move the beaters vigorously in step 4 to avoid underbeating the egg whites; see page 5 for more information on whipping egg whites. This pie is best on the day it's made.

1   recipe single-crust pie dough, fitted into a 9-inch pie plate and chilled (see note above)

FILLING

1¼   cups sugar

2   tablespoons grated fresh lemon zest and 1 cup fresh lemon juice (about 6 lemons)

½   cup water

¼   cup cornstarch

¼   teaspoon salt

8   large egg yolks (reserve 4 large egg whites for the meringue)

3   tablespoons unsalted butter, softened

MERINGUE

1 cup sugar

½ cup water

4 large egg whites (reserved from the filling)

½ teaspoon cream of tartar

Pinch salt

½ teaspoon vanilla extract

1. Adjust an oven rack to the middle position and heat the oven to 375 degrees. Following the photos on page 30, line the chilled crust with a double layer of aluminum foil and fill with pie weights. Bake until the pie dough looks dry and is light in color, 25 to 30 minutes. Remove the weights and foil and continue to bake the crust until deep golden brown, 10 to 12 minutes longer. Let cool on a wire rack to room temperature.

2. FOR THE FILLING: Whisk the sugar, lemon juice, water, cornstarch, and salt together in a large saucepan until the cornstarch is dissolved. Bring to a simmer over medium heat, whisking occasionally, until the mixture becomes translucent and begins to thicken, about 5 minutes. Whisk in the egg yolks until combined. Stir in the lemon zest and butter. Bring to a simmer and stir constantly until the mixture is thick enough to coat the back of a spoon, about 2 minutes. Strain through a fine-mesh strainer into the pie shell and scrape the filling off the underside of the strainer. Place plastic wrap directly on the surface of the filling and refrigerate until set and chilled, at least 2 hours or up to 1 day.

3. FOR THE MERINGUE: Adjust an oven rack to the middle position and heat the oven to 400 degrees. Combine the sugar and water in a small saucepan and bring to a boil over medium-high heat. Cook until the mixture is slightly thickened and syrupy, 3 to 4 minutes. Remove from the heat and set aside.

4. With an electric mixer on medium-low speed, whip the egg whites in a large bowl until foamy, about 1 minute. Whip in the cream of tartar and salt, gradually increasing the mixer speed to medium-high, until the whites are shiny and soft peaks form (see page 5), about 2 minutes. Reduce the mixer speed to medium and slowly add the hot syrup (avoid pouring the syrup onto the beaters or it will splash). Add the vanilla and beat until the mixture has cooled and is very thick and shiny, 5 to 9 minutes.

5. Following the photos below, use a rubber spatula to mound the meringue over the filling, making sure the meringue touches the edge of the crust. Use the spatula to create peaks all over the meringue. Bake until the peaks turn golden brown, about 6 minutes. Let the pie cool on a wire rack, about 2 hours. Serve at room temperature.

APPLYING THE MERINGUE

1. Spread the meringue onto the edge of the crust to prevent it from shrinking.

2. Use the spatula to make dramatic peaks and swirls all over the meringue.

Pumpkin-Praline Pie

What's not to like about a pie that combines the familiar spiced custard of a pumpkin pie with the pralinelike chew of a pecan pie? Most recipes for pumpkin-praline pie start with pumpkin pie as the base, but the placement of the pecan praline layer is more variable: it might be layered underneath the pumpkin custard or blanket the top of the pie. We preferred the latter—a topping that acted as the perfect crunchy foil to the sweet, creamy filling below.

After just a few tests, we realized that to hold up that crunchy topping, the pumpkin custard base would have to be pretty sturdy—more so than the usual Thanksgiving pie. To fortify the pumpkin base, we started by adding an extra egg (pumpkin pie recipes usually call for two eggs) to a can of plain pumpkin puree. Tasters preferred the richness of evaporated milk to either heavy cream or milk (the usual suspects when it came to the dairy) and the caramel flavor of dark brown sugar to granulated sugar.

While the filling tasted good, it was too loose to support the praline, and tasters didn't care for the stringy pumpkin fibers. Getting rid of the stringiness was as easy as a whirl in the food processor, and cooking the pureed filling on the stovetop evaporated the excess moisture, making for a sturdier pumpkin filling. (This last step also had the added benefit of reducing the baking time by 30 minutes.)

The pie was now ready for the praline topping. Some recipes have you follow the instructions for making authentic praline candy by boiling sugar, water, and pecans. This candy was good for snacking but much too complicated—and too sweet—for our pie. Other recipes included "shortcut" candy—pecans boiled in copious amounts of corn syrup. Sticky and insipid, this topping tasted nothing like rich praline.

We found a few recipes that didn't get into boiling sugar at all. Instead, they called for tossing chopped pecans with granulated sugar and a smidgen of corn syrup—just enough to make the topping clump like streusel; this uncooked mixture was

MAKING PUMPKIN-PRALINE PIE

1. Puree the pumpkin (with the brown sugar and spices) to break up any fibers.

2. Cook the pumpkin mixture to get rid of excess moisture.

3. Pour the hot filling into a warm pie crust to minimize baking time and promote even cooking.

4. Bake until the filling cracks on top, then add the praline topping and finish baking.

scattered on top of the still-hot, baked pumpkin pie. Intrigued by the apparent ease of this method, we topped our pumpkin pie with the crumbly nut mixture and popped it back into the oven. Ten minutes later the kitchen was filled with the smells of toasty sugar and pecans, and the topping bubbled enticingly around the edges.

The topping was now nearly perfect. All we wanted was a little more praline flavor, and we got it by replacing the granulated sugar with dark brown (just as we'd done with the pumpkin filling). We kept 2 teaspoons of granulated sugar for sprinkling on the top, as it helped to crisp the praline.

The last obstacle concerned timing: exactly when should we add the topping? If added too early—a few minutes before the center was set (as other recipes suggested)—the topping caused the filling to buckle under its weight. We turned to a visual cue that is the bane of many pumpkin pie bakers: the notorious cracking on top of the pie. As the pie just began to crack, it was perfectly set and ready to receive the topping, which covered any trace of the cracks. This worked like a charm every single time, and we now had a pie that would satisfy everyone.

PUMPKIN-PRALINE PIE

SERVES 8

You can use Single-Crust Pie Dough (page 10) or Easy Press-In Single-Crust Pie Dough (page 11) for this pie. Be sure to use pumpkin puree, not pumpkin pie filling, in this recipe. Leftover pie should be refrigerated.

1   recipe single-crust pie dough, fitted into a 9-inch pie plate and chilled (see note above)

FILLING

1   (15-ounce) can pumpkin puree (see note above)
¾   cup packed dark brown sugar
2   teaspoons ground cinnamon
1   teaspoon ground ginger
½   teaspoon ground allspice
    Pinch ground cloves
½   teaspoon salt
1   cup evaporated milk
3   large eggs
2   teaspoons vanilla extract

TOPPING

1   cup pecans, chopped fine
½   cup packed dark brown sugar
    Pinch salt
2   teaspoons dark corn syrup
1   teaspoon vanilla extract
2   teaspoons granulated sugar

1. Adjust an oven rack to the middle position and heat the oven to 375 degrees. Following the photos on page 30, line the chilled crust with a double layer of aluminum foil and fill with pie weights. Bake until the pie dough looks dry and is light in color, 25 to 30 minutes. Remove the pie shell from the oven, remove the weights and foil, and set aside. Reduce the oven temperature to 350 degrees. (The crust must still be warm when the filling is added.)

2. FOR THE FILLING: Puree the pumpkin, brown sugar, spices, and salt together in a food processor until smooth, about 1 minute. Cook the mixture in a large saucepan over medium-high heat until sputtering and thickened, about 4 minutes, and remove from the heat.

3. Whisk the evaporated milk into the pumpkin mixture, then whisk in the eggs and vanilla. Pour the filling into the warm pie shell and bake until the filling is puffed and cracked around the edges and the center barely jiggles when the pie is gently shaken, about 35 minutes.

4. FOR THE TOPPING: Meanwhile, toss the pecans, brown sugar, and salt together in a bowl. Add the corn syrup and vanilla, using your fingers to ensure that the ingredients are well blended.

5. Scatter the topping evenly over the puffed filling and sprinkle with the granulated sugar. Bake until the pecans are fragrant and the topping is bubbling around the edges, about 10 minutes. Let the pie cool on a wire rack until the filling has set, about 2 hours; serve slightly warm or at room temperature.

BLIND BAKING A PIE CRUST

1. Line the chilled pie crust with a double layer of aluminum foil, covering the edges to prevent burning.

2. Fill the crust with pie weights and bake in a 375-degree oven for 25 to 30 minutes. After baking, carefully remove the weights and foil.

Pecan Pie

The pecan pies of today bear little resemblance to their 19th-century inspiration. We wanted to re-create a traditional pecan pie without using modern-day processed corn syrup—a pie that boasted not just sweetness, but a deep, well-rounded flavor and lots of toasty pecans.

A bit of research revealed that corn syrup wasn't always the sweetener of choice—molasses, maple syrup, cane syrup, and sorghum syrup have all appeared in various recipes that date back to the 1800s. Because these predecessors of corn syrup were used abundantly in their day, we decided to try a handful to see what they could contribute to the flavor profile of our revamped pecan pie. Tasters were delighted by the range of flavors they offered, from full-bodied and molasses-y to light and buttery, and everything in between. Darker syrups overwhelmed the pies, but the more delicate ones were sensational, with far more flavor than we'd expected. Now that we knew what we were missing, we set out to approximate it using ordinary pantry ingredients.

We were able to piece together a working recipe of 3 eggs, 1 cup of sugar, 1 cup of corn syrup, 2 tablespoons of butter, and 1¼ cups of pecans, mixed together and baked in a 350-degree oven in an unbaked shell. We didn't want to call for any hard-to-find ingredients and so started our experimenting by creating a faux sugarcane syrup using sugar and some water. However, the results didn't much resemble the cane syrups we had tasted. After a few more syrup substitutions, we determined that maple syrup came the closest of all of them to what we'd tasted, but the maple flavor was too pronounced. After more tests, we discovered we could mellow the maple and achieve the flavors we sought by combining the syrup with light brown sugar, which added loads more flavor

than granulated sugar, and just a single table-spoon of molasses.

We heated the brown sugar, molasses, and maple syrup briefly, which dissolved the brown sugar, thus eliminating any graininess, then stirred in the butter. Our working recipe called for 2 tablespoons, but the resulting pie had little richness. We doubled the amount for appreciable buttery flavor without greasiness. Some pies we came across in our research included cream in the filling, so we tried adding ½ cup of cream with the brown sugar, molasses, and maple syrup. Tasters loved the creamy, custardy transformation it wrought. Unfortunately, the cream made the filling looser. The maple syrup, we learned, was also partly to blame; it has a higher water content than corn syrup. To better bind the filling and get a sliceable pie, we replaced the three whole eggs with six yolks, which have less water than whites, and so bind more firmly.

All that was left was the nuts. We tested pies made with whole pecan halves, chopped pecans, and a combination of chopped and whole nuts. We had no problem deciding our preference. We found whole pecans to be too much of a mouthful, and we had difficulty cutting through them with a fork. Chopped nuts were much easier to slice through and eat, and bringing out their flavor was as simple as toasting them before they went into the pie.

Most recipes suggest simply pouring the filling into an unbaked pie shell, but when we did so, the bottom crust came out soggy and undercooked. Apparently, as soon as the pie went into the oven, the uncooked bottom crust soaked up the uncooked liquid filling. We usually solve this problem by prebaking the crust, but pecan pie bakes for so long (most recipes specify close to an hour); couldn't we somehow use this long stretch of oven time to our advantage? Up to this point, we'd been baking the pie at a steady 350 degrees on the middle rack of the oven. What if we started it at a high temperature (450 degrees), then immediately turned down the dial to a gentle 325 degrees? We hoped the initial high heat would give the bottom crust a head start, and the subsequent low temperature (it took 15 minutes for the temperature inside the oven to come down to 325) would prevent the eggs from curdling. At the same time, we lowered the oven rack. The intense heat from below would help set the crust. The result was just as we'd hoped: a crisp, golden bottom crust.

To the dismay of our tasters, pecan pie needs to completely cool before you can eat it. Otherwise, the filling won't firm to the proper consistency, so the pie won't slice nicely and the filling will be too loose. Cooling took about 4 hours, at which point the filling was silky yet firm; the flavor a mild caramel with hints of molasses; and the nuts a toasty, crunchy counterpoint.

OLD-FASHIONED PECAN PIE

SERVES 8 TO 10

Regular or mild molasses tastes best in this pie. Serve with Bourbon Whipped Cream (recipe follows) or vanilla ice cream. Leftover pie should be refrigerated.

1	cup maple syrup
1	cup packed light brown sugar
½	cup heavy cream
1	tablespoon molasses (see note above)
4	tablespoons (½ stick) unsalted butter, cut into ½-inch pieces
½	teaspoon salt
6	large egg yolks, lightly beaten
1½	cups pecans, toasted (see page 130) and chopped
1	recipe Single-Crust Pie Dough (page 10), fitted into a 9-inch pie plate and chilled

1. Adjust an oven rack to the lowest position and heat the oven to 450 degrees. Combine the maple syrup, sugar, cream, and molasses in a medium saucepan and cook over medium heat, stirring occasionally, until the sugar dissolves, about 3 minutes. Remove from the heat and let cool, about 5 minutes. Whisk the butter and salt into the syrup mixture until combined. Whisk in the egg yolks until incorporated.

2. Scatter the pecans in the chilled pie shell. Carefully pour the syrup mixture over the pecans, place the pie in the oven, and immediately reduce the oven temperature to 325 degrees. Bake until the filling is set and the center jiggles slightly when the pie is gently shaken, 45 to 60 minutes. Let the pie cool on a wire rack for 1 hour, then refrigerate until set, about 3 hours and up to 1 day. Bring the pie to room temperature before serving.

BOURBON WHIPPED CREAM

MAKES ABOUT 2 CUPS

Though any style of whiskey will work here, we prefer the smoky sweetness of bourbon. For the most efficient whipping, make sure your heavy cream is as cold as possible.

1	cup heavy cream, chilled
2	tablespoons bourbon (see note above)
1½	tablespoons light brown sugar
½	teaspoon vanilla extract

With an electric mixer on medium speed, beat the cream, bourbon, sugar, and vanilla until stiff peaks form, about 2 minutes. (The whipped cream can be refrigerated for up to 4 hours.)

Jefferson Davis Pie

A definitively Dixie dessert, Jefferson Davis pie is a rich, caramel-y custard pie dressed up with dried fruit and nuts. Most recipes make a no-cook filling, a combination of brown sugar, egg yolks, butter, milk, warm spices, dried fruit, pecans, and a few tablespoons of flour; the mixture is poured into a raw pie shell and the pie is baked until the custard sets. This pie has a lot in common with pecan pie, another Southern classic, except for the fact that it hasn't gotten its share of the limelight. A sample of test recipes confirmed that Jefferson Davis suffers from the same pitfalls as pecan pie—the worst of the bunch had saccharine, loose fillings and soggy, watery crusts. We wanted to fix these problems so Jefferson Davis pie could take its rightful spot alongside other great Southern desserts.

Our first goal was to strike a good balance of sweetness and spice in the custard. Most recipes started out with 2 (or more) cups of brown sugar, but we found that 1 cup worked just fine, as less sugar let the flavors of the cinnamon and allspice (favored over common but imposing additions like cloves, nutmeg, and mace) shine through. Using heavy cream instead of milk gave the pie a silkier, thicker texture and much richer flavor.

Some recipes saddle this pie with 2 cups of raisins and dates and a cup of pecans. We started by halving those amounts and finely grinding them in the food processor for a more homogeneous filling. But our tasters weren't crazy about the bits of fruit and nuts suspended in the custard. Next, instead of folding them in, we pressed them into the bottom of the crust and poured the custard over the top. This pie boasted a thin layer of fruit and nuts topped by a creamy, smooth custard.

As for baking time and temperature, Jefferson Davis pies usually bake in a raw pie shell for about 45 minutes. The pies are typically started at a high temperature (about 425 degrees) to firm up the crust and then finished at a moderate temperature (about 350 degrees). But without fail, this method resulted in custards that completely dried out around the edges before they were totally set in the center. After several more tests, we found that a slightly longer bake (about an hour) in a gentle 325-degree oven allowed the crust to brown in the same time it took for the custard to set to the requisite firmness.

With a dollop of whipped cream—preferably spiked with bourbon—or a scoop of ice cream, this creamy, nutty, and fruity Southern pie was finally ready for its debut.

JEFFERSON DAVIS PIE

SERVES 8

You can use Single-Crust Pie Dough (page 10) or Easy Press-In Single-Crust Pie Dough (page 11) for this pie. Serve with Bourbon Whipped Cream (page 33) or vanilla ice cream. We prefer the mild flavor of golden raisins in this recipe, but regular raisins will work. Leftover pie should be refrigerated.

½	cup raisins (see note above)
½	cup chopped dates
½	cup pecans, toasted (see page 130) and chopped
1	recipe single-crust pie dough (see note above), fitted into a 9-inch pie plate and chilled
3	tablespoons all-purpose flour
1	teaspoon ground cinnamon
½	teaspoon salt
¼	teaspoon ground allspice
1	cup packed light brown sugar
8	tablespoons (1 stick) unsalted butter, softened
5	large egg yolks
1¼	cups heavy cream

1. Adjust an oven rack to the lowest position and heat the oven to 325 degrees. Pulse the raisins, dates, and pecans in a food processor until finely ground. Transfer the mixture to the chilled pie shell and gently press into an even layer.

2. Combine the flour, cinnamon, salt, and allspice in a small bowl. In a large bowl, beat the sugar and butter with an electric mixer on medium-low speed until just combined, about 1 minute. Mix in the egg yolks, one at a time, until incorporated. Add the flour mixture and cream and mix, scraping down the sides of the bowl as necessary, until just combined.

3. Pour the filling over the fruit and nuts and bake until the surface is deep brown and the center jiggles slightly when the pie is gently shaken, 55 to 65 minutes. Let the pie cool completely on a wire rack, about 4 hours.

SHOPPING WITH THE TEST KITCHEN

Pie Dishes: Although pie plates come in all sorts of materials (glass, ceramic, and aluminum) and with extra bells and whistles (scalloped edges, mesh bottoms, and crust protectors, for example), we recently tested eight plates and found that our old standby, the Pyrex 9-inch pie plate, still performs best. In our tests, the Pyrex yielded evenly browned, crisp crusts every time because of its glass construction, which provides slow, steady, insulating heat for even baking. Its shallow, angled sides prevent crusts from slumping, and it's just 1⅛ inches deep, which neatly fits a store-bought crust when we don't feel like making our own. Its basic, functional design and low price ($2.99) made it the clear winner.

Millionaire Pie

Millionaire pie may be unfamiliar to some, but it has been a staple at Furr's, a Southwestern chain of cafeterias, since 1946. The pie is so named because it's rich (from eggs and cream), it's gold (from lots of crushed pineapple), and it's supposed to taste "like a million bucks." In the original recipe a no-cook filling (raw eggs, confectioner's sugar, and butter) is topped with sweetened whipped cream studded with nuts and bits of pineapple. Most modern recipes avoid the raw eggs by using a mixture of cream cheese, whipped topping (such as Cool Whip), canned pineapple, and nuts in a graham cracker pie crust.

We knew we didn't want to make this pie with raw eggs, so we gathered a handful of the recipes based on cream cheese and whipped topping and got to work. These pies did not live up to their namesake—in fact, they were pretty poor, the filling little more than a pasty, cloyingly sweet frosting. Even worse, our tasters hated the soggy nuts and fibrous pineapple dispersed throughout the otherwise creamy topping.

Our first decision was to abandon the cream cheese and whipped topping of the modern impostors and instead create a pineapple chiffon filling from scratch—which was closer to the original. We started with a basic homemade pudding (sugar, cornstarch, half-and-half, and egg yolks), replacing the dairy with pineapple juice, folding in homemade whipped cream at the end, and pouring the mixture into a simple homemade graham cracker crust (ground crackers and melted butter). This filling was so loose that it was hard to cut a neat slice and was sorely lacking in pineapple flavor. Replacing the juice with pineapple juice concentrate was a step in the right direction, but for intense, complex pineapple flavor, we found that nothing worked better than cooking down a can of crushed pineapple until it was lightly browned and incredibly fragrant. We could then process the cooked pineapple into a smooth texture that tasters loved.

This filling tasted great, but it still wasn't slicing well, and our tasters didn't like chunks of nuts in the smooth filling. We tried adding more cornstarch to the filling to stabilize it, but that made the mixture too slippery. Plain gelatin firmed up the filling perfectly, and when we switched to pineapple-flavored gelatin we finally had a sliceable filling with plenty of pineapple punch.

Since we were already grinding up graham crackers for the crust, we tried adding the pecans to the food processor. Maybe we could move the nut flavor to the crust and eliminate those soggy nuts in the filling. This worked so well that we wondered if something other than graham crackers might work better as a foundation for this pie. Animal crackers and shortbread cookies were both OK, but not as flavorful as pecan shortbread cookies, which added another layer of sweet, rich pecan flavor to the crust. With one bite, we knew we'd created a pie that really did taste like a million bucks.

THE AMERICAN TABLE
FURR'S CAFETERIA

Brothers Roy and Key Furr started their namesake cafeteria chain in Hobbs, New Mexico, in 1946 with the promise of wholesome food "that you'd make every day if you could." There are now 54 Furr's Cafeterias scattered throughout New Mexico, Texas, Arizona, Colorado, Kansas, and Oklahoma. Their millionaire pie remains a best-seller to this day.

MILLIONAIRE PIE

SERVES 8

*Pecan Sandies, made by Keebler, are the test kitch-
en's favorite brand for making the crust; however,
any pecan shortbread cookie will work. If desired, top
the finished pie with ¼ cup of toasted and chopped
pecans or ½ cup of toasted sweetened flaked coconut.
Leftover pie should be refrigerated.*

CRUST

12	pecan shortbread cookies (see note above), broken into rough pieces (about 2½ cups)
½	cup pecans, chopped
2	tablespoons unsalted butter, melted and cooled

PIE

1	(20-ounce) can crushed pineapple packed in juice
½	cup plus 1 tablespoon sugar
	Salt
3	large egg yolks
1	(3-ounce) box pineapple-flavored gelatin
1	cup frozen pineapple juice concentrate, thawed
2	cups heavy cream, chilled

1. FOR THE CRUST: Adjust an oven rack to the middle position and heat the oven to 350 degrees. Process the cookies and pecans in a food proces-sor to fine crumbs. Add the butter and pulse until combined. Following the photo on page 44, use the bottom of a measuring cup to press the crumbs into an even layer on the bottom and sides of a 9-inch pie plate and refrigerate until firm, about 20 minutes. Bake until lightly browned and set, about 15 minutes. Let the crust cool to room tem-perature on a wire rack.

2. FOR THE PIE: Cook the pineapple, ¼ cup of the sugar, and pinch salt in a large nonstick skillet over medium-high heat, stirring occasionally, until the liquid evaporates and the pineapple is lightly browned, about 15 minutes. Scrape the mixture into the food processor and process until very smooth, about 1 minute; set aside.

3. Whisk the egg yolks, ¼ cup more sugar, and ¼ teaspoon salt in a medium bowl. Combine the gelatin and ½ cup of the pineapple juice con-centrate in a medium saucepan and let sit until the gelatin softens, about 5 minutes. Cook over medium heat until the gelatin dissolves and the mixture is very hot but not boiling, about 2 min-utes. Whisking vigorously, slowly add the gelatin mixture to the egg yolks. Return the mixture to the saucepan and cook, stirring constantly, until slightly thickened, about 2 minutes. Off the heat, stir in the remaining ½ cup pineapple juice concen-trate and processed pineapple mixture. Pour into a clean large bowl and refrigerate until set, about 1½ hours.

4. With an electric mixer on medium-high speed, whip the cream and remaining 1 tablespoon sugar to stiff peaks, about 3 minutes. Whisk 1 cup of the whipped cream into the gelatin mixture until com-pletely incorporated. Using a rubber spatula, fold 1 cup more whipped cream into the gelatin mixture until no streaks of white remain. Scrape the mix-ture into the cooled pie shell and smooth the top. Spread the remaining whipped cream evenly over the filling and refrigerate until chilled and set, at least 4 hours. Serve.

Coconut Cream Pie

Coconut cream pie evokes happy thoughts—a fluffy cloud of a dessert, a sweet finish to a satisfying home-cooked meal. But most coconut cream pies don't have the smooth, satiny fillings and crisp crusts we envision. Instead, they're heavy, leaden, pasty, overly sweet, bland vanilla puddings—with barely a whisper of coconut flavor—in soggy pie shells— definitely not a satisfying finish to any meal.

Looking to revitalize this classic dessert, we started with the crust. Though a plain pastry crust is typical of coconut cream pie, we were not the least bit wowed. We used a prebaked pie shell, which started out perfectly crisp, but when the filling went in, it quickly became soggy. We decided to try a graham cracker crust. Its crisp, sandy texture and sturdiness provided the perfect contrast to the creamy, smooth filling. To add even more flavor, we toasted some shredded coconut until it was golden brown, then processed it along with the graham crackers so that it could be broken down into fine bits. The coconut-enhanced crust was a hit with our tasters.

The filling for coconut cream pie usually consists of no more than eggs, sugar, cornstarch or flour, and cream or milk, and the method couldn't be easier (it's a basic stovetop pudding). The first thing we needed to do was find the right kind of cream or "milk" to use. We tried half-and-half and whole milk, but these fillings were just OK. Then we had the idea to try coconut milk; while this filling had a delicate coconut flavor and aroma, it was far too rich. We pulled back on the coconut milk and tried a filling made with both coconut milk and whole milk. This filling was less rich, but the coconut flavor was now too subtle. Simmering some unsweetened shredded coconut with the milk and coconut milk imparted good, pure coconut flavor. Tasters didn't complain about the pieces of coconut, so we decided to leave the tiny bits in the filling. One-half cup of coconut in the filling was perfect; any more and the filling became gritty.

Our next tests focused on getting the right level of thickness and creaminess in the filling. For thickness, we tried both cornstarch and flour but preferred the cornstarch because it gave the filling a light, natural feel while still allowing it to set up into a firm texture. Considering the eggs next, we noted that some recipes called for whole eggs, some for just yolks, and a few for both. Our preference was for yolks only (we used five), which gave us a filling with a smooth, lush texture and a full, deep flavor. Some butter whisked into the hot filling just before pouring it into the pie shell was the final touch that made the coconut cream creamy, rich, and silky.

With the crust ready, we added the coconut cream to the pie shell and refrigerated the pie so the filling would set up. Now all that was left to do was pile on the whipped cream topping (a simple combination of heavy cream, sugar, vanilla, and some rum) and a final garnish of toasted coconut. Finally, we had a truly memorable coconut cream pie that far exceeded our expectations.

COCONUT CREAM PIE

SERVES 8

You can find unsweetened shredded coconut in well-stocked supermarkets, natural foods stores, and Asian grocery stores. Leftover pie should be refrigerated.

CRUST

- 9 **whole graham crackers, broken into rough pieces**
- 4 **tablespoons unsweetened shredded coconut (see note above), toasted (see page 212)**
- 5 **tablespoons unsalted butter, melted and cooled**
- 2 **tablespoons sugar**

FILLING

- 1 (14-ounce) can coconut milk
- 1 cup whole milk
- 2/3 cup sugar
- 1/2 cup unsweetened shredded coconut (see note above)
- 1/4 teaspoon salt
- 5 large egg yolks
- 1/4 cup cornstarch
- 2 tablespoons unsalted butter, cut into 4 pieces
- 1 1/2 teaspoons vanilla extract

TOPPING

- 1 1/2 cups heavy cream, chilled
- 1 1/2 tablespoons sugar
- 1 1/2 teaspoons dark rum (optional)
- 1/2 teaspoon vanilla extract
- 1 tablespoon unsweetened shredded coconut (see note above), toasted (see page 212)

1. FOR THE CRUST: Adjust an oven rack to the middle position and heat the oven to 325 degrees. Pulse the graham cracker pieces and toasted coconut in a food processor until the crackers are broken down into coarse crumbs, about 10 pulses. Process the mixture to fine crumbs, about 12 seconds. Sprinkle the melted butter and sugar over the crumbs and pulse until combined. Sprinkle the mixture into a 9-inch pie plate and, following the photo on page 44, use the bottom of a measuring cup to press the crumbs into an even layer on the bottom and sides. Bake until the crust is deep golden brown, 20 to 25 minutes. Let the crust cool to room temperature on a wire rack.

2. FOR THE FILLING: Meanwhile, bring the coconut milk, milk, 1/3 cup of the sugar, shredded coconut, and salt to a simmer in a medium saucepan over medium-high heat, stirring occasionally. Whisk the egg yolks, remaining 1/3 cup sugar, and cornstarch together in a medium bowl until well combined and no lumps remain. Gradually whisk the milk mixture into the yolk mixture to temper, then return to the saucepan. Bring the mixture to a simmer over medium heat, whisking constantly, until thickened and a few bubbles burst on the surface, about 30 seconds. Off the heat, whisk in the butter and vanilla. Pour the filling into the cooled crust, place a sheet of plastic wrap directly on the surface of the filling, and refrigerate until the filling is chilled and set, at least 3 hours.

3. FOR THE TOPPING: Whip the cream, sugar, rum (if using), and vanilla together with an electric mixer on medium-low speed until frothy, about 1 minute. Increase the mixer speed to high and continue to whip until soft peaks form, 1 to 3 minutes. Spread the whipped cream over the top of the pie and sprinkle with the toasted coconut.

Black-Bottom Pie

Black-bottom pie is a chocolate cream pie—chocolate custard and sweetened whipped cream—with two added bonuses: an airy rum chiffon layer between the chocolate and whipped cream layers, and a chocolate cookie crust. Recipes for this pie first appeared in the early 20th century, but its popularity didn't take off until the late 1930s, when restaurant reviewer Duncan Hines wrote about experiencing the pie's "unbelievably light texture" at the Dolores Restaurant and Drive-In in Oklahoma City, Oklahoma.

But after preparing a few recipes, we realized why this pie is so rarely made. Between making the crust, chocolate custard, rum layer (which must be stabilized with gelatin, chilled, and lightened with

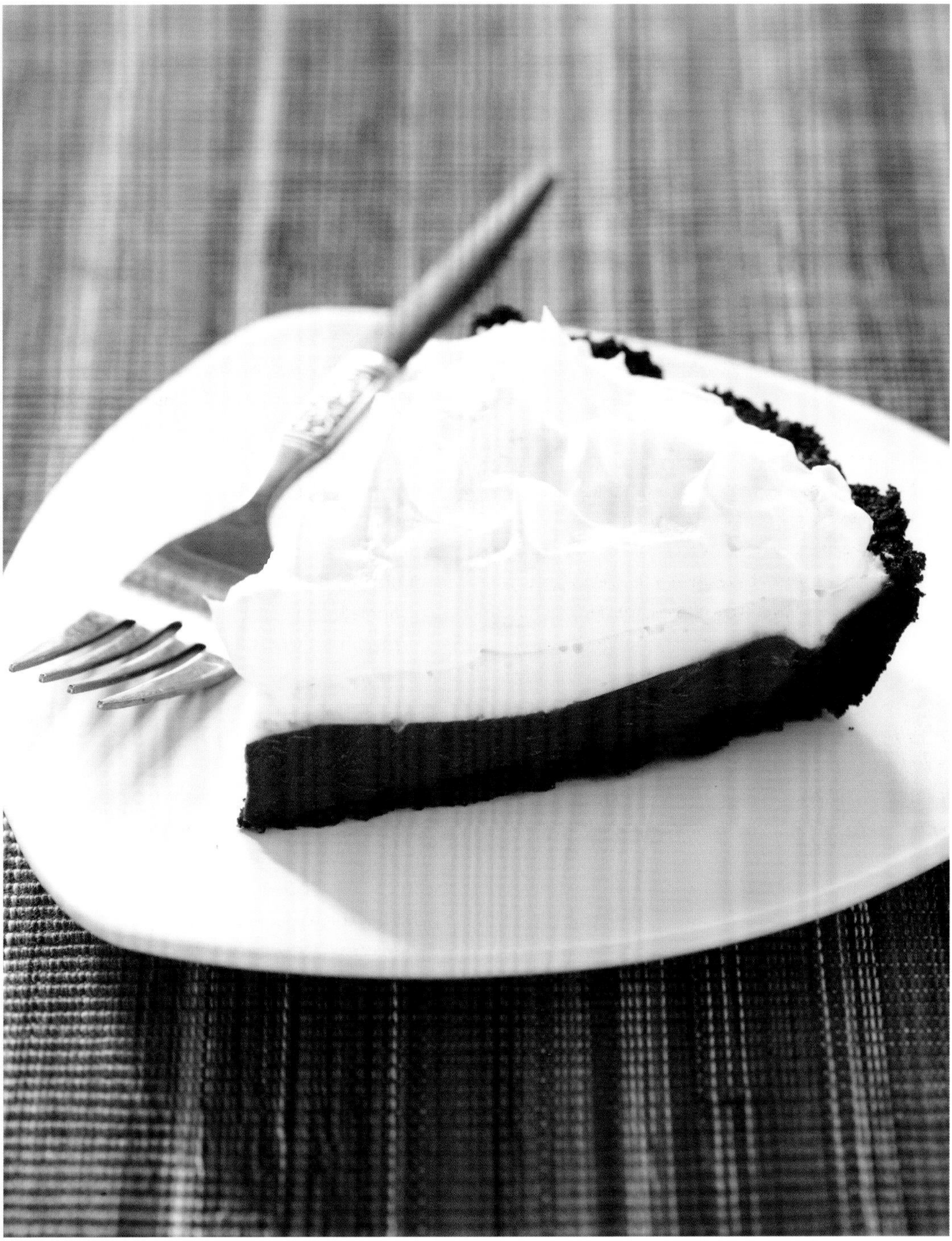

beaten raw egg whites to create a chiffon texture), and whipped cream, we dirtied three saucepans and seven bowls during 3 hours in the kitchen. But we had to admit, the contrast in texture and flavor between the chocolate custard, fluffy rum chiffon, and whipped cream was worth it.

We started our kitchen work at the bottom, with the crust. Although the pie was originally made with a gingersnap crust, by the 1940s, recipes began to shift to pastry or chocolate cookie crusts. We compared all three, and tasters agreed that the chocolate crust provided superior flavor— and actually lived up to the name "black-bottom." We crushed chocolate cookies, bound them with melted butter, pressed the mixture into a pie plate, and then baked the crust for 10 minutes to ensure a crisp foundation for our pie.

A few recipes saved time by using a large batch of custard as a base for both the chocolate and rum layers. This sounded promising, so we made a basic custard with sugar, half-and-half, egg yolks, and cornstarch. We combined half of the custard with chopped chocolate (which melted) then poured this portion into the crust to chill and set.

For the rum chiffon layer, our plan was to flavor the remaining custard with rum, stabilize it with a little gelatin, and then add whipped raw egg whites for the signature light and airy texture. We were disappointed to find that the whipped whites weren't quite sturdy enough to support the sweetened whipped cream on top. To make the egg whites sturdier, we cooked them, beating them with sugar, water, and cream of tartar over a double boiler, and then added this mixture to the rum-enhanced custard. This worked like a charm, producing a voluminous, sturdy, and flavorful chiffon that was well worth the effort. With a piping of whipped cream on top, it was easy to see why Duncan Hines was so impressed with black-bottom pie all those years ago.

BLACK-BOTTOM PIE

SERVES 8

Nabisco Famous Chocolate Wafers are the test kitchen's favorite brand for making the crust. This recipe makes a generous amount of filling; to prevent the filling from overflowing the pie crust, add the final ½ cup of the rum layer after the filling has set for 20 minutes. Leftover pie should be refrigerated.

CRUST

32	chocolate cookies (see note above), broken into rough pieces (about 2½ cups)
4	tablespoons (½ stick) unsalted butter, melted and cooled

PIE

⅔	cup plus 2 tablespoons sugar
2	cups half-and-half
4	teaspoons cornstarch
4	large egg yolks plus 1 large egg white
6	ounces semisweet chocolate, chopped fine
3	tablespoons golden or light rum
2	tablespoons water
1	teaspoon unflavored gelatin
¼	teaspoon cream of tartar
1½	cups heavy cream, chilled

1. FOR THE CRUST: Adjust an oven rack to the middle position and heat the oven to 350 degrees. Process the cookie pieces in a food processor until coarsely ground, about 15 pulses. Continue to process to fine crumbs, about 15 seconds. Add the butter and pulse until combined. Following the photo on page 44, use the bottom of a measuring cup to press the crumbs into an even layer on the bottom and sides of a 9-inch pie plate and refrigerate until firm, about 20 minutes. Bake until set, about 10 minutes. Let the crust cool to room temperature on a wire rack.

2. FOR THE PIE: Whisk together ⅓ cup of the sugar, half-and-half, cornstarch, and egg yolks in a saucepan. Cook over medium heat, stirring constantly, until the mixture comes to a boil, about 8 minutes.

3. Divide the hot custard evenly between two bowls. Whisk the chocolate into one bowl until smooth, then pour into the cooled pie crust; refrigerate. Whisk together the rum, 1 tablespoon of the water, and gelatin in a third bowl and let sit for 5 minutes; stir into the bowl with the plain custard and refrigerate, stirring occasionally, until the mixture is wobbly but not set, about 20 minutes.

4. Combine ⅓ cup more of the sugar, egg white, remaining 1 tablespoon water, and cream of tartar in a large heatproof bowl set over a medium saucepan filled with ½ inch of barely simmering water (don't let the bowl touch the water). With an electric mixer on medium-high speed, beat the egg white mixture to soft peaks, about 2 minutes; remove the bowl from the heat and beat the egg white mixture until very thick and glossy and cooled to room temperature, about 3 minutes.

5. Whisk the cooled egg white mixture into the chilled rum custard until smooth. Pour all but ½ cup of the rum custard into the chocolate custard–filled pie crust. Refrigerate for 20 minutes, then top with the remaining rum custard. Refrigerate until completely set, at least 3 hours or up to 24 hours. Before serving, whip the cream and remaining 2 tablespoons sugar together with an electric mixer on medium-low speed until frothy, about 1 minute. Increase the mixer speed to high and continue to whip until the cream forms soft peaks, 1 to 3 minutes. Spread the whipped cream over the top of the pie and serve.

French Silk Chocolate Pie

Don't let the name fool you: French Silk Pie is actually an American creation. The winning recipe from the third annual Pillsbury Bake-Off (in 1951), French Silk is an old-fashioned icebox pie— the exotic name reflects the international curiosity of postwar America and the Pillsbury contest. The original recipe was a cinch to make: the filling is just butter, sugar, three squares of melted and cooled unsweetened chocolate, and raw eggs whipped together until incredibly light and fluffy, poured into a homemade prebaked pie crust, and chilled until firm—no baking required. Served with dollops of whipped cream, French Silk Chocolate Pie was an instant hit.

We found a number of commercial versions of French Silk Pie in the freezer section at the supermarket and weren't surprised that they were completely mediocre and lacking in chocolate flavor. But we *were* shocked to find that the original prize-winning recipe also barely tasted like chocolate. It may have pleased eaters 60 years ago, but Americans today have become accustomed to ramped-up chocolate flavor. We wanted our own award-winning pie—one that tasted deeply of chocolate.

Right away, we nixed the raw eggs in the finished pie; the eggs in our pie would have to be cooked. To do so, we combined them with some sugar and water on the stovetop, beating until the mixture was light and thick—and cooked to a safe 160 degrees. We then continued whipping the mixture, off the heat, until it was cooled.

The original recipe called for 3 ounces of melted unsweetened chocolate. Wanting a more chocolaty pie, we tried doubling the amount. We folded the chocolate into the cooled egg and sugar mixture, but the unsweetened chocolate was acidic and harsh at that volume (and adding more sugar ruined the texture of the pie). Next we made pies with semi-sweet and bittersweet chocolate, in combination and alone. Across the board, tasters preferred the bold but balanced flavor of pies made with bittersweet chocolate; 8 ounces provided rich, potent flavor without going overboard.

Now the filling tasted terrific, but it was much too dense when we beat in the two sticks of softened butter called for in the original recipe. Cutting the amount of butter in half was better, but the filling wasn't quite silky or light enough.

Most recipes suggest serving the pie with whipped cream. We wondered if we could lighten the pie by incorporating whipped cream into the filling. We whipped 1 cup of cream, folded it into the chocolate mixture, and spooned the filling into the pie shell. We waited patiently for the pie to set (it took about 3 hours), sliced the pie, and dug in. The filling was light, but rich, thick, and chocolaty all at once. It was, finally, as smooth as French silk.

FRENCH SILK CHOCOLATE PIE

SERVES 8 TO 10

You can use Single-Crust Pie Dough (page 10) or Easy Press-In Single-Crust Pie Dough (page 11) for this pie. Serve with lightly sweetened whipped cream. Leftover pie should be refrigerated.

1	recipe single-crust pie dough, fitted into a 9-inch pie plate and chilled (see note above)
1	cup heavy cream, chilled
3	large eggs
¾	cup sugar
2	tablespoons water
8	ounces bittersweet chocolate, melted and cooled
1	tablespoon vanilla extract
8	tablespoons (1 stick) unsalted butter, cut into ½-inch pieces and softened

MAKING FRENCH SILK CHOCOLATE PIE

1. Beating the eggs and sugar together in a double boiler incorporates air and gives the filling a light, ethereal texture.

2. When the egg mixture reaches 160 degrees, it will be very thick. Remove it from the heat and continue beating until it is fluffy and cool.

3. After incorporating the melted chocolate, beat in softened butter to give the pie rich flavor and silky-smooth texture.

1. Adjust an oven rack to the middle position and heat the oven to 375 degrees. Following the photos on page 30, line the chilled crust with a double layer of aluminum foil and fill with pie weights. Bake until the pie dough looks dry and is light in color, 25 to 30 minutes. Remove the weights and foil and continue to bake the crust until deep golden brown, 10 to 12 minutes longer. Let the crust cool on a wire rack to room temperature.

2. With an electric mixer on medium-high speed, whip the cream to stiff peaks, 2 to 3 minutes.

Transfer the whipped cream to a small bowl and refrigerate.

3. Combine the eggs, sugar, and water in a large heatproof bowl set over a medium saucepan filled with ½ inch of barely simmering water (don't let the bowl touch the water). With an electric mixer on medium speed, beat until the egg mixture is thickened and registers 160 degrees on an instant-read thermometer, 7 to 10 minutes. Remove the bowl from the heat and continue to beat the egg mixture until fluffy and cooled to room temperature, about 8 minutes.

4. Add the chocolate and vanilla to the cooled egg mixture and beat until incorporated. Beat in the butter, a few pieces at a time, until well combined. Using a spatula, fold in the whipped cream until no streaks of white remain. Scrape the filling into the pie shell and refrigerate until set, at least 3 hours or up to 24 hours. Serve.

Icebox Key Lime Pie

Key lime pie was invented in the Florida Keys more than 100 years ago. The original recipe was considered an icebox pie because the filling of sweetened condensed milk, egg yolks, and lime juice wasn't cooked. Everything was simply stirred together and poured into a prebaked graham cracker crust. The pie was then refrigerated for several hours, where the lime's acid "cooked" the milk and yolks, creating a custardy filling bursting with lime flavor.

Because of concerns about eating raw eggs, today's Key lime pies fall into two distinct camps: uncooked pies in which the eggs are replaced with whipped cream or gelatin, and those whose egg-based filling is cooked on the stovetop. We tried a handful of uncooked pies and were consistently disappointed. Their texture was never custardy; the pies were either too fluffy from whipped cream or too rubbery from gelatin. We set our goal high: to create a Key lime pie as easy and custardy as the original without having to cook the filling.

We started with the lime juice. Most recipes don't use enough, and the resulting pie is too timid. We found that we needed a full cup of fresh lime juice (bottled lime juice tasted artificial) to produce a pie with bracing lime flavor. Lime zest added another layer of flavor, and processing the zest with sugar offset its sourness and chewiness.

To the juice and zest we added a can of sweetened condensed milk. We now needed something other than egg yolks to thicken this soupy mixture. Potato starch, nonfat dry milk, and store-bought

---

THE AMERICAN TABLE
KEY LIME PIE

Before Gail Borden invented sweetened condensed milk in 1856, drinking milk was a health risk, as there was no pasteurization or refrigeration for fresh milk. The shelf stability and safety of sweetened condensed milk made it especially popular in areas like the Florida Keys, where the hot climate promoted rapid spoilage of anything perishable.

Like many of our iconic foods, no one knows for sure when or by whom the first Key lime pie was made, but with canned milk in every pantry by the 1870s and an abundance of tiny Key limes throughout the area, it was only a matter of time. Most food historians trace the history of this pie back to the 1890s, but there are those—especially in the Keys—who claim the recipe is decades older.

lime curd failed miserably, producing weepy pies we could have drunk with a straw. Cream cheese had the opposite effect; it made the filling too dense—more cheesecake than custard pie. Then we tried instant pudding mix—not the cook-and-serve kind, but the stuff you just mix with milk, chill, and serve. Although we weren't crazy about the flavor (tasters rejected lemon and lime varieties, but vanilla was deemed acceptable), the texture was almost custardlike. The filling was still a little too thin, but it gave us a glimmer of hope.

Going back to the drawing board, we decided to try the instant vanilla pudding mix in combination with small amounts of gelatin and cream cheese—two ingredients that showed promise but had each caused textural problems when used as the sole thickener. After several days of trial and error, we finally hit on the right ratios to thicken our pie filling into custardy perfection. A block of cream cheese, ⅓ cup of instant vanilla pudding mix, and a mere 1¼ teaspoons of gelatin did the trick. After squeezing and scraping 250 limes into 29 pies, we'd discovered the secrets to a custardy no-cook, no-egg Key lime pie.

ICEBOX KEY LIME PIE

SERVES 8

Feel free to use Key limes if desired; note that you'll need about 40 Key limes to yield 1 cup of juice. Do not, however, use bottled Key lime juice or the pie will have a serious lack of flavor. Serve with lightly sweetened whipped cream. Leftover pie should be refrigerated.

CRUST

8	whole graham crackers, broken into rough pieces
5	tablespoons unsalted butter, melted and cooled
3	tablespoons sugar

MAKING A CRUMB CRUST

Press the crumb mixture evenly across the bottom of the pie plate, using a measuring cup. Then tightly pack the crumbs against the sides of the pie plate, using your thumb and the measuring cup simultaneously.

FILLING

¼	cup sugar
1	tablespoon grated fresh lime zest and 1 cup fresh lime juice (8 to 10 limes; see note above)
1	(8-ounce) package cream cheese, softened
1	(14-ounce) can sweetened condensed milk
⅓	cup instant vanilla pudding mix
1¼	teaspoons unflavored gelatin
1	teaspoon vanilla extract

1. FOR THE CRUST: Adjust an oven rack to the middle position and heat the oven to 325 degrees. Process the graham cracker pieces in a food processor to fine crumbs, about 30 seconds. Sprinkle the melted butter and sugar over the crumbs and pulse until combined.

2. Sprinkle the mixture into a 9-inch pie plate and wipe out the workbowl. Following the photo above, use the bottom of a measuring cup to press the crumbs into an even layer on the bottom and sides of the pie plate. Bake until the crust is fragrant and beginning to brown, 13 to 18 minutes.

3. FOR THE FILLING: Process the sugar and lime zest together in the food processor until the sugar turns bright green, about 30 seconds. Add the cream cheese and continue to process until combined, about 30 seconds. Add the condensed milk and pudding mix and continue to process until smooth, about 30 seconds. Scrape down the sides of the workbowl.

4. Stir the gelatin and 2 tablespoons of the lime juice together in a small bowl and microwave until warm (but not bubbling), about 15 seconds. Stir to dissolve the gelatin.

5. With the food processor running, pour the warm gelatin mixture, remaining lime juice, and vanilla through the feed tube and continue to process until thoroughly combined, about 30 seconds. Pour the lime filling into the cooled pie shell. Refrigerate the pie, uncovered, until chilled and set, about 6 hours. Serve chilled or at room temperature.

Icebox Strawberry Pie

With a red filling so bright it hurts, berries as big as plums, and poufy whipped cream, diner-style strawberry pies always look inviting. But these no-bake desserts often taste more like plastic than pie. We wondered if a bit of kitchen work could deliver a pie that lived up to its bright, tempting looks.

Most of the recipes we found in our research were virtually identical. A cup each of water and sugar were combined with a small amount of cornstarch until thickened, a pound of fresh whole berries and a few drops of red food coloring were stirred in, and the whole mixture was dumped into a pie shell. Some versions had one significant variation—namely, adding as much as a box of strawberry Jell-O to the filling. In our preliminary tests, the cornstarch-only version thickened nicely, but in the refrigerator, the filling began to

weep; the chill apparently loosened the starch's hold. At the other extreme, pie made with Jell-O was bouncy and, worse, had a fake strawberry taste. Both versions provided modest berry flavor at best. Meant to tempt the eye, these pies did little for the palate. We would start our testing from square one.

Right off the bat, we decided the red dye would have to go. That settled, we began to wonder about the generous measure of water (1 cup) added to the filling. Like most soft fruits, strawberries are naturally moist, so shouldn't we concentrate their juice? Instead, these recipes made a watery filling and then thickened it. We struck out in a new direction, beginning our testing by simmering 3 pounds of sliced fresh berries (what's strawberry pie if not a lot of strawberries?) in a dry saucepan. The berries released their juice, and after 20 minutes the mixture was thick, concentrated, and flavorful. All good, except for one thing: tasters missed the freshness of uncooked berries.

The next time we made the pie, we divided the fruit, cooking down 2 pounds of frozen berries—they worked equally well for cooking and cost less—and then stirring in 1 pound of fresh berries off the heat (we sliced the fresh berries first to make the pie easier to cut). We poured this mixture into the shell and chilled the pie. This pie had loads of berry flavor. As it chilled, however, the uncooked berries softened, making the filling watery.

Strawberries are low in pectin, a natural thickener found in citrus fruits and many other plants. To make up for the lack of pectin in strawberries, we started by adding some lemon juice, which also encourages thickening. It tightened the texture of the filling (and perked up the flavor), but not enough—the pie still wouldn't hold its shape when sliced. We thought back to the box of strawberry Jell-O that we had already unceremoniously dumped from our ingredient list—what if we replaced some

of the Jell-O with unflavored gelatin? We tested various quantities and found that 1 tablespoon produced a clean-slicing yet not bouncy pie.

Diner strawberry pies typically get a squirt of Reddi-wip, but we didn't intend to reach for the can now. Instead, we whipped cream with some cream cheese (along with vanilla and sugar) for a slightly tangy topping that balanced the sweetness of the berries. At last, we had on our hands a bright, fresh, very red, and very berry pie.

ICEBOX STRAWBERRY PIE

SERVES 8

You can use Single-Crust Pie Dough (page 10) or Easy Press-In Single-Crust Pie Dough (page 11) for this pie. In step 2, it is imperative that the cooked strawberry mixture measure 2 cups; any more than that and the filling will be too loose. If your fresh berries aren't fully ripe, you may want to add extra sugar to taste in step 3. Leftover pie should be refrigerated.

1   recipe single-crust pie dough, fitted into a 9-inch pie plate and chilled (see note above)

FILLING

2   pounds frozen strawberries
2   tablespoons fresh lemon juice
2   tablespoons water
1   tablespoon unflavored gelatin
1   cup sugar
     Pinch salt
1   pound fresh strawberries, hulled and sliced thin

TOPPING

4   ounces cream cheese, softened
3   tablespoons sugar
½   teaspoon vanilla extract
1   cup heavy cream, chilled

1. Adjust an oven rack to the middle position and heat the oven to 375 degrees. Following the photos on page 30, line the chilled crust with a double layer of aluminum foil and fill with pie weights. Bake until the pie dough looks dry and is light in color, 25 to 30 minutes. Remove the weights and foil and continue to bake the crust until deep golden brown, 10 to 12 minutes longer. Let the crust cool on a wire rack to room temperature.

2. FOR THE FILLING: Cook the frozen berries in a large saucepan over medium-low heat until they begin to release their juice, about 3 minutes. Increase the heat to medium-high and cook, stirring frequently, until thick and jamlike, about 25 minutes (the mixture should measure 2 cups).

3. Combine the lemon juice, water, and gelatin in a small bowl. Let sit until the gelatin softens and the mixture has thickened, about 5 minutes. Stir the gelatin mixture, sugar, and salt into the cooked berry mixture and return to a simmer, about 2 minutes. Transfer to a bowl and let cool to room temperature, about 30 minutes.

4. Fold the fresh berries into the filling, spread the filling evenly in the cooled pie shell, and refrigerate until set, about 4 hours. (The pie can be covered with plastic wrap and refrigerated for up to 24 hours.)

5. FOR THE TOPPING: With an electric mixer on medium speed, beat the cream cheese, sugar, and vanilla until smooth, about 30 seconds. With the mixer running, add the cream and whip until stiff peaks form, about 2 minutes. Dollop individual slices of pie with the topping and serve.

Raspberry Chiffon Pie

At its best, raspberry chiffon is light, billowy, and creamy. Rarely, however, is it intensely flavored. That's because the filling doesn't contain much fruit—it's mostly whipped egg whites and/or heavy cream, sugar, and gelatin. We wanted a raspberry chiffon pie that was more than pretty, and it had to have a truly fresh, sweet, and tart raspberry flavor.

Our first thought was that we needed to add more raspberries to the basic recipes we were finding. From our first tests, we learned that the usual protocol called for cooking the berries and sugar into a puree, which was strained to remove the seeds. Why not just add more of this puree? The solution was not so simple. Tasters preferred fillings made with gelatin-stabilized whipped cream to those made with gelatin-stabilized egg whites (the latter were billowy but not really creamy and smooth). Unfortunately, the cream filling could "hold" only so much fruit puree before it would collapse and refuse to set.

We had to find a way to help the chiffon filling stiffen so it could hold more fruit and more flavor. More gelatin helped (3 tablespoons was ideal), but there was a limit—we didn't want a bouncy Jell-O pie. A little cream cheese thickened the whipped cream and added more richness. In the end, these measures allowed us to add ⅓ cup of raspberry puree to the filling. A good start, but tasters wanted more fruit flavor.

Replacing the usual plain gelatin with raspberry-flavored gelatin bumped up the fruit flavor and gave the filling a vibrant color, but we were now officially out of ideas. Our filling had better flavor than the fillings most recipes produced, but it wasn't what we would call intense. We considered using lemon juice, which we hoped would both thicken the filling and heighten its flavor, but we

found its sharpness competed too much with the raspberry flavor. Thinking about the pure flavor of raspberry jam, we decided to try using pectin (which is used to turn fruit into jam). We wondered if we could use this kind of thickened, jammy filling as a thin base layer for our chiffon pie.

This idea worked perfectly. We cooked frozen berries (more affordable than fresh and available year-round) until they started to break down and then added the pectin, followed by the sugar. The mixture thickened beautifully and the flavor was intense. We set aside some of this smooth puree to flavor the chiffon filling and poured the rest (with fresh fruit added for texture and flavor) into a pre-baked pie shell. After about 10 minutes on the counter, this jamlike mixture set into a thin, dark red layer of pure raspberry flavor.

Next we prepared the chiffon filling (with the reserved berry mixture), spooned it over the fruit layer, and let the gelatin work its magic in the refrigerator. Three hours later, we had a perfectly set, sliceable pie with great color and intense raspberry flavor. With a crown of lightly sweetened whipped cream, our pie finally tasted as good as it looked.

RASPBERRY CHIFFON PIE

SERVES 8

You can use Single-Crust Pie Dough (page 10) or Easy Press-In Single-Crust Pie Dough (page 11) for this pie. The most common brand of pectin we found at the market is Sure-Jell, but any brand will work. The raspberry-flavored gelatin is important for the color and flavor of the chiffon layer; do not substitute unflavored gelatin. Leftover pie should be refrigerated.

1   **recipe single-crust pie dough, fitted into a 9-inch pie plate and chilled (see note above)**

FRUIT

2	cups (10 ounces) frozen raspberries
3	tablespoons pectin (see note above)
1½	cups sugar
	Pinch salt
1	cup fresh raspberries

CHIFFON

3	tablespoons raspberry-flavored gelatin (see note above)
3	tablespoons boiling water
3	ounces cream cheese, softened
1	cup heavy cream, chilled

TOPPING

1¼	cups heavy cream, chilled
2	tablespoons sugar

1. Adjust an oven rack to the middle position and heat the oven to 375 degrees. Following the photos on page 30, line the chilled crust with a double layer of aluminum foil and fill with pie weights. Bake until the pie dough looks dry and is light in color, 25 to 30 minutes. Remove the weights and foil and continue to bake the crust until deep golden brown, 10 to 12 minutes longer. Let the crust cool on a wire rack to room temperature.

2. FOR THE FRUIT: Cook the frozen raspberries in a medium saucepan over medium-high heat, stirring occasionally, until the berries begin to release their juice, about 3 minutes. Stir in the pectin and bring to a boil, stirring constantly. Stir in the sugar and salt and continue to boil, stirring constantly, until slightly thickened, about 2 minutes. Strain the mixture through a fine-mesh strainer into a medium bowl, pressing on the solids to extract as much puree as possible; discard the solids.

3. Transfer ⅓ cup of the raspberry puree to a small bowl and cool to room temperature. Gently fold the fresh raspberries into the remaining puree, then spread the mixture in the cooled pie shell.

4. FOR THE CHIFFON: Dissolve the gelatin in the boiling water in a large bowl. Add the cream cheese and reserved ⅓ cup raspberry puree and beat with an electric mixer on high speed until smooth, about 2 minutes. Add the cream and beat on medium-low until incorporated, about 30 seconds. Increase the mixer speed to high and beat until very thick, 1 to 2 minutes. Spread the chiffon evenly in the pie crust on top of the fruit. Cover the pie loosely with plastic wrap and refrigerate until the filling is chilled and set, about 3 hours.

5. FOR THE TOPPING: Before serving, whip the cream and sugar together with an electric mixer on medium-low speed until frothy, about 1 minute. Increase the mixer speed to high and continue to whip until soft peaks form, 1 to 3 minutes. Spread the whipped cream over the chiffon and serve.

Variation
STRAWBERRY CHIFFON PIE

Substitute frozen strawberries for the frozen raspberries, fresh strawberries, hulled and quartered, for the fresh raspberries, and strawberry-flavored gelatin for the raspberry-flavored gelatin.

CRANBERRY-APPLE CRISP

CHAPTER TWO

Old-Fashioned Fruit Desserts and Puddings

Berry Shortcakes

The combination of sweet-tart berries, airy whipped cream, and tender biscuits in a berry shortcake is one of the highlights of summer. Sadly, however, this dessert rarely measures up. The shortcakes typically turn to mush the second the berries are added, rendering the dessert gummy and starchy. We wanted to make craggy, sweet shortcakes with a crumb sturdy enough to support juicy berries and a healthy garnish of billowy whipped cream.

Shortcakes are basically biscuit dough enriched with sugar and fat, usually in the form of eggs or something richer than the usual milk or buttermilk. This fat adds heft and structure, creating a slightly more cakey texture that's perfect for soaking up the juice from the berries. Starting with a basic baking-powder biscuit recipe, we enriched the dough with an egg and half-and-half (milk was too thin, cream too heavy). This provided the density and crumb that we were after, but the flavor was muted. A fellow test cook suggested we try sour cream in place of the half-and-half, and this gave the shortcakes just the savory, tangy kick we were looking for. Replacing the usual granulated sugar with brown sugar added a welcome caramel note.

Although these shortcakes now tasted much better, they were squat and gummy on the inside; once we added the sour cream, they lost their tender, pillowy texture. We tried adding more baking powder to improve the rise, but this just gave the shortcakes a chemical flavor. Getting frustrated, we were about to remove the sour cream from the recipe when we realized that we were still treating these shortcakes like biscuits. Up to this point, we had been carefully rolling out the dough and using a biscuit cutter to punch out the rounds. But this dough, enriched with egg and sour cream, was more similar to a muffin or cake than a biscuit. What if we skipped the rolling and cutting?

We turned the oven down to a more cake-friendly 375 degrees (biscuits are usually baked at 425 or 450 degrees) and used an ice-cream scoop to portion the dough directly from the mixing bowl onto a parchment-lined baking sheet. The large, domed scoops solved our squat shortcake problem, and the oven's moderate heat gave the shortcakes plenty of time to cook through, creating a craggy, rustic exterior and a moist, fluffy interior. For one last touch, we tried brushing the unbaked domes of dough with melted butter and sprinkling them with granulated sugar. The crunchy, crystallized topping added another layer of texture and flavor.

As for the berries, we mashed some with brown sugar (preferred over granulated sugar for its more complex flavor) to release their juice but kept most of them whole because we liked their tartness and texture. To tie everything together, we dolloped our berry shortcakes with a tangy whipped topping made from heavy cream, brown sugar (again, everyone liked its caramel flavor), and sour cream. We now had the perfect way to showcase full, ripe summer berries.

BROWN SUGAR BERRY SHORTCAKES
SERVES 6

Depending on the sweetness of the berries, you may have to use more or less brown sugar. The shortcakes can be made up to a day in advance and stored, wrapped in plastic wrap, at room temperature. If you don't have a large ice-cream scoop, divide the dough into 6 equal portions and use your hands to form shortcakes in a rough semispherical shape. If you don't have a food processor, you can prepare the shortcakes by hand: Freeze the stick of butter until hard and then grate it into the dry ingredients using the large holes of a box grater. Toss gently to distribute the butter evenly and proceed with

the recipe. Each berry is prepared according to its size and structure—raspberries, blueberries, and currants can remain whole, but blackberries should be halved and strawberries should be hulled, halved, and sliced thin.

FRUIT

6	cups mixed fresh berries (see note above)
4–6	tablespoons light brown sugar (see note above)

SHORTCAKES

2	cups all-purpose flour
3	tablespoons light brown sugar
1	tablespoon baking powder
½	teaspoon salt
8	tablespoons (1 stick) unsalted butter, cut into ½-inch pieces and chilled, plus 2 tablespoons, melted (for brushing on the shortcakes)
1	large egg
½	cup sour cream
2	tablespoons granulated sugar

TOPPING

1	cup heavy cream
¼	cup sour cream
¼	cup packed light brown sugar

1. FOR THE FRUIT: Mash 2 cups of the berries with the brown sugar in a large bowl with a potato masher. Fold in the remaining 4 cups berries and let sit at room temperature until the sugar has dissolved and the berries are juicy, about 30 minutes.

2. FOR THE SHORTCAKES: Adjust an oven rack to the upper-middle position and heat the oven to 375 degrees. Pulse the flour, brown sugar, baking powder, and salt together in a food processor until no lumps of sugar remain. Scatter the chilled butter

pieces over the top and pulse until the mixture resembles coarse sand, about 7 pulses. Transfer to a large bowl.

3. Whisk the egg and sour cream together in a small bowl. Stir the egg mixture into the flour mixture with a rubber spatula until large clumps form. Using your hands, knead lightly until the dough comes together and no dry flecks of flour remain.

4. Using a large (#10) ice-cream scoop, scoop 6 dough rounds onto a parchment-lined baking sheet. Brush the tops with the melted butter and sprinkle with the granulated sugar. Bake until golden brown, 25 to 30 minutes, rotating the baking sheet halfway through baking. Let the shortcakes cool on the baking sheet for 10 minutes.

5. FOR THE TOPPING: With an electric mixer on medium speed, beat the heavy cream, sour cream, and brown sugar together until stiff peaks form. Split each shortcake in half using a serrated knife and place the bottoms on individual plates. Spoon a portion of the fruit over the bottoms, top with some of the whipped cream, and cap with the shortcake tops. Serve.

Blueberry Grunt

"Grunt" might seem like a funny name for a dessert, but one bite of the hot, comforting Yankee concoction just may win you over. This oddly named dessert promises juicy berries topped with biscuitlike dumplings—and no need to turn on the oven. But the reality is more often than not a washed-out, bland berry mess under soggy, dense biscuits. Because grunt is made entirely on the stovetop—ideal when you want a speedy yet satisfying fresh berry dessert (no messy rolling and fitting of pie dough necessary)—we figured this old-fashioned recipe was worth updating.

During our research, we learned that most grunts start with stewing fresh berries in water, sugar, and cinnamon. The fruit mixture is then topped with dollops of drop-biscuit dough (flour, milk, melted butter, sugar, baking powder, and salt), the pot is covered, and the whole concoction is simmered on the stove until the dumplings are cooked through. We found versions of this recipe that dated back to the early 1800s, when the dessert was named for the sound the fruit made as it bubbled beneath the dumplings. While grunt can be made with any manner of fruit, blueberry grunt became especially popular in New England. We got some fresh blueberries and headed into the test kitchen, planning to start on the filling first.

Dense fruit fillings for pies and cobblers are usually thickened with tapioca or cornstarch, but grunt filling is traditionally looser—it uses no thickeners (and up to ½ cup of water is added) to create a soupy filling that soaks into the dumplings. Our tasters, however, thought the filling was bland and made the dumplings too soggy. Balking at tradition, we set out to thicken our filling.

We started by cooking down the berries (with sugar, cinnamon, lemon zest, and a small amount of water) to a jamlike consistency. This concentrated the flavor, but our tasters missed the texture of whole berries. As a compromise, we cooked down half of the berries until jammy, then stirred in the remaining berries before topping the mixture with the dumplings. We found that just a little cornstarch (1 teaspoon) further tightened the filling without making it too thick.

Now the dumplings were less soggy without the watery filling beneath them, but they were still a little bland and dense. Replacing the milk with buttermilk added a nice tang, and adding a bit of baking soda made the dumplings much lighter. Tasters

noticed another problem, though: the tops of the cooked dumplings were strangely soggy. The cause was condensation dripping from the inside of the pot lid. We knew we had to somehow absorb the condensation before it could wreak havoc on our dumplings. To do this, we simply placed a clean kitchen towel under the lid to take in the excess liquid. Problem solved.

For a final burst of flavor and crunch, we sprinkled cinnamon sugar on the cooked dumplings before serving. At last, we had a grunt that could be appreciated for more than just its funny name.

SECRETS TO GREAT GRUNT

1. Use a small ice-cream scoop to drop evenly sized balls of dough over the warm filling.

2. Wrapping a kitchen towel around the lid of the pot helps to absorb condensation, keeping the dumplings light and fluffy.

3. Sprinkling cinnamon sugar over the top adds a crunchy contrast to the steamed dumplings.

BLUEBERRY GRUNT

SERVES 12

Do not use frozen blueberries here, as they will make the filling watery.

FILLING

8	cups fresh blueberries
½	cup sugar
2	tablespoons water
1	teaspoon grated fresh lemon zest and 1 tablespoon fresh lemon juice
½	teaspoon ground cinnamon
1	teaspoon cornstarch

TOPPING

¾	cup buttermilk
6	tablespoons (¾ stick) unsalted butter, melted and cooled
1	teaspoon vanilla extract
2¼	cups all-purpose flour
½	cup sugar
1½	teaspoons baking powder
½	teaspoon baking soda
½	teaspoon salt
½	teaspoon ground cinnamon

1. FOR THE FILLING: Cook 4 cups of the blueberries, sugar, water, lemon zest, and cinnamon in a Dutch oven over medium-high heat, stirring occasionally, until the mixture is thick and jam-like, 10 to 12 minutes. Whisk the lemon juice and cornstarch together in a small bowl, then stir into the blueberry mixture. Add the remaining 4 cups blueberries and cook until heated through, about 1 minute. Remove the pot from the heat, cover, and keep warm.

2. FOR THE TOPPING: Combine the buttermilk, butter, and vanilla in a measuring cup. Whisk the flour, 6 tablespoons of the sugar, baking powder,

baking soda, and salt together in a large bowl. Slowly stir the buttermilk mixture into the flour mixture until a dough forms.

3. Using a small ice-cream scoop or 2 large spoons, spoon golf ball–size dumplings on top of the warm berry mixture (you should have 14 dumplings). Wrap the lid of the Dutch oven with a clean kitchen towel (keeping the towel away from the heat source) and cover the pot. Simmer gently until the dumplings have doubled in size and a toothpick inserted into the center comes out clean, 16 to 22 minutes.

4. Combine the remaining 2 tablespoons sugar and cinnamon in a small bowl. Remove the lid and sprinkle the cinnamon sugar over the dumplings. Serve immediately.

Peach Brown Betty

Although pies and crisps seem to hog the stage when it comes to baked fruit desserts, the less common brown betty deserves a second look. This super-simple homey sweet is made by layering slices of fruit and buttery bread crumbs in a deep dish and baking them until the fruit is tender and the crumb topping is crisp. Apples are the usual star of brown betty, but we wanted something different (apples get enough attention as it is) and thought juicy, ripe peaches would make for a brightly flavored yet still old-fashioned dessert.

We knew that what makes ripe, in-season peaches so satisfying—that rich juice that drips off the chin when enjoying the fruit out of hand—would make our betty too watery if we weren't careful. We tried the usual tactics for dealing with excess fruit juice but didn't have much luck. Adding cornstarch or flour to the peaches dulled their flavor. Tossing the peaches with sugar to draw out their liquid and draining them worked but took about an hour, more time than we were willing to devote to what should be an uncomplicated dessert. Casting about for another solution, we thought maybe easiest would prove best and simply precooked the peaches in a skillet. As fast as they released their juice into the pan, the juice evaporated. Even better, the natural sugars began to deepen and caramelize, intensifying the peach flavor. We wondered if sprinkling in more sugar would magnify the effect. It did just that. In fact, without constant stirring, the juice on the bottom of the skillet began to scorch. So we opted to wait until after the sauté to add sugar (white for pure sweetness, brown for deeper flavor).

Although brown betty is usually made in a baking dish, we thought our large skillet would work just as nicely (and cut down on extra dishes). We sprinkled fresh bread crumbs over the fruit and put the skillet into the oven to brown them. However, when we pulled the pan out of the oven, we found the topping had drowned in the bubbling juice, rendering a mushy, bland mess. We had to find a way to get rid of the moisture released by the peaches during baking and decided to stir in a portion of the bread crumbs to absorb the liquid. Happily, the filling thickened nicely. To brighten the flavor, we added a little lemon juice; a splash of vanilla extract brought the flavor of the peaches into focus.

Now, with the peach juice reined in, the topping was dry enough to turn golden brown, but it still wasn't crisp enough for contrast with the tender peaches. A sprinkling of cinnamon sugar improved the situation slightly, but it was clear we had to revisit the bread-crumb situation. Up to this point, we'd been tossing fresh bread crumbs (made in the food processor) with melted butter. We tried using dried crumbs, but they were too fine and sank into the peaches in seconds. Toasting the fresh crumbs first made the topping too dark and the filling too dry. Going back to untoasted bread crumbs, we wondered if the melted butter was weighing them down. Next time around, we processed the crumbs with cold butter, stirred some of the coarse, shaggy mixture into the peaches and sprinkled the rest on top, then placed our betty in the oven. About a half-hour and one

PEELING PEACHES

1. With a paring knife, score a small X at the base of each peach.

2. Lower the peaches into boiling water and simmer until the skins loosen, 30 to 60 seconds.

3. Transfer the peaches immediately to ice water and let cool for about 1 minute.

4. Use a paring knife to remove strips of loosened peel, starting at the X on the base of each peach.

bowl of Peach Brown Betty later, tasters were thrilled—our super-crisp topping was a suitable match for the juicy, fragrant peach filling.

PEACH BROWN BETTY

SERVES 6

You can substitute 3 pounds of thawed and drained frozen sliced peaches for fresh peaches. If you don't have an ovensafe skillet, transfer the peach filling to a 2-quart baking dish at the end of step 2 and continue with the recipe as directed.

TOPPING

4	slices high-quality white sandwich bread, torn into quarters
5	tablespoons unsalted butter, cut into ½-inch pieces and chilled
1	tablespoon granulated sugar
¼	teaspoon ground cinnamon

FILLING

2	tablespoons unsalted butter
3½	pounds peaches, peeled (see page 57), pitted, and sliced ½ inch thick (see note above)
⅓	cup granulated sugar
⅓	cup packed light brown sugar
1	tablespoon fresh lemon juice
1	teaspoon vanilla extract
⅛	teaspoon salt

1. FOR THE TOPPING: Adjust an oven rack to the middle position and heat the oven to 400 degrees. Pulse the bread and butter in a food processor until coarsely ground and set aside. Combine the sugar and cinnamon in a small bowl.

2. FOR THE FILLING: Melt the butter in a large nonstick ovensafe skillet over medium-high heat.

BUILDING A BETTER BROWN BETTY

1. Pulse the bread with chilled butter in a food processor for fluffy, crisp crumbs.

2. After caramelizing the peaches, stir in some crumbs to absorb excess juice and to support the topping.

3. Sprinkle the remaining crumbs on top, sprinkle with the cinnamon sugar, and bake so the top can brown and crisp.

Cook the peaches, stirring occasionally, until they begin to caramelize, 8 to 12 minutes. Off the heat, stir in 1 cup of the bread-crumb mixture, granulated sugar, brown sugar, lemon juice, vanilla, and salt.

3. Top the peach mixture with the remaining bread-crumb mixture. Sprinkle with the cinnamon sugar and bake until the topping is golden brown and the juice is bubbling, 20 to 25 minutes. Let cool for 10 minutes. Serve warm.

Baked Apple Dumplings

Apple dumplings, with their tender pastry, concentrated apple flavor, and warm spice notes, are the perfect ending to dinner on a cool autumn evening. But although these homespun treats used to make frequent appearances on farmhouse tables across the country, they seem to have fallen out of favor. Sure, they're relatively easy to make (you're basically wrapping dough around an apple), but they can also easily go awry. Potential pitfalls include crunchy apples inside overcooked crusts, apples that turn to mush, gummy dough, and soggy bottoms. We wanted to bring back this American classic and see if we could improve on tradition.

Many recipes take a shortcut and utilize store-bought pie dough. While store-bought dough might be acceptable in a pie, where the filling is the star, it was a letdown in dumplings. There was no question about it: we'd be making our own dough. Our first real decision, then, was pie dough versus biscuit dough. We tried pie dough first, but the raw dough tore, and baking ruptured it at the seams and sent it sliding down the side of the fruit. Meanwhile, steam from the baking apple had turned the dough gluey.

Moving on to biscuit dough, we started with a basic recipe that included both butter (for flavor) and shortening (for tenderness). We gradually increased the amounts of both from 8 tablespoons of butter and 4 tablespoons of shortening to 10 tablespoons and 5 tablespoons, respectively. Mixed with 2½ cups of flour, 2 teaspoons of baking powder, and ¾ cup of buttermilk, the butter and shortening yielded a sturdy yet tender dough that was easy to wrap around the apples. Baked in a 425-degree oven, this dough formed tender, fluffy

biscuits that absorbed the apples' juice and a bottom crust that was crisp. Unfortunately, so were the apples.

We'd been using Granny Smiths, because the test kitchen likes them for baking. We couldn't be sure if they were to blame, but either way, tasters complained they were too tart. After a series of tests, tasters picked sweeter Golden Delicious apples, which held up during baking. In fact, they held up too well—they were still crisp.

Another complaint our tasters had was that the individual servings were too large (a dessert complaint we don't hear too often). We hit on the notion of cutting the apples in half—this move, we hoped, would give us cooked-through dumplings that were a reasonable size. We seeded and cored the apple halves and filled the hollows with cinnamon sugar, raisins, and butter. We wrapped each half, cut a hole in the top to let steam escape, brushed the dumplings with beaten egg white, and sprinkled them with more cinnamon sugar for a crisp, browned topping.

Twenty-five minutes later, after the apple juice had started to bubble and the kitchen smelled fantastic, we pulled the dumplings from the oven. The apples were tender, the biscuits tender and buttery, and tasters could even finish a serving. Drizzled with a simple apple cider sauce, our old-fashioned dumplings are sure to be a welcome addition to the modern-day dinner table.

BAKED APPLE DUMPLINGS

SERVES 8

Use a melon baller or a metal teaspoon to core the apples. We like to serve the dumplings warm with vanilla ice cream and Cider Sauce (recipe follows). For sweet apples, we recommend Golden Delicious, Braeburn, and Gala.

DOUGH

2½	cups all-purpose flour
3	tablespoons sugar
2	teaspoons baking powder
¾	teaspoon salt
10	tablespoons (1¼ sticks) unsalted butter, cut into ½-inch pieces and chilled
5	tablespoons vegetable shortening, cut into ½-inch pieces and chilled
¾	cup buttermilk, chilled

DUMPLINGS

6	tablespoons sugar
1	teaspoon ground cinnamon
3	tablespoons unsalted butter, softened
3	tablespoons golden raisins, chopped
4	firm sweet apples (see note above)
2	egg whites, lightly beaten

1. FOR THE DOUGH: Process the flour, sugar, baking powder, and salt together in a food processor until combined. Scatter the butter and shortening over the top and pulse until the mixture resembles wet sand. Transfer to a bowl and stir in the buttermilk until a dough forms. Turn out onto a lightly floured work surface and knead briefly until the dough is cohesive. Press the dough into an 8 by 4-inch rectangle. Cut the dough in half, wrap each half tightly in plastic wrap, and refrigerate until firm, about 1 hour.

2. FOR THE DUMPLINGS: Adjust an oven rack to the middle position and heat the oven to 425 degrees. Combine the sugar and cinnamon in a small bowl. In a second bowl, combine the butter, raisins, and 3 tablespoons of the cinnamon sugar. Peel the apples and halve them through the equator. Following the photos, remove the core and divide the butter mixture among the apple halves.

3. On a lightly floured work surface, roll each dough half into a 12-inch square. Cut each 12-inch square into four 6-inch squares. Working with one at a time, lightly brush the edges of each dough square with the egg white and place one apple half, cut side up, in the center of each square. Gather the dough one corner at a time on top of the apple and crimp the edges to seal. Using a paring knife, cut vent holes in the top of each dumpling.

MAKING APPLE DUMPLINGS

1. Scoop out the core and seeds, taking care not to pierce the bottoms of the apple halves.

2. Divide the butter mixture among the apple halves, filling the hollows.

3. Fold the corners of the dough up to enclose the apple halves, overlapping and crimping to seal.

4. Arrange the dumplings on a parchment-lined baking sheet, brush with the egg white, and sprinkle with the cinnamon sugar.

4. Arrange the dumplings on a parchment-lined baking sheet, brush the tops with the egg white, and sprinkle with the remaining cinnamon sugar. Bake until the dough is golden brown and the juice is bubbling, 20 to 25 minutes. Let the dumplings cool on the baking sheet for 10 minutes. Serve.

CIDER SAUCE

MAKES ABOUT 1½ CUPS

This sauce can be made up to 2 days in advance; reduce the cider mixture as directed, then refrigerate it in an airtight container. When ready to serve, return the mixture to a simmer and whisk in the butter and lemon juice off the heat.

1	cup apple cider
1	cup water
1	cup sugar
½	teaspoon ground cinnamon
2	tablespoons unsalted butter
1	tablespoon fresh lemon juice

Bring the cider, water, sugar, and cinnamon to a simmer in a saucepan and cook over medium-high heat until thickened and reduced to 1½ cups, about 15 minutes. Off the heat, whisk in the butter and lemon juice.

Cranberry-Apple Crisp

We love a warm bowl of apple crisp, topped with a scoop of vanilla ice cream, but thought we could improve upon this dessert by adding sweet-tart cranberries. In spite of our enthusiasm, we soon had doubts. Our crisp had no balance of flavors; one bite tasted super-tart and overloaded with cranberries, and the next tasted of apples, with no cranberry flavor at all. Also, the soggy topping was not crisp at all. We had our work cut out for us.

At the start, we ran across a crisp recipe that called for canned cranberry sauce. The idea of using canned cranberries when our supermarket was overflowing with bags of fresh berries seemed ridiculous, but what if we made our own cranberry sauce with fresh cranberries? That way we could get even cranberry distribution (a sauce would be easy to stir into the apples) and sweeten the cranberries before they met the apples.

We cooked fresh cranberries with sugar and a little water until they burst and thickened into a homemade sauce. We then added the mixture to diced Granny Smith apples and topped the fruit with the classic combination of butter, flour, sugar, cinnamon, and oats.

After an hour and a half in the oven, when the fruit juices started to bubble up from underneath, we thought we had a winner. The scarlet filling looked like it was packed with cranberry flavor, but it actually tasted pretty dull and the consistency was soupy.

A colleague suggested that dried cranberries might be the answer to deeper cranberry flavor. Adding a cup of dried berries gave our crisp a one-two punch of concentrated cranberry flavor and added a welcome textural hit that tasters loved. And as the dried berries rehydrated, they absorbed some of the excess juices, making for a drier topping. Adding some tapioca to the filling (better than either flour or cornstarch) also helped to thicken the fruit juices.

Now that we had the berries sorted out, we took another look at the apples. We liked the way Granny Smiths held their shape in the oven, but our tasters thought they were awfully tart in the crisp. To get a better balance of flavors, we tried combining the Grannies with sweeter apples like Gala, Golden Delicious, Red Delicious, and Braeburn. The Braeburns were tasters' favorite, followed by Golden Delicious.

The crisp was taking nearly 90 minutes to bake. Any less time and the apples were too firm, but in 90 minutes the topping turned almost as hard as a stale granola bar. Since we were already dirtying a pot to make the cranberry sauce, we thought we'd use the same pot to jump-start the apples on the stovetop. Just 5 minutes of stovetop cooking was all it took to reduce the baking time from 90 to 30 minutes. The apples now cooked evenly in the baking dish and the topping was no longer a dark, hard shell.

After peeling our way through bushels of apples and puckering up to pounds of cranberries, we had finally found the path to perfect cranberry-apple crisp.

CRANBERRY-APPLE CRISP

SERVES 12

If you can't find Braeburn apples, Golden Delicious will work. Serve with vanilla ice cream or whipped cream.

TOPPING

- ¾ cup all-purpose flour
- 12 tablespoons (1½ sticks) unsalted butter, cut into ½-inch pieces and chilled
- ½ cup packed light brown sugar
- ½ cup granulated sugar
- 1 teaspoon ground cinnamon
- ¾ cup old-fashioned oats

FILLING

- 1 pound fresh or frozen cranberries (about 4 cups)
- 1¼ cups granulated sugar
- ¼ cup water
- 2½ pounds Granny Smith apples (5 to 7 apples), peeled, cored, and cut into ½-inch pieces

- 2½ pounds Braeburn apples (5 to 7 apples; see note above), peeled, cored, and cut into ½-inch pieces
- 1 cup dried sweetened cranberries
- 3 tablespoons Minute tapioca

1. FOR THE TOPPING: Adjust an oven rack to the middle position and heat the oven to 400 degrees. Pulse the flour, butter, brown sugar, granulated sugar, and cinnamon together in a food processor until coarse crumbs form (some pea-size pieces of butter will remain), about 10 pulses. Transfer to a medium bowl, stir in the oats, and, using your fingers, pinch the topping into peanut-size clumps. Refrigerate while preparing the filling.

2. FOR THE FILLING: Bring the cranberries, ¾ cup of the sugar, and water to a simmer in a Dutch oven over medium-high heat and cook until the cranberries are completely softened and the mixture is jamlike, about 10 minutes. Scrape the mixture into a bowl. Add the apples, dried cranberries, and remaining ½ cup sugar to the Dutch oven and cook over medium-high heat until the apples begin to release their juice, about 5 minutes.

3. Off the heat, stir the cranberry mixture and tapioca into the apple mixture. Pour into a 13 by 9-inch baking dish set on a rimmed baking sheet and smooth the surface.

4. Scatter the topping evenly over the filling and bake until the juices are bubbling and the topping is a deep golden brown, about 30 minutes. (If the topping is browning too quickly, loosely cover with a piece of aluminum foil.) Let cool on a wire rack. Serve warm.

Banana Pudding

In the early 1900s, English trifle took a detour; it jumped the pond and morphed into banana pudding, with cookies and bananas replacing the cake and jam. Today, banana pudding is on the menu of almost every Southern diner and barbecue joint, and it's even starting to gain some ground in the national restaurant arena. It's easy to see why creamy, sweet, cold, and fruity banana pudding is so popular. And making it couldn't be easier: vanilla pudding is layered with sliced bananas and vanilla wafers. However, bad banana pudding is a nightmare—the banana slices turn brown and slimy, the cookies are soggy, and the pudding itself is bland or overly sweet. Not to mention that the whole shebang can be totally lacking in banana flavor. We wanted a banana pudding that avoided these problems and, most important, put the banana back into banana pudding.

We tested a half-dozen recipes that ranged from the gourmet—using bourbon and homemade praline—to the pedestrian—involving instant vanilla pudding and Cool Whip. Most homemade puddings were made with the standard method: gently cooking custards of milk or half-and-half, sugar, egg yolks, cornstarch, and flavorings. Then the puddings were passed through a fine-mesh strainer to make them silky smooth and the desserts were assembled, using either crushed cookies or whole cookies, and refrigerated overnight. We decided right away to use half-and-half, not milk, for more richness and creaminess. Also, real whipped cream was in, and the fake stuff was out. Finally, since the crushed cookies disintegrated in the pudding, we'd use whole ones.

We knew that to combine the bananas with the pudding, we'd have to cook them first so they'd break down. We sautéed them in butter and sugar, pureed them, and stirred them into the pudding.

This version tasted great. But though the bananas were soft in the skillet, they never broke down entirely, so the pudding was mealy. We tried steaming the bananas in the microwave; this fixed the texture but the flavor wasn't as deep or rich as when we had cooked the bananas on the stovetop.

Finally, we tried roasting, which intensifies the flavors and sugars of fruits. We put the bananas in a 325-degree oven until their skins turned black (this took about 20 minutes), then placed the peeled bananas in the food processor. It occurred to us that we could go ahead and process the vanilla pudding right in there with the bananas and skip the cumbersome step of pushing the pudding through the fine-mesh strainer.

We layered the banana pudding with wafers and refrigerated it. The next day, we looked at it in horror: the pudding had turned an ugly beige because the bananas had oxidized. In our next test, we added a squeeze of lemon juice to the pudding; this minimized the browning and at the same time brightened and lightened the rich, sweet pudding. For more banana flavor, we sliced extra bananas into the pudding.

It was time to turn to the cookies, which were still sodden and pasty. Sure, the cookies would soften somewhat after being covered by the pudding, but we didn't want them to be mushy and fall apart in the finished dessert. To fix that, we first tried using stale cookies, and next crisping fresh cookies in the oven. Neither version succeeded. After a few more tests, we realized that it was the hot pudding that was causing the cookies to turn sodden. To prevent the mushiness, all we had to do was cool the pudding before constructing the layers—problem solved.

Finally, we did a series of tests on the pudding-to-cookie ratio; tasters weren't satisfied until we were using an entire box of wafers, double the number called for in a typical recipe. We carefully assembled

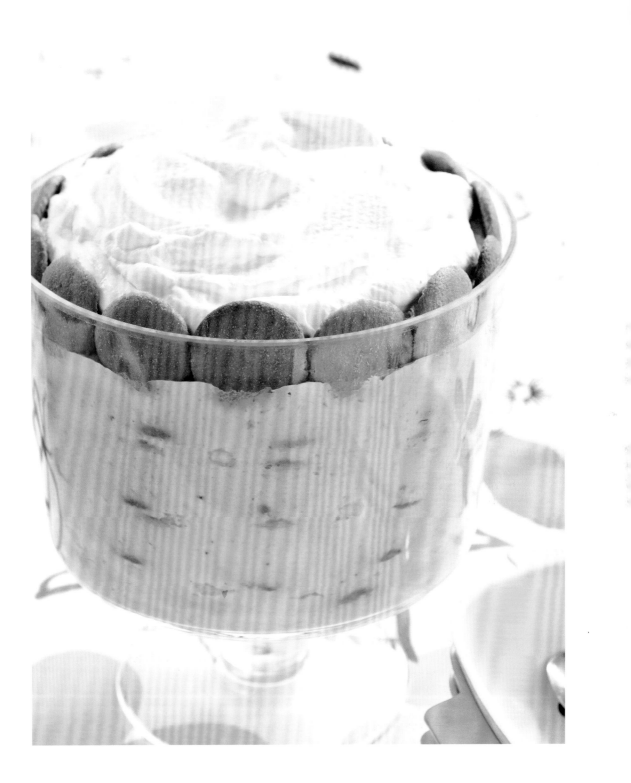

the dessert and left this banana pudding to chill overnight. The next day, we sampled the pudding. With a dollop of whipped cream on top, this was undeniably the best banana pudding we'd ever had.

BANANA PUDDING

SERVES 12

If your food processor bowl holds less than 11 cups, puree half of the pudding with the roasted bananas and lemon juice in step 3, transfer the puree to a large bowl, and whisk in the rest of the pudding.

PUDDING

7	slightly underripe large bananas
1½	cups sugar
8	large egg yolks
6	tablespoons cornstarch
6	cups half-and-half
½	teaspoon salt
3	tablespoons unsalted butter
1	tablespoon vanilla extract
3	tablespoons fresh lemon juice
1	(12-ounce) box vanilla wafers

TOPPING

1	cup heavy cream, chilled
1	tablespoon sugar
½	teaspoon vanilla extract

1. FOR THE PUDDING: Adjust an oven rack to the upper-middle position and heat the oven to 325 degrees. Place 3 unpeeled bananas on a baking sheet and bake until the skins are completely black, about 20 minutes. Let cool for 5 minutes.

2. Meanwhile, whisk together ½ cup of the sugar, egg yolks, and cornstarch in a medium bowl until smooth. Bring the half-and-half, remaining 1 cup sugar, and salt to a simmer over medium heat in a large saucepan. Whisk ½ cup of the simmering

half-and-half mixture into the egg yolk mixture to temper. Slowly whisk the egg yolk mixture into the saucepan. Cook, whisking constantly, until the mixture is thick and large bubbles appear on the surface, about 2 minutes. Off the heat, stir in the butter and vanilla.

3. Transfer the pudding to a food processor. Peel the roasted bananas, add them to the food processor with 2 tablespoons of the lemon juice, and process until smooth. Scrape the pudding into a large bowl and press plastic wrap directly onto the surface of the pudding. Refrigerate until slightly cool, about 45 minutes.

4. Cut the remaining 4 bananas into ¼-inch slices and toss with the remaining 1 tablespoon lemon juice. Spoon one-quarter of the pudding into a 3-quart trifle dish and top with a layer of cookies, a layer of sliced bananas, and another layer of cookies. Repeat twice more, ending with the pudding. Press plastic wrap directly onto the surface of the pudding and refrigerate until the cookies have softened, at least 8 hours or up to 2 days.

5. FOR THE TOPPING: With an electric mixer on medium speed, beat the cream, sugar, and vanilla until stiff peaks form, about 2 minutes. (The whipped cream can be refrigerated for up to 4 hours.) Top the banana pudding with the whipped cream. Serve.

Variations
TOASTED COCONUT–BANANA PUDDING

Substitute 1 (16-ounce) can coconut milk for 2 cups of the half-and-half. Sprinkle ¼ cup sweetened shredded coconut, toasted (see page 212), over the whipped cream–topped pudding before serving.

PEANUTTY BANANA PUDDING

In step 4, make cookie sandwiches by placing 1 banana slice and ½ teaspoon creamy peanut butter between 2 vanilla wafers (you'll need ½ cup peanut butter to make about 50 cookie sandwiches). Assemble the pudding by alternating layers of pudding and peanut butter–banana sandwiches, ending with the pudding. Sprinkle ¼ cup chopped salted dry-roasted peanuts over the whipped cream–topped pudding before serving.

New Orleans Bourbon Bread Pudding

The best bourbon bread pudding is a rich, scoopable custard that envelops the bread with a perfect balance of sweet spiciness and musky bourbon flavor. The history behind New Orleans's most famous dessert is as eclectic as the city itself. The basic custard and bread combination is of English origin. The bread—which in New Orleans is almost always a baguette—is from France. The addition of raisins to the custard can be credited to German settlers, and it was the Irish who infused the cream base with various liquors. The bourbon, of course, originally came from Kentucky traders.

We began our tests by preparing and sampling a number of published recipes—all were awful. We, along with tasters, encountered a wide range of problems, from harsh bourbon flavor to curdled eggs to rock-hard raisins to slimy bread swimming in a river of custard. These bread puddings were nothing like our New Orleans ideal.

In some recipes the bread was cubed and staled overnight, but these bread puddings looked more like the cobblestone streets in the French Quarter than something we'd like to eat for dessert. We wanted a more rustic look and had much

THE AMERICAN TABLE
THE HISTORY OF BOURBON

How did Kentucky bourbon (the name given to whiskey distilled from at least 51 percent corn) end up playing such an important role in New Orleans's signature dessert? Right after the Revolutionary War, settlers in what eventually became Kentucky planted significant amounts of corn. Because there weren't many passable roads on which to transport this much grain back over the mountains to populated areas along the East Coast, many farmers distilled their crop to make whiskey. Bottles were packed in crates (stamped with the words Old Bourbon, after the region of Kentucky where this liquor was produced) and shipped down the Ohio and Mississippi rivers to New Orleans and, eventually, the rest of the world.

better results tearing the baguette into ragged pieces. Toasting the torn pieces to a deep golden brown enriched their flavor and gave the bread a crispness that helped to prevent the finished dish from turning soggy.

We found a ratio of 1 egg to ½ cup dairy worked well when it came to the composition of the custard and decided that a mixture of 3 parts cream to 1 part milk was rich but not over the top. Tasters preferred the caramel flavor of brown sugar (rather than the usual white sugar) to sweeten the custard. Now it was time to tackle the most problematic aspect of our bread pudding: the curdling custard.

Setting the baking dish with the pudding in a roasting pan filled with hot water (called a water bath) was one way to moderate the oven heat and keep the eggs from curdling, but this method is quite cumbersome for a simple recipe born out of the desire to use up day-old bread. We found that replacing the traditional whole eggs with just egg yolks helped stave off curdling. (We later found out that's because the whites set faster than the yolks.) Also helpful in curdle-proofing the pudding was lowering the oven temperature (to 300 degrees).

Our bread pudding was now plenty rich and creamy (and not curdled), but tasters wanted some contrast in texture. Taking inspiration from our Blueberry Grunt (page 56) and Peach Brown Betty (page 58), in which cinnamon and sugar are sprinkled on top to form a crunchy topping, we adapted this idea for our bread pudding. Once the custard had set up in the oven, we added cinnamon, sugar, and some butter and let the pudding bake for another 20 minutes. Now the topping caramelized and formed a golden crust. To protect the bread pudding from drying out, we simply covered it with foil until we sprinkled the cinnamon-sugar mixture on top, then baked it uncovered the rest of the time.

Last, we addressed the bourbon in our pudding. There's no doubt that bourbon bread pudding is an adult dessert. It should have enough robust bourbon flavor to warm you up, but not so much that it knocks you down. One-half cup to plump the raisins (which solved the rock-hard raisin problem from earlier tests) and another ¼ cup in the custard gave our bread pudding just enough bourbon punch. And for a real taste of New Orleans, we drizzled servings of the pudding with a warm bourbon-based cream sauce.

NEW ORLEANS BOURBON BREAD PUDDING

SERVES 8 TO 10

A French baguette from a bakery rather than the supermarket makes this pudding even better.

PUDDING

1	(18- to 20-inch) French baguette, torn into 1-inch pieces (about 10 cups)
1	cup golden raisins
¾	cup bourbon
8	large egg yolks

SECRETS TO NEW ORLEANS BOURBON BREAD PUDDING

1. Toasting the torn French baguette enhances its flavor and texture.

2. Soaking the bread for 30 minutes in the custard softens the bread without turning it soggy.

3. Covering the bread pudding with aluminum foil allows the custard to set without drying out.

4. Sprinkling the half-baked pudding with a sugary topping adds a crisp crust.

1½	cups packed light brown sugar
3	cups heavy cream
1	cup whole milk
1	tablespoon vanilla extract
1½	teaspoons ground cinnamon
¼	teaspoon ground nutmeg
¼	teaspoon salt
3	tablespoons granulated sugar
6	tablespoons (¾ stick) unsalted butter, cut into ¼-inch pieces and chilled

SAUCE

1½	teaspoons cornstarch
¼	cup bourbon
¾	cup heavy cream
2	tablespoons granulated sugar
2	teaspoons unsalted butter, cut into ¼-inch pieces
	Pinch salt

1. FOR THE PUDDING: Adjust an oven rack to the middle position and heat the oven to 450 degrees. Arrange the bread in a single layer on a baking sheet and bake, stirring occasionally, until golden and crisp, about 12 minutes, rotating the baking sheet halfway through baking. Let the bread cool. Reduce the oven temperature to 300 degrees. Grease a 13 by 9-inch baking pan.

2. Meanwhile, heat the raisins with ½ cup of the bourbon in a small saucepan over medium-high heat until the bourbon begins to simmer, 2 to 3 minutes. Strain the mixture over a bowl, reserving the bourbon and raisins separately.

3. Whisk the egg yolks, brown sugar, cream, milk, vanilla, 1 teaspoon of the cinnamon, nutmeg, and salt together in a large bowl. Whisk in the

remaining ¼ cup bourbon and the bourbon used to plump the raisins. Fold in the toasted bread until evenly coated. Let the mixture sit until the bread begins to absorb the custard, about 30 minutes, tossing occasionally. (If the majority of the bread is still hard when squeezed, soak for another 15 to 20 minutes.)

4. Pour half of the bread mixture into the prepared baking pan and sprinkle with half of the reserved raisins. Pour the remaining bread mixture into the pan and sprinkle with the remaining raisins. Cover with aluminum foil and bake for 45 minutes.

5. Meanwhile, mix the granulated sugar and the remaining ½ teaspoon cinnamon in a small bowl. Using your fingers, combine the butter and cinnamon sugar until the mixture is the size of small peas. Remove the foil from the pudding, sprinkle with the butter mixture, and bake the pudding, uncovered, until the custard is just set, 20 to 25 minutes. Increase the oven temperature to 450 degrees and bake until the top of the pudding forms a golden crust, about 2 minutes. Transfer the pudding to a wire rack and let cool for at least 30 minutes or up to 2 hours.

6. FOR THE SAUCE: Meanwhile, whisk the cornstarch and 2 tablespoons of the bourbon together in a small bowl. Heat the cream and granulated sugar in a small saucepan over medium heat until the sugar dissolves. Whisk in the cornstarch mixture and bring to a boil. Reduce the heat to low and cook until the sauce thickens, 3 to 5 minutes. Off the heat, stir in the remaining 2 tablespoons bourbon, butter, and salt. Drizzle the warm sauce over individual servings of the bread pudding.

Chocolate Bread Pudding

The simplest versions of bread pudding consist of stale or toasted bread soaked in a mixture of eggs, sugar, and dairy (cream or milk) and baked. Adding chocolate to bread pudding sounds like a winning proposition, but the reality isn't always so rosy, with the resulting dessert often lacking in deep chocolaty flavor and richness.

We tested a number of recipes uncovered in our research and had a hard time deciding which one was the best of the bunch (they were all horrible). Recipes in which cocoa powder was simply stirred into the custard base were pale and lacking chocolate punch. Recipes with melted chocolate tasted better, but the dense chocolate thickened the base so it never fully permeated the bread, making for bland, dry bread cubes suspended in chocolate custard.

We started from scratch with a basic bread pudding recipe. We soaked cubed, toasted white sandwich bread in a custard base of egg yolks, heavy cream, milk, and sugar. For fully developed chocolate flavor, we used both cocoa powder and melted chocolate; Dutch-processed cocoa gave the mixture a good foundation of chocolate flavor and melted semisweet chocolate (preferred over too-sweet milk chocolate) added richness. Just a tablespoon of instant espresso powder enhanced the chocolate flavor without being identifiable on its own.

The first thing we noticed about this bread pudding was that the sandwich bread was a little light for the chocolaty custard; for the next test, we used toasted challah, a richer bread that suited the chocolate base better.

Now we were having issues with the base. While it definitely tasted chocolaty, it was so thick that it wasn't fully soaking into the bread. To thin it, we made a batch without the melted chocolate (which we would add back later) and were happy to find that the base now soaked through the toasted challah more efficiently. To further loosen the liquid, we removed the egg yolks (again, we'd add them back later) from the soaking mixture, which was now just cream, milk, cocoa, espresso powder, and sugar. Without the yolks, we could heat the mixture to better dissolve the cocoa and sugar and to promote a deeper soak.

With the bread cubes fully saturated with the hot cocoa powder mixture, we could combine the egg yolks and melted chocolate with more cream and sugar to make a rich chocolate custard for the bread pudding. We poured this thick mixture over the soaked bread and baked the pudding in a gentle 325-degree oven for 45 minutes. When it came out of the oven, it smelled incredible. To make it even more tempting, we drizzled a little reserved chocolate sauce (just melted chocolate and cream) over the warm bread pudding. Judging from the way our tasters enthusiastically crowded around for seconds, we knew that this chocolate bread pudding recipe was a winner.

CHOCOLATE BREAD PUDDING

SERVES 10 TO 12

Challah can be found in most bakeries and many supermarkets. It is important to use Dutch-processed cocoa in this recipe. Natural cocoa will make the bread pudding too bitter.

1	(12-inch) loaf challah, cut into ½-inch cubes (about 12 cups) (see note above)
4	cups heavy cream
2	cups whole milk
1	cup sugar
½	cup Dutch-processed cocoa powder (see note above)
1	tablespoon instant espresso powder
8	ounces semisweet chocolate, chopped
10	large egg yolks

1. Adjust an oven rack to the middle position and heat the oven to 300 degrees. Arrange the bread in a single layer on a baking sheet and bake, stirring occasionally, until golden and crisp, about 30 minutes, rotating the baking sheet halfway through baking. Let the bread cool and transfer to a large bowl. Increase the oven temperature to 325 degrees.

2. Grease a 13 by 9-inch baking pan. Heat 1½ cups of the cream, milk, ½ cup of the sugar, cocoa, and espresso powder in a saucepan over medium-high heat, stirring occasionally, until steaming and the sugar dissolves. Pour the warm cream mixture over the toasted bread and let sit, tossing occasionally, until the liquid has been absorbed, about 10 minutes.

3. Meanwhile, bring 1 cup more cream to a simmer in a saucepan over medium-high heat. Off the heat, stir in the chocolate until smooth. Transfer 1 cup of the chocolate mixture to a medium bowl and let cool for 5 minutes; cover the remaining chocolate mixture and reserve for serving. Add the egg yolks, remaining 1½ cups cream, and remaining ½ cup sugar to the bowl with the chocolate mixture and whisk to combine.

4. Pour the bread mixture into the prepared pan and pour the chocolate custard mixture evenly over the top. Bake until the custard is just set and the surface is slightly crisp, about 45 minutes. Let cool for 30 minutes. Warm the reserved chocolate mixture over low heat, then pour over the bread pudding and serve.

Caramel Bread Pudding

With its soft, creamy interior and slightly crunchy crust, bread pudding seemed like it would be the perfect match for the rich, luscious flavor of caramel. We hoped that we could introduce caramel flavor by simply adding store-bought caramel sauce to the egg custard, but that made the custard too heavy. Worse, the custard was so sweet that the caramel flavor was barely detectable. We wanted the whole package—silky interior, crisp top, and deep caramel flavor throughout—and we had a long way to go to get there.

We started with the bread. Tasters thought French bread was too chewy for this pudding, and challah and brioche were too rich. White sandwich bread (dried in the oven so it would absorb more custard) was preferred for its light texture and mild flavor. As for the custard, taking the sugar out of the recipe and relying on the caramel sauce to sweeten the pudding was a step in the right direction, but the egg yolks were muting the flavor of the caramel sauce. We switched to whole eggs, which lightened the custard enough to allow more of the caramel flavor to come through. At the same time, we also decided to streamline things and replace the heavy cream and milk with half-and-half.

We were making progress, but the flavor of the jarred caramel sauce was still too weak. For our next test, we made a traditional, from-scratch caramel by carefully boiling sugar and water to 350 degrees (measured on a candy/deep-fry thermometer) and adding cream; although better, the caramel flavor was too subtle and the overall dish was too sweet. Because brown sugar is more flavorful than white, our next test was to make a quick caramel (technically more of a butterscotch sauce) with brown sugar, butter, cream, and corn syrup, and it worked much better: the caramel flavor was more prominent in the pudding, and the method was much less fussy than making a true caramel sauce.

We were almost there, but tasters wanted still more caramel pop. Topping the baked pudding with extra caramel was a nice touch, but starting with an additional layer of caramel sauce under the bread pudding elevated the caramel flavor to new heights. Finally, tasters were treated to a caramel bread pudding that truly lived up to its name.

CARAMEL BREAD PUDDING

SERVES 8 TO 10

Firm-textured breads such as Arnold Country Classic White or Pepperidge Farm Farmhouse Hearty White work best here.

15	slices high-quality white sandwich bread, cut into 1-inch pieces (about 16 cups) (see note above)
2	cups packed light brown sugar
12	tablespoons (1½ sticks) unsalted butter
1	cup heavy cream
¼	cup light corn syrup
5	teaspoons vanilla extract
3	cups half-and-half
5	large eggs
¼	teaspoon salt

1. Adjust the oven racks to the upper-middle and lower-middle positions and heat the oven to 450 degrees. Arrange the bread in a single layer on two baking sheets. Bake, stirring occasionally, until golden and crisp, about 12 minutes, switching and rotating the sheets halfway through baking. Let the bread cool. Reduce the oven temperature to 325 degrees.

2. Grease a 13 by 9-inch baking pan. Melt the brown sugar and butter in a large saucepan over medium-high heat, stirring often, until bubbling and straw-colored, about 4 minutes. Off the heat, whisk in the cream, corn syrup, and 2 teaspoons of the vanilla. Pour 1 cup of the caramel over the bottom of the prepared pan; set aside. Reserve 1 cup of the caramel for serving, then whisk the half-and-half into the remaining caramel.

3. Whisk the eggs and salt together in a large bowl. Whisk in the half-and-half mixture, a little at a time, until incorporated, then stir in the remaining 3 teaspoons vanilla. Fold in the toasted bread and let sit, stirring occasionally, until the bread is saturated, about 20 minutes. (If the majority of the bread is still hard when squeezed, soak for another 15 to 20 minutes.)

4. Pour the bread mixture into the caramel-coated pan and bake on the lower-middle rack until the top is crisp and the custard is just set, about 45 minutes. Let cool for 30 minutes. Drizzle with ½ cup of the reserved caramel sauce and serve, passing the remaining sauce at the table.

TENNESSEE STACK CAKE

CHAPTER THREE

Great American Cakes

Tunnel of Fudge Cake

In 1966, Ella Helfrich of Houston, Texas, won second place—and $5,000—in the annual Pillsbury Bake-Off for her tunnel of fudge cake recipe. Ella's glazed, nutty, and brownielike cake was baked in a Bundt pan, but its most distinguishing feature was the ring (or "tunnel") of creamy fudge that formed inside the cake as it baked. Intrigued, we aimed to develop our own version.

To start, we dusted off the old Pillsbury recipe, which specifies creaming three sticks of butter with 1½ cups of granulated sugar, then mixing in eggs, flour, and nuts along with a secret ingredient: a package of powdered Pillsbury Two Layer Double-Dutch Fudge Buttercream Frosting mix. This mix was the key to the cake, as it contained large amounts of cocoa powder and confectioners' sugar, which separated out during baking—this cake was always slightly underbaked—and came together to help form the fudgy center. Pillsbury no longer sells this frosting mix, but the company does offer an updated recipe on its website.

We had high hopes as we pulled the cake made from the new Pillsbury recipe out of the oven. Sadly, it was lacking in chocolate flavor, and even worse, it had no fudgy center. Other modern

recipes attempt to replace the frosting mix with ingredients like instant chocolate pudding and homemade chocolate ganache, but they hardened into a ring in the middle of the batter. Some recipes include chunks of chocolate inserted in the batter, but these cakes baked up with a liquid interior that gushed when the cake was sliced. A proper tunnel of fudge cake has a creamy, frostinglike filling that holds its shape when the cake is cut. We decided to see if we could fix the updated Pillsbury recipe.

To add more chocolate flavor, we switched from natural cocoa powder (which can be sour) to less acidic Dutch-processed cocoa. Adding melted chocolate to the batter made the cake more moist and contributed big chocolate punch. As for the tunnel, even when we slightly underbaked the cake, the interior was still too dry.

To add moisture (as well as flavor), we swapped out almost half of the granulated sugar

PREPARING A BUNDT CAKE PAN

To ensure a clean release, make a simple paste from 1 tablespoon melted butter and 1 tablespoon flour (or cocoa powder for chocolate cakes) and apply it to the pan with a pastry brush.

for brown sugar. But the big key was adjusting the amounts of two base ingredients: flour and butter. Cutting back on the flour made the cake much more moist, and using less butter helped the cakey exterior set more quickly. Finally, after two dozen failed cakes, the "tunnel" was back—and better than ever.

TUNNEL OF FUDGE CAKE

SERVES 12

Do not use a cake tester, toothpick, or skewer when testing this cake for doneness because the fudgy interior will look just like undercooked cake batter; when the cake is done, the sides will begin to pull away from the pan and the top will feel springy when pressed with a finger.

CAKE

½	cup boiling water
2	ounces bittersweet chocolate, chopped
2	cups all-purpose flour
2	cups pecans or walnuts, chopped fine
2	cups confectioners' sugar
¾	cup Dutch-processed cocoa powder plus extra for the pan
1	teaspoon salt
20	tablespoons (2½ sticks) unsalted butter, softened
1	cup granulated sugar
¾	cup packed light brown sugar
1	tablespoon vanilla extract
5	large eggs, room temperature

GLAZE

4	ounces bittersweet chocolate, melted
⅓	cup heavy cream, hot
2	tablespoons light corn syrup
¼	teaspoon vanilla extract
	Pinch salt

1. FOR THE CAKE: Adjust an oven rack to the lower-middle position and heat the oven to 350 degrees. Prepare a 12-cup nonstick Bundt pan following the photo on page 76.

2. Whisk the boiling water and chocolate together in a small bowl until melted and smooth; let the mixture cool slightly. In a medium bowl, whisk the flour, nuts, confectioners' sugar, cocoa, and salt together.

3. In a large bowl, beat the butter, granulated sugar, brown sugar, and vanilla together with an electric mixer on medium speed until light and fluffy, 3 to 6 minutes. Beat in the eggs, one at a time, until combined, about 1 minute. Beat in the chocolate mixture until combined, about 30 seconds. Reduce the mixer speed to low and slowly beat in the flour mixture until just incorporated, about 30 seconds.

4. Scrape the batter into the prepared pan and smooth the top. Wipe any drops of batter off the sides of the pan and gently tap the pan on the work surface to settle the batter. Bake the cake until the edges begin to pull away from the sides of the pan and the top feels springy when pressed with a finger, about 45 minutes.

5. FOR THE GLAZE: Whisk all the glaze ingredients together in a medium bowl until smooth and let sit until thickened, about 25 minutes.

6. Let the cake cool in the pan for 10 minutes, then flip it out onto a wire rack set inside a rimmed baking sheet. Let the cake cool completely, about 2 hours. Drizzle the chocolate glaze over the top and sides of the cake. Let the glaze set, about 25 minutes, before serving.

Wacky Cake

During the First World War, butter, sugar, milk, and eggs were often in short supply, leading American women to devise a variety of "make-do" cakes. During World War II, American women revived and improved upon the make-do cake recipes their mothers had used a generation earlier. Several sources suggest that Wacky Cake was invented during the 1940s, but we couldn't understand how it earned its name until we read a recipe in *The Time Reader's Book of Recipes*, a collection of reader recipes compiled by the editors of *Time* magazine in 1949.

Mrs. Donald Adam of Detroit, Michigan, submitted this strange recipe, which called for mixing the dry ingredients—flour, cocoa powder, sugar, salt, and baking soda—right in the baking pan. If that wasn't strange enough, three holes—two small and one large—were made in the dry mix. Into the large hole went melted vegetable shortening and vanilla and vinegar were placed in the smaller holes. Cold water was poured over everything, then the whole mess was stirred and popped into the oven.

Back in the test kitchen, we followed the instructions, and right before our eyes the batter began to bubble and rise—even before it hit the oven. It was the easiest cake we'd ever made. And it was surprisingly good.

How does this recipe work? Without eggs, this cake depends on the last-minute reaction of vinegar and baking soda to lift the thick batter. The three holes ensure that the dry ingredients remain dry until the last possible second. Mixing in the pan might seem like a gimmick, but when we combined the ingredients in a bowl and scraped the batter into a pan, the cake did not rise as well. The lift provided by the reaction of the baking soda and vinegar is fleeting, and the recipe's odd mixing method ensures that the batter gets into the oven quickly.

The 1949 recipe we had found needed little improvement. To simplify things, we replaced the melted shortening with vegetable oil, and to boost the chocolate flavor we added another tablespoon of cocoa. The cake was a bit sweet, so we trimmed a little sugar, and because several tasters complained about a slight "soapy" flavor, we decreased the amount of baking soda.

On a whim, we decided to try this cake with more "modern" ingredients. We replaced the oil with melted butter and used milk instead of water. This cake was less chocolaty and more crumbly; we honestly felt that the original was better. Hard times gave rise to a not-so-wacky recipe that still deserves a place in the American kitchen.

WACKY CAKE

SERVES 6 TO 8

This easy chocolate cake can be served as is or with a dollop of whipped cream.

1½	cups all-purpose flour
¾	cup granulated sugar
¼	cup Dutch-processed cocoa powder
¾	teaspoon baking soda
½	teaspoon salt
5	tablespoons vegetable oil
1	tablespoon white vinegar
1	teaspoon vanilla extract
1	cup water
	Confectioners' sugar, for dusting

1. Adjust an oven rack to the middle position and heat the oven to 350 degrees. Grease an 8-inch square baking pan.

2. Whisk the flour, granulated sugar, cocoa, baking soda, and salt together in the prepared pan.

MIXING WACKY CAKE

1. Make one large and two small craters in the dry mix. Pour the oil into the large crater, and the vinegar and vanilla into the smaller craters. Pour the water over everything.

2. Using a wooden spoon or spatula, mix the batter, taking care not to overmix; the batter should still contain a few streaks of flour.

Make one large and two small craters in the dry ingredients. Add the oil to the large crater and the vinegar and vanilla separately to the small craters. Pour the water into the pan and mix until just a few streaks of flour remain. Immediately put the pan in the oven.

3. Bake until a toothpick inserted in the center of the cake comes out with a few moist crumbs attached, about 30 minutes, rotating the pan halfway through baking. Let the cake cool in the pan, set on a wire rack, then dust with confectioners' sugar before serving.

Wellesley Fudge Cake

Unbelievable as it may sound, roughly 100 years ago, fudge (along with other sweets) was a contraband treat coveted by Wellesley College students. But the students rebelled, as students do, and held secret fudge-making parties in their dorm rooms. Cut to 10 years later, when several tearooms in the town of Wellesley offered on their menus Wellesley fudge cake, a mild chocolate layer cake filled and frosted with an unusually thick layer of fudge frosting. The cake was made from unsweetened chocolate, brown sugar, pastry flour, and "thick, sour milk," all of which resulted in a cake with a tender, spongy crumb. It was baked in two square pans, unusual for a layer cake. But it was the frosting that truly distinguished Wellesley fudge cake. Chocolate, milk, and sugar were boiled to what candy makers refer to as the soft-ball stage; the warm fudge was then spread on the cake and the cake left to sit until the frosting set up.

Over the years, Wellesley fudge cake has become just another chocolate layer cake with chocolate buttercream frosting. We made the original recipe plus several other versions and were dismayed by pale cakes with marginal chocolate flavor topped with gritty or thin frostings. We wanted to honor the spirit of the original—its singular square shape and barely granular fudge frosting—while adjusting it for modern tastes.

The thick frosting is spread so lavishly on Wellesley fudge cake that the cake has to be sturdier than the delicate original in order not to tear. We replaced the pastry flour with all-purpose flour, giving the cake more gluten formation, and therefore more structure. To simulate the "thick, sour milk," we used buttermilk. Tasters preferred the deep flavor of cocoa powder to bar chocolate, and the hot water in the original recipe that had melted the chocolate now handily "bloomed" the cocoa; the heat deepened the cocoa's flavor and rid it of any dustiness. Finally, we replaced the brown sugar with granulated sugar, which didn't interfere with the chocolate flavor.

On to the showstopper: the frosting. Right away, we eliminated any recipes in which melted

chocolate, confectioners' sugar, and milk were simply stirred together—that's not fudge. But the true fudge icings we tested were alternately hard and grainy, thin and soupy, or incredibly difficult to make. We were after the milky, nearly achy sweetness and slight crystalline crunch that mark real fudge. And, sticking with the humble origins of the recipe, we didn't want to have to break out the candy thermometer to make it.

In our research, we'd come across an old advertisement for evaporated milk that included a simple fudge recipe: butter was combined with granulated sugar and evaporated milk and the mixture was boiled until it was caramel-like, about 5 minutes. We were encouraged, except that after a few tries, we found that the granulated sugar crystallized unpredictably. Switching to brown sugar stabilized the base, but when we added the chopped chocolate, the mixture turned dry and grainy. After researching the science behind this misstep, we learned that the hot sugar mixture was causing the fat in the chocolate to separate. So after our next batch thickened, we took it off the heat, then added more butter and more evaporated milk to cool it slightly, and finally stirred in the chopped chocolate. Problem solved.

Now, however, we had a new problem on our hands: the frosting was too loose. To fix this issue, we added confectioners' sugar (sifted, to eliminate lumps) and cooled the mixture for about an hour, stirring periodically. After we iced the cake, we chilled it in the refrigerator. One hour later, we sliced it and were rewarded—the frosting was sweet and deeply fudgy with the luscious texture of barely softened butter and the faintest sugar crunch. Wellesley fudge cake tasted as satisfying to us as it must have to students a century ago.

WELLESLEY FUDGE CAKE

SERVES 12

This cake is traditionally baked in two 8-inch square cake pans, but two 9-inch round cake pans will also work.

CAKE

2½	cups all-purpose flour
2	teaspoons baking soda
1	teaspoon baking powder
½	teaspoon salt
¾	cup hot water
½	cup Dutch-processed cocoa powder
16	tablespoons (2 sticks) unsalted butter, cut into 16 pieces and softened
2	cups granulated sugar
2	large eggs
1	cup buttermilk, room temperature
2	teaspoons vanilla extract

FROSTING

1½	cups packed light brown sugar
1	cup evaporated milk
8	tablespoons (1 stick) unsalted butter, cut into 8 pieces and softened
½	teaspoon salt
8	ounces bittersweet chocolate, chopped
1	teaspoon vanilla extract
3	cups confectioners' sugar, sifted

1. FOR THE CAKE: Adjust an oven rack to the middle position and heat the oven to 350 degrees. Grease and flour two 8-inch square baking pans, then line the bottoms with parchment paper (see page 88). Combine the flour, baking soda, baking powder, and salt in a bowl; set aside.

2. In a small bowl, whisk the hot water and cocoa together until smooth; set aside. In a large bowl, beat the butter and granulated sugar together with an electric mixer on medium-high speed until light and fluffy, 3 to 6 minutes. Beat in the eggs, one at a time, until incorporated. Mix in one-third of the flour mixture, followed by ½ cup of the buttermilk. Repeat with half of the remaining flour mixture and

the remaining ½ cup buttermilk. Add the remaining flour mixture and mix until combined. Reduce the mixer speed to low and slowly add the cocoa mixture and vanilla until incorporated.

3. Give the batter a final stir with a rubber spatula to make sure it is thoroughly combined. Scrape the batter into the prepared pans, smooth the tops, and gently tap the pans on the work surface to settle the batter. Bake the cakes until a toothpick inserted in the center comes out with a few crumbs attached, 25 to 30 minutes, rotating the pans halfway through baking. Let the cakes cool in the pans for 15 minutes. Run a small knife around the edges of the cakes, then flip them out onto a wire rack. Peel off the parchment paper, flip the cakes right side up, and let cool completely before frosting, about 2 hours. (The cakes can be wrapped tightly in plastic wrap and stored at room temperature for up to 2 days.)

MAKING FUDGE FROSTING

1. Heat the brown sugar, ½ cup evaporated milk, 4 tablespoons butter, and salt until small bubbles begin to appear around the edge of the saucepan, 4 to 8 minutes.

2. Reduce the heat and simmer until large bubbles form and the mixture has thickened and turned deep golden brown, about 6 minutes longer.

3. Transfer the mixture to a bowl and stir in the remaining butter and evaporated milk until the mixture has cooled slightly, then add the chocolate and vanilla.

4. Whisk in the confectioners' sugar. Let the frosting cool to room temperature, stirring occasionally, until it thickens to a spreadable consistency.

4. FOR THE FROSTING: Stir together the brown sugar, ½ cup of the evaporated milk, 4 tablespoons of the butter, and salt in a large saucepan and cook over medium heat until small bubbles appear around the edge of the pan, 4 to 8 minutes. Reduce the heat to low and simmer, stirring occasionally, until large bubbles form and the mixture has thickened and turned deep golden brown, about 6 minutes. Transfer to a large bowl. Stir in the remaining ½ cup evaporated milk and remaining 4 tablespoons butter until the mixture has cooled slightly. Add the chocolate and vanilla and stir until smooth. Whisk in the confectioners' sugar until incorporated. Let the frosting cool to room temperature, stirring occasionally, about 1 hour.

5. Line the edges of a cake platter with strips of parchment paper to keep the platter clean while you assemble the cake. Place one of the cake layers on the platter. Spread 1 cup of the frosting over the cake, right to the edges. Place the second cake layer on top, press lightly to adhere, and spread the remaining frosting evenly over the top and sides of the cake. Refrigerate the cake until the frosting is set, about 1 hour. Remove the parchment strips from the platter before serving.

Chocolate Blackout Cake

Mention Ebinger's to most Brooklynites over the age of 40 and you'll see a sparkle of nostalgia in their eyes. Bring up chocolate blackout cake and you might actually see a tear or two. When the Brooklyn-based chain of bakeries closed its doors, the borough went into mourning. On that fateful day, August 27, 1972, the *New York Times* ran a story titled "Tears Replace the Coffee Cakes." Of all the lost Ebinger's recipes, none has received more attention in the last 30-plus years than its chocolate blackout cake.

A forerunner of "death by chocolate" confections, chocolate blackout cake is decidedly decadent, marrying fudgy, dark chocolate layers with a rich, creamy chocolate pudding that acts as both filling and frosting. But what really sets this cake apart is yet another dimension of chocolate flavor—its signature shaggy coating of chocolate cake crumbs.

Blackout cake got its name from the blackout drills performed by the Civilian Defense Corps during World War II. When the navy sent its ships to sea from the Brooklyn Navy Yard, the streets of the borough were "blacked out" to avoid silhouetting the battleships against the cityscapes of Brooklyn and Manhattan. The cake was so named because of its darkly chocolate—practically black—appearance.

Ebinger's original recipe was never published, leaving cookbook authors and Brooklyn grandmothers to rely on their taste buds to reproduce "authentic" versions. We compiled a folder of promising recipes, but the only things they had in common were long ingredient lists and complicated cooking techniques. We wanted a great-tasting cake, but it also had to be simple and easy to make.

We started with the cake layers. For big chocolate flavor, most recipes rely on natural cocoa powder, but we found it too astringent. The less acidic Dutch-processed cocoa was better, but we wanted even more chocolate flavor. We tried adding melted chocolate, but the cake became dense and gummy.

We had better luck when we used a few test-kitchen tricks to bring out the subtleties of the cocoa. The tang of buttermilk carried the chocolate flavor; other dairy products seemed to mute it. Adding brewed coffee to the batter enhanced the nuances of the cocoa, as did a combination of brown and granulated sugar. But still we pined

---

THE AMERICAN TABLE
A LOST ICON

Ebinger's Baking Company opened in 1898 on Flatbush Avenue in Brooklyn and grew into a chain of more than 60 stores before going bankrupt in 1972. Started by Arthur Ebinger, a baker who emigrated from Germany with a vast collection of recipes, the business grew to include his wife and their three sons. During its heyday, Ebinger's was a point of bragging rights for Brooklynites, as celebrities and the well-to-do from Manhattan never went to Brooklyn without taking home a cake or one of Ebinger's other specialties, such as challah, rye bread, pumpkin pie, Othellos (filled mini sponge cakes covered in chocolate), and crumb buns.

MAKING THE CRUMB COATING

1. Using your hands, crumble one cake layer into medium-size crumbs.

2. Sprinkle the cake crumbs all over the top of the cake, then use your hands to gently press the crumbs onto the sides.

for more depth. Borrowing a technique used with chilis and curries where spices are cooked in melted butter to bloom them and intensify their flavor, we decided to bloom the cocoa powder. We added the cocoa to the butter that we were already melting for the cake. As the pungent aroma of cocoa filled the kitchen, we knew we were on the right track. The cake made with the bloomed cocoa was dark and rich, with a distinct chocolate flavor.

To keep things simple, we decided to mix the cake batter right in the saucepan with the butter and cocoa. Although unconventional, this stream-lined method yielded a perfect cake and saved time.

The traditional pudding component of the cake should be velvety, with a chocolate tang, and rich enough to cling to the cake like frosting. Some rec-ipes achieve this with a mixture of cocoa, chocolate, cornstarch, and water. Given the pronounced choc-olate flavor in our cake, tasters preferred a sweeter, more dairy-rich chocolate flavor in the pudding. A combination of half-and-half and milk gave the pudding a satiny feel, and unsweetened chocolate gave the pudding depth of flavor.

Once the two cake layers and the pudding had cooled, it was time to assemble this skyscraper. We divided the cakes along their equators, planning to use three of the four resulting rounds as layers and the fourth for the crumbled cake topping. We spread a generous amount of pudding between the layers and coated the exterior of the cake with the rest. To finish it off, we crumbled the reserved cake layer, sprinkled it over the top of the cake, and pressed more crumbs into the sides. After just one bite, we realized why Brooklynites still talk about this cake more than 35 years after the closing of Ebinger's.

CHOCOLATE BLACKOUT CAKE

SERVES 8 TO 10

Be sure to give the pudding and the cake enough time to cool or you'll end up with runny pudding and gummy cake.

PUDDING

1¼	cups granulated sugar
¼	cup cornstarch
½	teaspoon salt
2	cups half-and-half
1	cup whole milk
6	ounces unsweetened chocolate, chopped
2	teaspoons vanilla extract

CAKE

¾	cup Dutch-processed cocoa powder, plus extra for dusting the pans
1½	cups all-purpose flour
2	teaspoons baking powder
½	teaspoon baking soda
½	teaspoon salt
8	tablespoons (1 stick) unsalted butter
1	cup strong brewed coffee, room temperature
1	cup buttermilk, room temperature
1	cup packed light brown sugar

1 cup granulated sugar
2 large eggs, room temperature
1 teaspoon vanilla extract

1. FOR THE PUDDING: Whisk the granulated sugar, cornstarch, and salt together in a medium saucepan, then slowly whisk in the half-and-half and milk. Bring the mixture to a simmer over medium heat, whisking constantly, until it thickens, 2 to 3 minutes. Stir in the chocolate and cook, stirring constantly, until melted and smooth, about 1 minute. Off the heat, stir in the vanilla. Transfer the pudding to a large bowl and press plastic wrap directly onto the surface. Refrigerate the pudding until cold, about 4 hours.

2. FOR THE CAKE: Adjust an oven rack to the middle position and heat the oven to 325 degrees. Grease two 8-inch cake pans, then dust with cocoa and line the bottoms with parchment paper (see page 88). In a medium bowl, whisk the flour, baking powder, baking soda, and salt together.

3. Melt the butter in a large saucepan over medium heat. Stir in the remaining ¾ cup cocoa and cook until fragrant, about 1 minute. Off the heat, whisk in the coffee, buttermilk, brown sugar, and granulated sugar until dissolved. Whisk in the eggs and vanilla, then slowly whisk in the flour mixture until no streaks remain. (The batter will be very loose.)

4. Give the batter a final stir with a rubber spatula to make sure it is thoroughly combined. Scrape the batter into the prepared pans, smooth the tops, and gently tap the pans on the work surface to settle the batter. Bake the cakes until a toothpick inserted in the center comes out with a few crumbs attached, 30 to 35 minutes, rotating the pans halfway through baking.

5. Let the cakes cool in the pans for 10 minutes. Run a small knife around the edges of the cakes, then flip them out onto a wire rack. Peel off the parchment paper, flip the cakes right side up, and let cool completely before filling and frosting, about 2 hours.

6. Line the edges of a cake platter with strips of parchment paper to keep the platter clean while you assemble the cake. Following the photos on page 95, slice each cake into two even layers using a long serrated knife. Crumble one of the cake layers into medium-size crumbs following the photo on page 84.

7. Place one of the cake layers on the platter. Spread 1 cup of the pudding over the cake right to the edges. Top with a second cake layer and spread with 1 cup more pudding. Place the remaining cake layer on top and press lightly to adhere. Frost the cake with the remaining pudding. Sprinkle the cake crumbs evenly over the top and press them onto the sides of the cake following the photo on page 84. Remove the parchment strips from the platter before serving.

Lady Baltimore Cake

With three layers of tender white cake, stripes of dried fruit and nut filling, and mounds of sticky meringuelike frosting, Lady Baltimore cake makes quite the dazzling centerpiece. Although the roots of this Southern confection are a bit hazy (the cake was most likely handed down from British colonists), it gained in popularity when a writer, Owen Wister, named his 1906 romance novel after the cake. The book became a best-seller, and bakers started making Lady Baltimore cakes with a fury.

KEEPING THE CAKE PLATTER CLEAN

 To keep the cake platter clean when frosting a cake, cover the edges of the platter with strips of parchment paper, then slide the pieces of parchment out from under the cake once the frosting job is done.

An old-fashioned cake, Lady Baltimore is composed of a delicate American-style white cake and seven-minute boiled frosting. We prepared a few existing recipes and found none that offered tender cake, a bold yet balanced filling that wasn't overly sweet, and light, airy frosting, so we started working on our own recipe.

White cake is an egg-white-only cake flavored with vanilla, sugar, and butter—lots of butter. White cakes are prepared in an interesting fashion: softened butter is beaten into the dry ingredients, after which the wet ingredients are beaten in. It's easy and quite quick, too—it takes longer to prepare the pans than it does to make the batter.

With the mixing method established, we had to nail down each of the ingredients. For flour, we quickly found that cake flour was a must to ensure a delicate texture. Higher-protein all-purpose flour made for a dense, slightly rubbery cake. One cup of milk and a half-dozen egg whites proved just right, and a generous 2 teaspoons of vanilla lent the cake enough flavor to stand up to the robust filling and frosting.

In some Lady Baltimore cakes the filling ingredients are kept to a bare minimum, with just figs and pecans; in others the cake is filled with numerous dried fruits. We tried both styles, and tasters much preferred the cake when it was jam-packed with a variety of fruits. A single cup of fruit and ¼ cup of toasted pecans provided the right amount of filling to separate the three levels of cake, and a food processor ground the mixture to the perfect consistency. To sharpen the flavor of the filling, we stirred in some bourbon (rum or water can be substituted), a common ingredient in many Lady Baltimore cakes.

Before being slathered across the layers of cake, the filling is typically mixed with a portion of the frosting, so it was about time to try our luck with seven-minute frosting. Its odd name refers to the time it takes to "cook" the water, sugar, and egg whites that form the frosting's base. The mixture is whipped while being warmed over simmering water, which effectively cooks the mixture and makes a thick, frothy, and glossy meringue. A pinch of cream of tartar helps to stabilize the meringue. With a splash of vanilla and pinch of salt, the frosting tasted great and looked even better.

Although the billowy, glossy frosting looks attractive enough on its own, we found it was easy to up the ante by making impressive swirls in the glossy coat using the back of a spoon. For a little more oomph and to echo the crunchiness in the nut filling, we decorated the cake with sugared pecans. After just one bite, tasters were swooning—and we had to assume Lady Baltimore herself would, too.

LADY BALTIMORE CAKE

SERVES 8 TO 10

Any combination of cherries, dates, figs, pineapple, and raisins will work here. Note that you must have a hand-held mixer to make the frosting.

CAKE

1	cup whole milk, room temperature
6	large egg whites, room temperature
2	teaspoons vanilla extract
2¼	cups cake flour
1¾	cups sugar
4	teaspoons baking powder
1	teaspoon salt
12	tablespoons (1½ sticks) unsalted butter, softened

FROSTING

1¼	cups sugar
4	large egg whites
3	tablespoons water
1	teaspoon cream of tartar
	Pinch salt
1	teaspoon vanilla extract

FILLING

1	cup mixed dried fruits (see note above)
¼	cup pecans, toasted (see page 130)
2	tablespoons bourbon, rum, or water
1	recipe Sugared Pecans (recipe follows)

PREPARING CAKE PANS

1. Trace the outline of the bottom of the pan on a piece of parchment paper. Then cut out the outline, cutting on the inside of the line so that the paper fits snugly inside the pan.

2. Grease the inside of the pan evenly with a thin coating of butter or vegetable shortening.

3. Sprinkle flour in the cake pan, then shake and rotate to coat evenly with the flour; shake out any remaining flour.

4. Fit the trimmed piece of parchment into the pan. The butter or shortening, along with the flour, will help the parchment adhere.

1. FOR THE CAKE: Adjust an oven rack to the middle position and heat the oven to 350 degrees. Grease and flour three 8-inch cake pans, then line the bottoms with parchment paper. Whisk the milk, egg whites, and vanilla together in a large measuring cup.

2. In a large bowl, whisk the flour, sugar, baking powder, and salt together. Using an electric mixer on low speed, beat the butter into the flour mixture until the mixture resembles moist crumbs, with no powdery streaks remaining.

3. Beat in all but ½ cup of the milk mixture, then increase the mixer speed to medium and beat until smooth, light, and fluffy, 1 to 3 minutes. Reduce the mixer speed to low and slowly beat in the remaining ½ cup milk mixture until the batter looks slightly curdled, about 15 seconds.

4. Give the batter a final stir with a rubber spatula to make sure it is thoroughly combined. Scrape the batter into the prepared pans, smooth the tops, and gently tap the pans on the work surface to settle the batter. Arrange the pans at least 3 inches from the oven walls and 3 inches apart. (If the oven is small, place the pans on the upper-middle and lower-middle racks in a staggered fashion to allow for air circulation.) Bake the cakes until a toothpick inserted in the center comes out clean, 20 to 25 minutes, rotating the pans halfway through baking.

5. Let the cakes cool in the pans for 10 minutes. Run a small knife around the edges of the cakes, then flip them out onto a wire rack. Peel off the parchment paper, flip the cakes right side up, and let cool completely before filling and frosting, about 2 hours. (The cakes can be wrapped tightly in plastic wrap and stored at room temperature for up to 2 days.)

6. FOR THE FROSTING: Combine the sugar, egg whites, water, cream of tartar, and salt in a large heatproof bowl set over a medium saucepan filled with 1 inch barely simmering water (don't let the bowl touch the water). Using an electric mixer, beat the mixture on medium-high speed until stiff peaks form (see page 5), 6 to 8 minutes. Remove the bowl from the heat, add the vanilla, and continue to beat until the mixture is cooled to room temperature and the frosting is very thick and stiff, about 8 to 10 minutes longer; set aside.

7. FOR THE FILLING: Process the dried fruits and nuts in a food processor until finely chopped, about 20 seconds. Transfer to a medium bowl and stir in the bourbon. Stir 2 cups of the frosting into the fruit and nut mixture.

8. Line the edges of a cake platter with strips of parchment paper to keep the platter clean while you assemble the cake. Place one of the cake layers on the platter. Following the photos, spread half of

MAKING LADY BALTIMORE CAKE

1. Place one of the cake layers on a cake platter and spread half of the fruit and frosting mixture over the cake. Repeat with the second layer.

2. Top with the third cake layer and spread frosting on the top and sides of the cake.

3. Use a spoon to create decorative swirls in the frosting.

4. Decorate the cake with the sugared pecans.

the fruit and frosting mixture over the cake, right to the edges. Repeat with another cake layer and the remaining fruit and frosting mixture. Top with the remaining cake layer, press lightly to adhere, and spread the remaining plain frosting over the top and sides of the cake, using the back of a spoon to create attractive swirls. Decorate with the sugared pecans and remove the parchment strips from the platter before serving.

SUGARED PECANS

MAKES 2 CUPS

Choose pecan halves that are not broken. Depending on how many pecans you use to decorate the cake, you may have some left over.

2	tablespoons granulated sugar
½	teaspoon kosher salt
1	tablespoon bourbon, rum, or water
1	tablespoon unsalted butter
2	teaspoons vanilla extract
1	teaspoon light brown sugar
2	cups pecan halves (see note above), toasted (see page 130)

1. Combine the granulated sugar and salt in a medium bowl.

2. Bring the bourbon, butter, vanilla, and brown sugar to a boil in a medium saucepan over medium-high heat, whisking constantly. Stir in the pecans and cook, stirring constantly, until the nuts are shiny and almost all the liquid has evaporated, about 1½ minutes.

3. Add the pecans to the sugar and salt mixture and toss to combine. Transfer to a baking sheet to cool completely, about 15 minutes. (The nuts can be stored in an airtight container at room temperature for up to 5 days.)

Strawberry Cream Cake

Strawberry shortcake is the usual way to showcase sweet, ripe strawberries, but its homespun nature doesn't suit fancier occasions. Enter the strawberry cream cake. We found no shortage of recipes for strawberry cream cakes that looked good, but we were left broken-hearted by their lackluster taste and texture. Either the cake itself collapsed under the weight of the filling, or the whipped cream squirted out the sides of the cake when we cut slices. But worst of all, the strawberry flavor often took a backseat to the cake and cream. We wanted a sturdy cake, a firm filling, and strawberry flavor fit for a starring role.

With multiple layers, we needed a cake that was structurally sound. Butter cakes are rich but somewhat fragile, so we moved on to sponge cakes. But tasters found the various sponge cakes we prepared too lean and dry. We realized that what we wanted was the structure of a sponge cake coupled with the richness of a butter cake. We decided to try a chiffon cake, an American invention introduced at Hollywood's Brown Derby restaurant in the 1920s and popularized by Betty Crocker in the 1940s. Similar in texture to an angel food cake, a chiffon cake has more fat (in the form of egg yolks and vegetable oil) than most sponge cakes, making it high and light but also moist and tender.

When we baked the test-kitchen recipe for chiffon cake in a round cake pan (instead of the traditional tube pan), there was no way to hang it upside down while cooling, as is done with angel food cake, to help the cake maintain its shape. The result was a sunken center and retracted sides. We tried increasing the flour and decreasing the liquid. The cake no longer sank, but tasters felt it wasn't rich enough. The answer was to switch out the oil for butter, which produced a richer, fuller flavor. Now that we had a deeper cake (for the multiple layers), we also had to switch out the regular round cake pan for a slightly taller springform pan (although a 9-inch cake pan with straight sides that are at least 2 inches high will work, too).

For the strawberry filling, most recipes call for folding sliced strawberries into whipped cream. Tasters deemed this filling one-dimensional and boring. We decided to treat the berries as a separate layer and began focusing on enhancing their flavor. First, we macerated the berries in sugar to draw out their juice, mashed a portion, and then combined the mashed and whole berries. While this helped bind the berries, it also decreased their volume, requiring us to use 4 pints instead of the 2 we'd started with. The problem was that the macerated sliced berries became soft and were not visually appealing once added to the cake layers. The solution? Dividing the berries in half: one portion was sliced and used around the edge of the filling for visual appeal, and the other half was macerated, pulsed in a food processor, and spread over the center.

But we found that these processed berries exuded too much juice, which made the cake soggy. We tried straining off the excess liquid, but this was vital berry flavor going down the drain. Our next step was to boil down the strained juice to evaporate the excess water, then add the syrupy remains back to the berries. This provided the perfect amount of soak for the cake, with no berry flavor lost. The final adjustment to flavor was to add some sweet liqueur (kirsch, cherry brandy, was the favorite), which we cooked along with the strained juice to eliminate any boozy overtones.

With the strawberry and cake components securely in place, all we needed to fix was the whipped cream layer so it had more flavor and texture and could stand up to the strawberries. We experimented with sour cream, yogurt, and cream cheese, all of which offered a nice tangy flavor, but only cream cheese provided a boost in texture. When whipped with the heavy cream, cream cheese produced a stiff yet silky-smooth blend that helped anchor the cake layers. Even when sliced, the cake remained cohesive.

At last, we had a layered cake that met all our expectations—sturdy yet moist chiffon cake, vibrant berries, and a robust, tangy cream.

MAKING STRAWBERRY CREAM CAKE

1. Place 20 strawberry halves evenly around the edge of the cake (they will be visible once the layers are assembled).

2. Cover the center of the cake completely with half of the pureed berry mixture.

3. Spread 1½ cups of the whipped cream over the berry mixture, leaving a ½-inch border. Repeat the layering of cake, berries, berry mixture, and whipped cream.

4. Press the last cake layer into place, spread with the remaining whipped cream, and decorate with the remaining berry halves.

STRAWBERRY CREAM CAKE

SERVES 8 TO 10

You can use either a 9-inch springform pan or a 9-inch cake pan; if using a cake pan, you will need one with straight sides that are at least 2 inches high. Depending on the sweetness of the berries, you may have to use more or less sugar. Leftover cake should be refrigerated.

CAKE

1¼	cups cake flour
1	cup sugar
1½	teaspoons baking powder
¼	teaspoon salt
3	large eggs, separated, plus 2 large eggs, room temperature
6	tablespoons (¾ stick) unsalted butter, melted and cooled
2	tablespoons water
2	teaspoons vanilla extract

FILLING

2	quarts strawberries, hulled
4–6	tablespoons sugar (see note above)
2	tablespoons kirsch
	Pinch salt

WHIPPED CREAM

1	(8-ounce) package cream cheese, softened
½	cup sugar
1	teaspoon vanilla extract
⅛	teaspoon salt
2	cups heavy cream

1. FOR THE CAKE: Adjust an oven rack to the lower-middle position and heat the oven to 325 degrees. Grease and flour a 9-inch springform pan or 9-inch cake pan, then line the bottom with parchment paper (see page 88). Whisk the flour, all but 3 tablespoons of the sugar, baking powder, and salt together in a large bowl. Whisk in the egg yolks, whole eggs, butter, water, and vanilla until smooth.

2. With an electric mixer on medium-low speed, whip the egg whites until foamy, about 1 minute. Gradually add the remaining 3 tablespoons sugar, increase the mixer speed to medium-high, and continue to whip until soft peaks form (see page 5), 1 to 3 minutes longer. Stir one-third of the whites into the batter to lighten. Gently fold the remaining whites into the batter until no white streaks remain.

3. Scrape the batter into the prepared pan, smooth the top, and gently tap the pan on the work surface to settle the batter. Bake the cake until a toothpick inserted in the center comes out clean, 30 to 40 minutes, rotating the pan halfway through baking. Let the cake cool in the pan for 10 minutes. Run a small knife around the edge of the cake, then flip it out onto a wire rack. Peel off the parchment paper, flip the cake right side up, and let cool completely before assembling, about 2 hours.

4. FOR THE FILLING: Halve 24 of the prettiest berries and reserve. Quarter the remaining berries, toss with the sugar, and let sit for 1 hour, stirring occasionally. Strain the juice from the berries and reserve (you should have about ½ cup). In a food processor, pulse the macerated berries until coarsely chopped, about five pulses (you should have about 1½ cups). In a small saucepan over medium-high heat, simmer the reserved juice and kirsch until syrupy and reduced to about 3 tablespoons, 3 to 5 minutes. Pour the reduced syrup over the pulsed berries, add the salt, and toss to combine. Set aside.

5. FOR THE WHIPPED CREAM: Before serving, in a large bowl, whip the cream cheese, sugar, vanilla, and salt together with an electric mixer on medium-high speed until light and fluffy, 1 to 2 minutes. Reduce the mixer speed to low and add the cream in a slow, steady stream. Increase the mixer speed to medium-high and beat until the mixture forms stiff peaks, 2 to 3 minutes (you should have about 4½ cups).

6. Following the photos on page 95, slice the cake into three even layers with a long serrated knife. Line the edges of a cake platter with strips of parchment paper to keep the platter clean while you assemble the cake. Place one of the cake layers on the platter and arrange a ring of 20 strawberry halves, cut sides down and stem ends facing out, around the perimeter of the cake layer, following the photos on page 91. Pour half of the pureed berry mixture into the center, then spread to the edges. Gently spread about one-third of the whipped cream (about 1½ cups) over the berry layer, leaving a ½-inch border at the edge. Place the second cake layer on top and press down gently. Repeat with 20 more strawberry halves, the remaining berry mixture, and half of the remaining whipped cream; gently press the remaining cake layer on top. Spread the remaining whipped cream over the top and decorate with the remaining cut strawberries. Remove the parchment strips from the platter before serving.

Coconut Layer Cake

Too often, coconut cake is just plain white cake with plain white frosting and thin shreds of coconut slapped on—beyond the garnish, there's zero coconut flavor to be had. We wanted a cake infused inside and out with the tropical aroma and flavor of coconut. We also wanted a tender cake with a delicate crumb and a silky, gently sweetened icing. We set out to develop the coconut cake of our dreams.

Considering the cake first, we thought a basic white cake was in order. We began by doctoring the batter with coconut milk and a bit of coconut extract. Tasters praised its buttery flavor and its tender, fine crumb, but we found that, from batch to batch, coconut milk could produce varying results. Sometimes we ended up with a flat cake, sometimes a mounded cake, sometimes a heavy, greasy cake. We discovered that the source of the problem was the variation in fat content—as much as 33 percent—among brands of coconut milk. Cream of coconut, on the other hand, seemed to be a more consistent product, perhaps because there are fewer brands on the market (Coco López being the best known). We decided to swap the coconut milk for cream of coconut (thinned with a little water); because cream of coconut is sweetened, we had to cut back on the sugar to prevent the cake from being overly sweet. To enhance the richness contributed by the cream of coconut, we added an egg yolk to the traditional roster of egg whites found in a white cake. Our cake now boasted a rich, full flavor and—best of all—actually tasted like coconut.

Now it was time to work on the frosting. We sampled several styles—everything from seven-minute icing to butter and confectioners' sugar frosting to an egg white buttercream. All of them garnered applause, but the egg white buttercream was the winner. Creamy and smooth, this frosting clung to the tender white cake perfectly.

Egg white buttercream begins with a meringue, into which softened butter is beaten. We tried two approaches to building the meringue. First, we beat the egg whites and sugar to soft peaks. But this meringue fell quickly when we added the butter, and the resulting icing was heavy. Then we tried whisking the egg whites and sugar together over a double boiler until the sugar dissolved. This meringue was much more stable. Although it fell when butter was added, the completed frosting was soft and creamy. (Note that the mixture does not become hot enough to eliminate the unlikely presence of salmonella bacteria in the eggs.)

Now we could slice our cakes into two layers each to build a sky-high four-level cake. Spread with creamy, coconutty frosting and garnished with toasted shredded coconut, this cake was undeniably decadent and loaded with coconut flavor.

CUTTING A CAKE INTO LAYERS

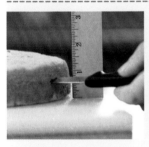

1. To cut a cake into two or three even layers, measure the height and determine the layers' thickness. Using a knife, mark the thickness of the layers at several points.

2. Using the marks as a guide, score the entire edge of the cake with a long serrated knife.

3. Following the scored lines, continue to run the knife around the cake several more times, slowly cutting inward, to slice the layers apart.

4. Carefully separate the layers by gently slipping your fingers between them and lifting the top layer away.

COCONUT LAYER CAKE

SERVES 8 TO 10

Be sure to use cream of coconut, not coconut milk. One 15-ounce can is enough for both the cake and the frosting; stir it well before using because it separates upon standing.

CAKE

¾	cup cream of coconut (see note above)
¼	cup water
5	large egg whites plus 1 large egg, room temperature
1	teaspoon coconut extract
1	teaspoon vanilla extract
2¼	cups cake flour
1	cup sugar
1	tablespoon baking powder
¾	teaspoon salt
12	tablespoons (1½ sticks) unsalted butter, cut into 12 pieces and softened

FROSTING

1	cup sugar
4	large egg whites
	Pinch salt
1	pound (4 sticks) unsalted butter, each stick cut into 6 pieces and softened
¼	cup cream of coconut (see note above)
1	teaspoon coconut extract
1	teaspoon vanilla extract
2	cups sweetened shredded coconut, toasted (see page 212)

1. FOR THE CAKE: Adjust an oven rack to the lower-middle position and heat the oven to 325 degrees. Grease and flour two 9-inch cake pans, then line the bottoms with parchment paper (see page 88). Whisk the cream of coconut, water, egg whites, whole egg, coconut extract, and vanilla together in a large measuring cup.

2. Whisk the flour, sugar, baking powder, and salt together in a large bowl. With an electric mixer on low speed, beat the butter into the flour mixture, one piece at a time, about 30 seconds. Continue to beat the mixture until it resembles coarse meal, with butter bits no larger than small peas, 1 to 3 minutes longer.

3. With the mixer still running, add 1 cup of the egg mixture to the flour mixture. Increase the mixer speed to medium-high and beat until light and fluffy, about 45 seconds. With the mixer still running, add the remaining egg mixture in a steady stream (this should take about 15 seconds). Stop the mixer and scrape down the bowl with a rubber spatula, then beat at medium-high speed to combine, about 15 seconds. (The batter will be thick.)

4. Give the batter a final stir with a rubber spatula to make sure it is thoroughly combined. Scrape the batter into the prepared pans, smooth the tops, and gently tap the pans on the work surface to settle the batter. Bake the cakes until a toothpick inserted in the center comes out clean, about 30 minutes, rotating the pans halfway through baking.

5. Let the cakes cool in the pans for 10 minutes. Run a small knife around the edges of the cakes, then flip them out onto a wire rack. Peel off the parchment paper, flip the cakes right side up, and let cool completely before frosting, about 2 hours.

6. FOR THE FROSTING: Combine the sugar, egg whites, and salt in a large heatproof bowl set over a medium saucepan filled with 1 inch barely simmering water (don't let the bowl touch the water). Whisk constantly until the mixture is opaque and registers 120 degrees on an instant-read thermometer, about 2 minutes. Remove from the heat.

7. Using an electric mixer on high speed, beat the mixture until barely warm (about 80 degrees), glossy, and sticky, about 7 minutes. Reduce the mixer speed to medium-high and beat in the butter, one piece at a time. Beat in the cream of coconut, coconut extract, and vanilla. Stop the mixer and scrape the bottom and sides of the bowl with a rubber spatula. Continue to beat at medium-high speed until well combined, about 1 minute longer.

8. Following the photos on page 95, slice each cake into two even layers with a long serrated knife. Line the edges of a cake platter with strips of parchment paper to keep the platter clean while you assemble the cake. Place one of the cake layers on the platter. Spread a generous ½ cup of the frosting over the cake, right to the edges. Place the second cake layer on top and press lightly to adhere. Repeat twice more with 1 cup more frosting and the remaining two cake layers. Spread the remaining frosting over the top and sides of the cake. Sprinkle the toasted coconut on the top and press into the sides of the cake. Remove the parchment strips from the platter before serving.

Tennessee Stack Cake

This eight-layer cake, an Appalachian specialty, is known by various names, including Apple Stack Cake, Pioneer Stack Cake, and Washday Stack Cake. The last name refers to how the cookielike layers were often baked on washday and then layered with an apple filling and left to sit for a day or two before being served. As the cake sits, the cookielike layers soak up moisture from the apple filling and soften, becoming tender and cakelike in the process. We'd never seen a cake quite like this before and were eager to start research to develop our own version.

Starting with the filling, we found that recipes most often relied on applesauce or apple butter. We prepared recipes using each. The applesauce tasted fine, but it was too fluid and turned the cake mushy, rather than just softening it. Apple butter was best—fluid, but not too much so. Next we tried apple butter made with fresh apples and apple butter made with dried apples (dried apples were a common mountain staple). The flavor of the butter made with dried apples was intense and a winner with tasters. We pitted jarred apple butter, hoping to take advantage of its convenience, against our own homemade version, but everyone preferred the homemade butter spiced with cinnamon, cloves, and allspice.

With our filling set, we turned to the cake layers. The cake batter is more akin to cookie dough—stiff enough to roll out. But the mixing method is very much like that of a cake: butter and sugar are creamed together, and then the dry ingredients (flour, baking powder, baking soda) are incorporated in stages, alternating with the wet ingredients (buttermilk, eggs, and vanilla). Once the dough comes together, it's divided into portions and rolled out. We found that using a cake pan as a template ensures that the layers line up perfectly.

It didn't take us long to determine the proportions of the ingredients, but we did wrestle with spicing our cake layers. Traditionally, the layers are flavored with ginger, or sometimes cinnamon, but we decided to leave the spices out and simply let the spiced apple butter infuse the cake with its warm flavor.

Once the layers cooled, we spread them with the apple butter, stacked them, and then set the cake aside in the refrigerator to set up. We hoped we didn't have to wait 2 days to enjoy the cake (as is tradition), but we did have to wait 24 hours—any sooner and the cake layers weren't sufficiently softened.

TENNESSEE STACK CAKE

SERVES 10 TO 12

This cake takes a while to create, but each step is simple and the dough rounds that form each layer are sturdy and easy to handle. Be sure to let the cake set at least 24 hours, as the moisture from the filling transforms the texture of the cookielike layers into a tender apple-flavored cake.

FILLING

3	(6-ounce) bags dried apples
1	cup packed light brown sugar
1½	teaspoons ground cinnamon
½	teaspoon ground cloves
½	teaspoon ground allspice

LAYERS

6	cups all-purpose flour
1	tablespoon baking powder
1	teaspoon baking soda
¼	teaspoon salt
½	cup buttermilk
2	large eggs
1	teaspoon vanilla extract
16	tablespoons (2 sticks) unsalted butter, softened
2	cups granulated sugar
	Confectioners' sugar, for dusting

1. FOR THE FILLING: Bring the apples and water to cover to a boil in a large saucepan. Reduce the heat and simmer until the apples are completely softened, about 10 minutes. Drain the apples and let cool until just warm, about 15 minutes. Puree the apples in a food processor until smooth. Transfer to a bowl and stir in the brown sugar, cinnamon, cloves, and allspice. (The filling can be refrigerated in an airtight container for up to 2 days.)

MAKING TENNESSEE STACK CAKE

1. After dividing the dough into eight equal portions, roll out each piece of dough into a 10-inch circle.

2. Using a 9-inch cake pan as a template, cut out a neat circle from each piece of dough.

3. Gently slide each dough round onto a removable tart pan bottom and transfer to one of the baking sheets.

4. To assemble the cake, place one layer on a serving plate and spread with filling. Repeat, leaving the top layer plain.

2. FOR THE LAYERS: Adjust the oven racks to the upper-middle and lower-middle positions and heat the oven to 350 degrees. Grease two baking sheets. Whisk the flour, baking powder, baking soda, and salt together in a medium bowl. Whisk the buttermilk, eggs, and vanilla together in a large measuring cup.

3. In a large bowl, beat the butter and granulated sugar together with an electric mixer on medium-high speed until light and fluffy, 3 to 6 minutes.

Beat in half of the flour mixture, followed by half of the buttermilk mixture. Repeat with the remaining flour mixture and the remaining buttermilk mixture, beating until combined. (The dough will be thick.)

4. Divide the dough into eight equal portions. Following the photos, work with two portions at a time on a lightly floured surface, rolling out each into a 10-inch circle about ⅛ inch thick. Using a 9-inch cake pan as a template, trim away the excess dough to form two perfectly round 9-inch disks. Transfer the disks to the prepared baking sheets and bake until golden brown, 10 to 12 minutes, switching and rotating the baking sheets halfway through baking. Transfer the disks to wire racks and cool completely, at least 1 hour. Repeat with the remaining dough. (The layers can be wrapped tightly in plastic wrap and stored at room temperature for up to 2 days.)

5. Place one layer on a serving platter and spread with ¾ cup of the filling. Repeat six times. Top with the final layer, wrap tightly in plastic wrap, and refrigerate until the layers soften, at least 24 hours or up to 2 days. Dust with confectioners' sugar and serve.

Cranberry Upside-Down Cake

You'd be hard-pressed to find someone who isn't familiar with pineapple upside-down cake, but its cranberry counterpart is far less famous. And that's a shame. This ruby-crowned cake is a visual stunner, and the delicate balance of sweet-tart cranberry topping and tender butter cake makes it every bit as appealing as the pineapple version. But the fruit topping is often thin and runny or, worse, a

super-sticky candied mess that won't leave the pan at all. As for the cake itself, though a sturdy texture is a must to support the fruit, most recipes overcompensate and the cakes bake up dry and dense.

We baked a lineup of cakes that ranged from fluffy to leaden in texture, but one coarse-crumbed cake stood out as the tasters' favorite. This cake featured ground almonds, which lent a moist richness and hearty texture to the crumb. The cake was a little heavy, so rather than beating whole eggs into the batter, we added the yolks and then whipped the egg whites separately. Folding the fluffy beaten whites into the finished batter produced a beautiful cake—light and tender but still sturdy enough to support the heavy fruit topping.

Recipes that called for lining the cake pan with berries tossed with sugar produced watery, runny toppings. Precooking the cranberries and sugar on the stovetop to evaporate some of the fruit's moisture proved to be a better option. To make the topping more cohesive, we strained out the berries after a few minutes and continued to reduce the juice to a thick syrup.

The topping now had the right consistency, but it was a little too tart. Increasing the amount of sugar made the topping taste like candy, and after trying sweeteners like honey, maple syrup, and corn syrup, tasters settled on raspberry jam, which perfectly rounded out the tartness of the cranberries and enhanced the fruit flavor of the topping. After about 40 minutes in the oven, we had a cranberry upside-down cake that wowed both the eyes and the palate.

CRANBERRY UPSIDE-DOWN CAKE

SERVES 8

To prevent this cake from sticking, be sure to spray the parchment-lined cake pan with vegetable oil spray and do not let the cake cool in the pan for more than 10 minutes before turning it out.

TOPPING

- 6 tablespoons unsalted butter
- 3 cups fresh or defrosted frozen cranberries
- ¾ cup sugar
- 2 tablespoons seedless raspberry jam
- ½ teaspoon vanilla extract

CAKE

- ¼ cup blanched slivered almonds
- 1 cup all-purpose flour
- 1 teaspoon baking powder
- ¼ teaspoon salt
- ½ cup whole milk
- ½ teaspoon vanilla extract
- ½ teaspoon almond extract
- 6 tablespoons (¾ stick) unsalted butter, softened
- ¾ cup sugar
- 3 large eggs, separated

1. FOR THE TOPPING: Adjust an oven rack to the middle position and heat the oven to 350 degrees. Grease and flour a 9-inch cake pan, line the bottom with parchment paper (see page 88), and spray with vegetable oil spray. Melt the butter in a large nonstick skillet over medium heat. Add the cranberries, sugar, and jam and cook until the cranberries are just softened, about 4 minutes. Strain the cranberry mixture over a bowl, reserving the juice.

2. Add the strained juice to the empty skillet and simmer over medium heat until syrupy and reduced to 1 cup, about 4 minutes. Off the heat, stir in the vanilla. Arrange the strained berries in a single layer in the prepared pan. Pour the juice mixture over the berries and refrigerate for 30 minutes.

3. FOR THE CAKE: Process the almonds and ¼ cup of the flour in a food processor until finely ground. Add the remaining ¾ cup flour, baking powder, and salt and pulse to combine. Whisk the milk, vanilla, and almond extract together in a measuring cup. In a large bowl, beat together the butter and sugar with an electric mixer on medium speed until light and fluffy, 3 to 6 minutes. Beat in the egg yolks, one at a time, until combined. Reduce the mixer speed to low and add one-third of the flour mixture, followed by half of the milk mixture. Repeat with half of the remaining flour mixture and the remaining milk mixture. Beat in the remaining flour mixture.

4. Using a clean bowl and beaters, beat the egg whites on medium-high speed until they hold soft peaks (see page 5), about 2 minutes. Whisk one-third of the whites into the batter, then fold in the remaining whites. Pour the batter over the chilled cranberry mixture and bake until a toothpick inserted in the center comes out clean, 35 to 40 minutes, rotating the pan halfway through baking. Let cool on a wire rack for 10 minutes, then run a small knife around the edge of the cake and invert onto a serving platter. Serve.

Lemon Buttermilk Sheet Cake

When cookouts and barbecues demand an easy bake-and-take dessert, nothing smacks of summer more than lemon sheet cake. A single bite should offer a punch of bright and sweet lemon flavor—like a gulp of great lemonade. But most recipes we tried missed the mark. The lemon flavor was either too fleeting or overpowering.

Before we addressed flavor issues, we needed a solid foundation. We started by preparing batches of the test kitchen's white and yellow sheet cakes (white cakes use only egg whites, whereas yellow

MAKING LEMON SUGAR

1. Beat the sugar with the lemon zest to release the flavorful oils in the zest. Using the lemon sugar in the cake provides a foundation of lemon flavor.

2. For added flavor and crunch, sprinkle the extra lemon sugar over the glazed cake.

cakes employ whole eggs), replacing a few tablespoons of the milk in each recipe with lemon juice. Tasters much preferred the denser yellow cake, as the richness of the whole eggs balanced the acidity of the lemon. This recipe uses cake flour for a fine, velvety crumb and utilizes the traditional creaming method (beating butter and sugar before adding the wet and dry ingredients) to develop structure and height in the cake.

Tasters liked the flavor of this cake, but we weren't pleased with the domed top and sloping sides. Adding the lemon juice had changed the chemistry of the recipe. Replacing some of the baking powder with baking soda helped, as did reducing the baking temperature from 350 to 325 degrees—the slower baking meant that the edges and interior of the cake set at the same time, resulting in a perfectly flat top.

We had already started down the path to bright, clean lemon flavor—swapping out some of the milk for freshly squeezed lemon juice. But we could only go up to ¼ cup before the cake started tasting medicinal. We added the grated zest from three lemons to round out the lemon flavor and used a test-kitchen trick of beating the zest with sugar to create a homemade lemon sugar that lent a wallop of lemony richness to the cake. Replacing the remaining milk with buttermilk (and once again adjusting the ratio of baking powder to baking soda) added extra tang that reinforced the lemon flavor.

Tasters passed over both buttercream and cream cheese frostings in favor of a simple glaze made with confectioners' sugar, buttermilk, and lemon juice. A sprinkle of some reserved lemon sugar added crunch and a final flourish of lemon flavor and color.

LEMON BUTTERMILK SHEET CAKE

SERVES 15 TO 18

We recommend using an offset spatula to evenly glaze the warm cake.

CAKE

2½	cups cake flour
1	teaspoon baking powder
½	teaspoon baking soda
½	teaspoon salt
¾	cup buttermilk, room temperature
3	tablespoons grated fresh lemon zest and ¼ cup fresh lemon juice (3 lemons)
1	teaspoon vanilla extract
1¾	cups granulated sugar
12	tablespoons (1½ sticks) unsalted butter, softened
3	large eggs plus 1 large egg yolk, room temperature

GLAZE

3	cups confectioners' sugar
3	tablespoons fresh lemon juice
2	tablespoons buttermilk

1. FOR THE CAKE: Adjust an oven rack to the middle position and heat the oven to 325 degrees. Grease and flour a 13 by 9-inch baking pan. Combine the flour, baking powder, baking soda, and salt in a medium bowl. Combine the buttermilk, lemon juice, and vanilla in a large measuring cup.

2. In a large bowl, beat together the lemon zest and granulated sugar with an electric mixer on medium speed until moist and fragrant, about 1 minute. Transfer ¼ cup of the sugar mixture to a small bowl, cover, and reserve. Add the butter to the remaining sugar mixture and beat until light and fluffy, about 2 minutes. Beat in the eggs and the yolk, one at a time, until combined. Reduce the mixer speed to low. Mix in one-third of the flour mixture, followed by half of the buttermilk mixture. Repeat with half of the remaining flour mixture and the remaining buttermilk mixture. Add the remaining flour mixture and mix until smooth, about 30 seconds. Give the batter a final stir with a rubber spatula to make sure it is thoroughly combined.

3. Scrape the batter into the prepared pan, smooth the top, and gently tap the pan on the work surface to settle the batter. Bake until the cake is golden brown and a toothpick inserted into the center comes out clean, 25 to 35 minutes, rotating the pan halfway through baking. Transfer the pan to a wire rack and let the cake cool for 10 minutes.

4. FOR THE GLAZE: Meanwhile, whisk all the glaze ingredients together until smooth. Gently spread the glaze over the warm cake and sprinkle evenly with the reserved sugar mixture. Let the cake cool completely, at least 2 hours. Serve.

Tres Leches Cake

Tres leches cake is a sponge cake soaked with a mixture of "three milks" (heavy cream, evaporated milk, and sweetened condensed milk), then topped with whipped cream. This tender, creamy cake is especially popular in south Texas, where the Mexican American community has been making it for generations. We aimed to develop a tres leches cake that was moist (but not mushy) and not overly sweet. We gathered together several recipes found in our cookbook library and got to work.

Most of the cakes we sampled in our tests failed and were mushy and too sweet. Some recipes produced decent tres leches cakes, but nothing remarkable. One test cook recalled enjoying a tres leches cake spread with a caramel topping called dulce de leche. This sounded intriguing, so we regrouped to develop a caramel-accented tres leches cake that was truly moist without being soggy.

Although some make tres leches cake into a layered affair, we preferred the convenience of baking, soaking, and serving the cake all in one 13 by 9-inch baking pan. Many sources suggested that the crumb of a sponge cake did the best job of absorbing the milk mixture, so we started with a basic sponge cake recipe, which gets its lift from beaten egg whites. It emerged from the oven puffed and golden but sank in the center when we poured on the milk mixture. In search of a sturdier sponge cake, we tried several other recipes, with no success. A colleague finally suggested a "hot milk" sponge, made by heating milk and butter and then pouring the mixture into whipped whole eggs (which are sturdier than just whites). This cake baked up tall and sturdy enough to handle the milk mixture.

Most recipes use one can each of evaporated and sweetened condensed milk (12 and 14 ounces, respectively) and an equal amount of cream. Cutting back the amount of cream to just 1 cup produced a thicker mixture that didn't oversaturate the cake. Many of the recipes we reviewed in our research warned us that the specifics of adding the milk mixture were critical, and they were right. After many tests, we found that pouring room-temperature milk over warm cake worked best. Poking holes in the cake first allowed all of the milk mixture to be totally absorbed by the tender crumb.

We next focused on the dulce de leche aspect of our cake. A common shortcut method for making this type of caramel calls for boiling an unopened can of sweetened condensed milk for about an hour; since we were already using sweetened condensed milk, we wondered if we could cook it down a little to get the dulce de leche flavor inside our cake. Since boiling the can seemed too dangerous, we poured the milk into a bowl and microwaved it until it became slightly thickened and straw-colored. We mixed this with the other milks that we poured over the cake.

With a hint of rich caramel in each custard-laden bite, this was the tres leches cake we had been looking for.

TRES LECHES CAKE

SERVES 15 TO 18

If using a stand mixer to beat the eggs in step 3, be sure to use the whisk attachment. The cake becomes more moist and dense as it sits. Leftover cake should be refrigerated.

MILK MIXTURE

1   (14-ounce) can sweetened condensed milk
1   (12-ounce) can evaporated milk
1   cup heavy cream
1   teaspoon vanilla extract

CAKE

- 2 **cups all-purpose flour**
- 2 **teaspoons baking powder**
- 1 **teaspoon salt**
- ½ **teaspoon ground cinnamon**
- 1 **cup whole milk**
- 8 **tablespoons (1 stick) unsalted butter, cut into chunks and softened**
- 2 **teaspoons vanilla extract**
- 4 **large eggs, room temperature**
- 2 **cups sugar**

FROSTING

- 1 **cup heavy cream**
- 3 **tablespoons corn syrup**
- 1 **teaspoon vanilla extract**

1. FOR THE MILK MIXTURE: Pour the condensed milk into a microwave-safe bowl and cover tightly with plastic wrap. Microwave on medium-low, stirring often and replacing the plastic wrap several times, until slightly darkened and thickened, 9 to 15 minutes. Gradually whisk in the evaporated milk, cream, and vanilla. Set the mixture aside to cool to room temperature, about 30 minutes.

2. FOR THE CAKE: Adjust an oven rack to the middle position and heat the oven to 325 degrees. Grease and flour a 13 by 9-inch baking pan. Whisk the flour, baking powder, salt, and cinnamon together in a medium bowl. Heat the milk, butter, and vanilla together in a small saucepan over low heat until the butter is melted.

3. In a large bowl, whip the eggs with an electric mixer on medium-high speed and gradually add the sugar, about 1 minute. Continue to whip the mixture until very thick and voluminous, 4 to 8 minutes longer.

4. Reduce the mixer speed to low and add the melted butter mixture until combined, about 30 seconds. Add the flour mixture, in two additions, until incorporated, about 30 seconds. Increase the mixer speed to medium and whip the batter until fully combined and smooth, about 30 seconds.

5. Scrape the batter into the prepared pan, smooth the top, and gently tap the pan on the work surface to settle the batter. Bake the cake until a toothpick inserted in the center comes out with a few crumbs attached, 30 to 35 minutes, rotating the pan halfway through baking. Let the cake cool in the pan for 10 minutes.

6. Using a skewer, poke about 50 holes in the warm cake (you do not need to poke all the way through). Slowly pour the cooled milk mixture over the cake. Let the cake cool for about 15 minutes, then refrigerate it until the milk mixture is completely absorbed and the cake has cooled completely, about 3 hours.

7. FOR THE FROSTING: Let the cake sit at room temperature for 30 minutes. With an electric mixer on medium speed, beat the cream, corn syrup, and vanilla together in a medium bowl to soft peaks, 1 to 2 minutes. Spread the frosting evenly over the top of the cake and serve.

Southern Caramel Cake

With its toffee-flavored frosting draped over tender yellow cake, caramel cake is a favorite all over the South. The unique frosting starts out creamy but quickly firms to a fudgelike consistency, and its exterior develops a thin, crystalline crust while remaining silky and smooth underneath.

While the appeal of this Dixieland dessert is clear, it's easy to understand why few bakers make it, even in the South. Caramel frosting is notoriously tricky. Traditional recipes call for cooking granulated sugar (sometimes with water) in a saucepan until dark amber, carefully adding cream while it violently sputters, then beating in butter and confectioners' sugar. Some recipes shortcut the process by starting with brown sugar, but usually a candy thermometer is still required to recognize when the caramel has reached the right stage. If these challenges aren't enough, the frosting can harden at lightning speed. Our goal was an easier, foolproof caramel icing that would stay creamy long enough to frost a two-layer cake.

We first needed a sturdy cake with enough flavor to stand up to the sweet frosting. We started with the test kitchen's recipe for classic yellow cake, which relies on the "reverse creaming" mixing method. In standard creaming, butter and sugar are beaten until fluffy, then the wet and dry ingredients are added. The result is a tender, fluffy cake. Reverse creaming means beating the butter (followed by dairy) into the dry ingredients. Less air is beaten into the batter, and the crumb is finer and less fluffy.

Tests confirmed that reverse creaming produced a somewhat sturdier cake better suited to the caramel frosting. Switching from cake flour to higher-protein all-purpose flour gave the cake yet more

structure to handle the heavy frosting. To temper the cake's sweetness, we tried cutting back on the standard 1½ cups of sugar, but even a slight reduction made the cake dry. We had better luck replacing the milk with tangy buttermilk.

Next, we researched "easy" caramel frostings made with brown sugar. In the most promising recipe, 2 cups of brown sugar, 12 tablespoons of butter, and ½ cup of heavy cream were cooked over medium heat; when bubbles formed around the edge of the saucepan, the mixture was transferred to a mixer and confectioners' sugar was beaten in. This method was easy, but because the brown sugar was cooking in so much liquid, it never developed enough caramelized flavor. For our next test we simmered just the sugar and butter before adding the cream; now the flavor of caramel was unmistakable.

But the icing still stiffened before we finished frosting the cake. Upping the amount of butter kept the mixture soft for longer, but it also made the frosting greasy. Thinking of how creamy buttercream frostings are made of softened butter whipped with confectioners' sugar, we tried beating a little softened butter into the finished frosting. This frosting was rich and silky, and the fat from the butter kept the frosting soft and spreadable for a few precious extra minutes. And the best part was that the signature of a Southern caramel cake, the crystalline crust, formed in just half an hour—which really pleased our tasters.

SOUTHERN CARAMEL CAKE

SERVES 8 TO 10

In step 6, the cooled frosting stays soft and spreadable longer than in other recipes, but it will harden over time. If the frosting does begin to stiffen, you can microwave it for about 10 seconds (or until it returns to a spreadable consistency).

CAKE

½	cup buttermilk, room temperature
4	large eggs, room temperature
2	teaspoons vanilla extract
2¼	cups all-purpose flour
1½	cups granulated sugar
1½	teaspoons baking powder
½	teaspoon baking soda
¾	teaspoon salt
16	tablespoons (2 sticks) unsalted butter, cut into 16 pieces and softened

FROSTING

12	tablespoons (1½ sticks) unsalted butter, cut into 12 pieces and softened
2	cups packed dark brown sugar
½	teaspoon salt
½	cup heavy cream
1	teaspoon vanilla extract
2½	cups confectioners' sugar, sifted

1. FOR THE CAKE: Adjust an oven rack to the middle position and heat the oven to 350 degrees. Grease and flour two 9-inch cake pans, then line the bottoms with parchment paper (see page 88). Whisk the buttermilk, eggs, and vanilla together in a large measuring cup.

2. Whisk the flour, granulated sugar, baking powder, baking soda, and salt together in a bowl. With an electric mixer on low speed, beat in the butter, one piece at a time, until only pea-size pieces remain. Pour in half of the buttermilk mixture and beat on medium-high speed until light and fluffy, about 1 minute. Slowly add the remaining buttermilk mixture to the bowl and beat until incorporated, about 15 seconds.

3. Scrape the batter into the prepared pans, smooth the tops, and gently tap the pans on the work surface to settle the batter. Bake the cakes until golden and a toothpick inserted in the center comes out clean, 20 to 25 minutes. Let the cakes cool in the pans for 10 minutes. Run a small knife around the edges of the cakes, then flip them out onto a wire rack. Peel off the parchment paper, flip the cakes right side up, and let cool completely before frosting, about 2 hours.

4. FOR THE FROSTING: Heat 8 tablespoons of the butter, brown sugar, and salt together in a large saucepan over medium heat until small bubbles appear around the edge of the pan, 4 to 8 minutes. Whisk in the cream and cook until the ring of bubbles reappears, about 1 minute. Off the heat, whisk in the vanilla.

5. Transfer the hot frosting mixture to a bowl and, with an electric mixer on low speed, gradually mix in the confectioners' sugar until incorporated. Increase the mixer speed to medium and beat until the frosting is pale brown and just warm, about 5 minutes. Add the remaining 4 tablespoons butter, one piece at a time, and beat until light and fluffy, about 2 minutes.

6. Line the edges of a cake platter with strips of parchment paper to keep the platter clean while you assemble the cake. Place one of the cake layers on the platter. Spread ¾ cup of the frosting over the cake, right to the edges. Place the second cake layer on top, press lightly to adhere, and spread the remaining frosting evenly over the top and sides of the cake. Remove the parchment strips from the platter before serving.

Pecan-Bourbon Bundt Cake

Cakes spiked with liquor are an old-fashioned holiday favorite—especially in the South. We're not talking fruitcake, but a pecan-rich yellow cake spiked with bourbon and baked in a Bundt pan for its festive presentation. But there's no doubt about it—flavoring cakes with liquor can be tricky. Add too little, and its flavor is barely noticeable; add too much, and the cake might as well be served in a glass. The cake itself can be overly sweet, with the nuts merely taking up real estate and not actually contributing any of their rich flavor. We decided we were up for a challenge and set out to create a pecan-laced Bundt cake with robust, but not overwhelming, bourbon flavor and a great texture.

We started out by baking a number of Bundt cake recipes and found these cakes were either too dense or too light. We cobbled together a basic working recipe and proceeded to tweak the proportions of ingredients before nailing down flavorings.

A fairly high ratio of fat to flour combined with a large number of eggs proved to be a good start. As for liquid, most Bundt cakes include an acid to balance the cake's sweetness. Sour cream and yogurt are common, but we found that buttermilk did a great job of making the crumb tangy without weighing it down. For leaveners, we tested the usual suspects; the best results came about with a combination of baking powder and baking soda. Baked at a moderate 350 degrees, the cake had the firm, but not overly dense, texture we sought.

Next, we moved on to the bourbon. In most recipes we found it was either added as part of the cake's liquid component or used to douse the cake once baked. We tried both styles, and tasters preferred the cakes with the bourbon in them, not on them. With ¼ cup, our cake tasted decidedly

of bourbon, but because it was in the batter, any bitterness from the alcohol baked off. To amplify the rich caramel flavors of the bourbon, we added some molasses to the batter.

We had focused our attention on the cake's texture and flavor, but now it was time to give the nuts their due. Nut-flavored cakes have nuts either stirred into the batter or added to a streusel of sorts that ribbons throughout the cake's middle. We found that mixing the nuts into the batter made them taste steamed because of the cake's long cooking time. A streusel, then, seemed like the better option. Within a few tests, we decided that simple was best so as not to detract from the cake's overall flavor. We settled on a mix of chopped pecans, light brown sugar, and melted butter. We simply sandwiched the mixture between layers of the batter.

While we liked the overall flavor and texture of the cake at this point, we couldn't help but think that the cake could use more of a bourbon punch. Revisiting our previous tests, we thought of drizzling a little raw bourbon over the cake in the form of a glaze. Just a couple of tablespoons blended with confectioners' sugar, more molasses, and a little water made for a full-flavored glaze that contributed both big flavor and an attractive sheen to our cake.

PECAN-BOURBON BUNDT CAKE

SERVES 12

We recommend using light or mild molasses so it won't overpower the subtle bourbon flavor.

FILLING

  1   **cup pecans, toasted (see page 130) and chopped fine**

  ½   **cup packed light brown sugar**

  2   **tablespoons unsalted butter, melted and cooled**

CAKE

- 3 cups all-purpose flour
- 1 teaspoon salt
- 1 teaspoon baking powder
- ½ teaspoon baking soda
- ½ cup buttermilk, room temperature
- ¼ cup light molasses (see note above)
- ¼ cup bourbon
- 1 tablespoon vanilla extract
- 18 tablespoons (2¼ sticks) unsalted butter, cut into chunks and softened
- 1¾ cups granulated sugar
- 3 large eggs plus 1 large egg yolk, room temperature

GLAZE

- 1¾ cups confectioners' sugar
- 2 tablespoons bourbon
- 1 tablespoon light molasses
- 1 tablespoon water
- Pinch salt

1. FOR THE FILLING: Combine all the filling ingredients in a medium bowl. Set aside.

2. FOR THE CAKE: Adjust an oven rack to the lower-middle position and heat the oven to 350 degrees. Prepare a 12-cup nonstick Bundt pan following the photo on page 76. Whisk the flour, salt, baking powder, and baking soda together in a medium bowl. In a small bowl, whisk the buttermilk, molasses, bourbon, and vanilla together.

3. In a large bowl, beat the softened butter and granulated sugar together with an electric mixer on medium speed until light and fluffy, 3 to 6 minutes. Beat in the eggs and egg yolk, one at a time, until combined, about 1 minute.

4. Reduce the mixer speed to low and beat in one-third of the flour mixture, followed by half of the buttermilk mixture. Repeat with half of the remaining flour mixture and the remaining buttermilk mixture. Beat in the remaining flour mixture until just incorporated.

5. Scrape half of the batter into the prepared pan, smooth the top, and sprinkle evenly with the nut filling. Scrape the remaining batter over the nut filling and smooth the top. Wipe any drops of batter off the sides of the pan and gently tap the pan on the work surface to settle the batter. Bake the cake until a toothpick inserted in the center comes out with a few moist crumbs attached, 50 to 60 minutes, rotating the pan halfway through baking.

6. Let the cake cool in the pan for 10 minutes, then flip it out onto a wire rack set inside a rimmed baking sheet. Let the cake cool completely, about 2 hours.

7. FOR THE GLAZE: Whisk all the glaze ingredients together in a bowl until smooth, then let sit until thickened, about 25 minutes. Drizzle the glaze over the top and sides of the cake. Let the glaze set, about 25 minutes, before serving.

SHOPPING WITH THE TEST KITCHEN

Bundt Pans: Bundt pans come in a wide variety of shapes, finishes, and capacities (and can cost anywhere from $9 to $40 or more). We decided to find out which pan would deliver a cake with a good shape and even browning that would also release easily from the pan. Our winner, the Nordic Ware Original Bundt Pan ($36), produced the best cake with even browning every time. Its nonstick surface ensured easy release of cakes, and clearly defined ridges made for an attractive presentation.

Gingerbread Cake

Come early December, when the turkey and pies are long gone, we find ourselves tempted by the thick slices of gingerbread that show up in bakery and coffee shop display cases. But there's no reason to buy it—traditional gingerbread cake is easier to make than you might think. In most recipes butter, sugar, eggs, flour, leavener, warm spices, molasses, and water are combined, and the batter is poured into a square pan and baked. Sadly, the recipes we tried produced cakes that were dry and far too sweet, with unbalanced spicing dominated by the dusty burn of powdered ginger. Without overly complicating the recipe, we wanted to turn this classic holiday treat into a moist, boldly flavored yet balanced cake.

The first thing to go was the square baking pan; for more substantial slices, we decided to bake our gingerbread in a Bundt pan. We found that 2½ cups of all-purpose flour, 16 tablespoons of butter, and 4 eggs filled the pan nicely. Creaming the butter and sugar in a mixer made the cake a little too light and fluffy. Searching for a denser, moister texture, we tried a dump-and-stir mixing method, replacing the butter with an equal volume of vegetable oil, but that made the cake greasy and lacking in richness. We tried the same method using melted butter, which proved the best path to a moist, dense, richer cake.

The standard liquid combination of mild molasses and water seemed lackluster, so we switched to robust molasses. In place of water, we tried milk and buttermilk; both were fine but didn't add much. We tested unexpected liquids like coffee (too bitter) and orange juice (too sour) before we recalled a recipe we'd seen in our research—it used stout as an ingredient. Willing to try anything, we stirred in some beer and were shocked that it gave the cake a deep, malty tang that tasters loved.

Powdered ginger gave the cake some bite, and cinnamon and allspice supported the ginger nicely (tasters nixed nutmeg, cloves, and cardamom). A surprising ingredient, black pepper, helped draw out more of the ginger's pleasing burn.

Ground spices used in large quantities gave the cake a dusty texture. Rather than increasing the amounts for flavor, we tried cooking the spices in melted butter, a technique we use in the test kitchen for savory spiced dishes like curry and chili. The flavors bloomed, but tasters still wanted more ginger. Trading in the powdered ginger, we went to the real McCoy and found that 4 teaspoons of grated fresh ginger added an unmistakable element that the dried spices couldn't muster.

With a glaze of confectioners' sugar, ginger, and ginger ale, we'd finally managed to put the ginger back into gingerbread.

BOLD AND SPICY GINGERBREAD CAKE

SERVES 12

Guinness is the test kitchen's favorite brand of stout. An equal amount of orange or lemon juice can be substituted for the ginger ale in the glaze. Be sure to use finely ground black pepper here.

CAKE

2½	cups all-purpose flour
2	teaspoons baking powder
¾	teaspoon baking soda
¾	teaspoon salt
16	tablespoons (2 sticks) unsalted butter
2	tablespoons ground ginger
2	teaspoons ground cinnamon
1	teaspoon ground allspice
¼	teaspoon pepper (see note above)
4	large eggs, room temperature
1½	cups sugar
4	teaspoons grated fresh ginger

¾ cup robust or dark molasses

¾ cup stout beer (see note above)

GLAZE

1¾ cups confectioners' sugar

3 tablespoons ginger ale (see note above)

1 teaspoon ground ginger

1. FOR THE CAKE: Adjust an oven rack to the middle position and heat the oven to 375 degrees. Prepare a 12-cup nonstick Bundt pan following the photo on page 76. Whisk the flour, baking powder, baking soda, and salt together in a large bowl.

2. Melt the butter in a medium saucepan over medium heat until bubbling. Stir in the ground ginger, cinnamon, allspice, and pepper and cook until fragrant, about 30 seconds. Remove from the heat and let cool slightly.

3. Whisk the eggs, sugar, and fresh ginger together in a large bowl until light and frothy. Stir in the melted butter mixture, molasses, and stout until incorporated. Whisk the flour mixture into the egg mixture until no lumps remain.

4. Pour the batter into the prepared pan and smooth the top. Wipe any drops of batter off the sides of the pan and gently tap the pan on the work surface to settle the batter. Bake the cake until a toothpick inserted in the center comes out clean, about 45 minutes. Let the cake cool in the pan for 20 minutes, then flip it out onto a wire rack set inside a rimmed baking sheet. Let the cake cool completely, about 2 hours.

5. FOR THE GLAZE: Whisk all the glaze ingredients together in a bowl until smooth. Pour the glaze over the top and sides of the cooled cake. Let the glaze set, about 15 minutes, before serving.

Classic Lemon Pound Cake

A perfect pound cake is hard to find. Most of the time, pound cake turns out either heavy, leaden, and dry or spongy and rubbery. Worst still, lemon pound cakes often have no hint of citrus whatsoever. We wanted to retool the pound cake so we had tender, velvety, buttery cake with bold lemon flavor.

The traditional ingredient list for pound cake is 1 pound each of butter, sugar, eggs, and flour. And the instructions couldn't be easier: beat softened butter and sugar until fluffy, add eggs, and finish with flour. Since this classic cake predates the widespread availability of chemical leaveners by about 150 years, traditional recipes don't contain baking powder. As a result, the only air in the batter comes from creaming the butter and sugar. If the butter is too warm or too cold (and there's little margin for error), the cake turns out not airy and tender but dense and tough. In the past, we've found that melting the butter and using a food processor for creaming ensure even incorporation of the butter, but not everyone has a big food processor. We set out to replace the processor with an electric mixer so we could have a reliable pound cake recipe that any home baker could make.

To lighten the density of the cake, many modern recipes include baking powder. Some of the recipes we tested went overboard with this ingredient, and the texture of the resulting cakes was like that of a fluffy layer cake. In the end, we found that ½ teaspoon of baking powder was enough to lighten the texture. The crumb was still fine and compact, but it wasn't quite so leaden.

The texture still needed help. We decided to try something bolder and wondered if a dairy ingredient (usually not part of the pound cake formula) would help. Milk turned the cake springy and layer-cakelike, and cream cheese imparted an odd flavor that reminded tasters of a breakfast Danish. Sour cream, however, made the crumb tender and moist. Creaming the butter and sugar was still important, but now the recipe was no longer so fickle.

It was time to introduce lemon into the equation. Lemon juice alone was losing most of its punch in the oven, so we determined that a mix of juice and zest was a must. Beating the zest with the sugar helped to release its flavorful oils. But even hefty amounts of juice and zest got us only so far, and too much juice (highly acidic) began to affect the texture of the cake adversely. Some recipes resort to lemon extract, but this gave the cake an artificial flavor. Lemon syrup (nothing more than lemon juice simmered with sugar), brushed over the cake once it emerged from the oven, was a better option. We added another blast of lemon by replacing the milk in the glaze with lemon juice.

Tasters were pleased—this pound cake was tender and moist, and it boasted a definite citrusy burst. We were happy, too—we had developed a foolproof recipe that relied on a straightforward mixing method.

CLASSIC LEMON POUND CAKE

SERVES 8

This cake is more moist the day after it is baked.

CAKE

1 ¾	cups all-purpose flour
½	teaspoon baking powder
½	teaspoon salt
¼	cup sour cream
1 ½	tablespoons grated fresh lemon zest and 1 ½ tablespoons fresh lemon juice (2 lemons)
1	cup plus 2 tablespoons granulated sugar
16	tablespoons (2 sticks) unsalted butter, softened
5	large eggs, room temperature

SYRUP

| ¼ | cup granulated sugar |
| ¼ | cup fresh lemon juice (2 lemons) |

GLAZE

| ½ | cup confectioners' sugar |
| 1 | tablespoon fresh lemon juice |

1. FOR THE CAKE: Adjust an oven rack to the middle position and heat the oven to 325 degrees. Grease and flour a 9 by 5-inch loaf pan. Sift the flour, baking powder, and salt into a bowl. Stir the sour cream and lemon juice together in a second bowl.

2. Using your fingers, toss the granulated sugar and lemon zest together in a large bowl until the clumps are gone. Add the butter and beat with an electric mixer on medium-high speed until light and fluffy, 3 to 6 minutes. Scrape down the sides of the bowl. Beat the eggs in a small bowl and add them in three additions, mixing until smooth and scraping down the bowl after each addition (the mixture will begin to look curdled). Reduce the mixer speed to low and add one-third of the flour mixture, followed by half of the sour cream mixture. Repeat with half of the remaining flour mixture and the remaining sour cream mixture. Beat in the remaining flour mixture until combined. Scrape down the bowl, then mix on low speed until smooth, about 30 seconds. Give the batter a final stir with a rubber spatula to make sure it is thoroughly combined.

3. Scrape the batter into the prepared pan, smooth the top, and gently tap the pan on the work surface to settle the batter. Bake until golden brown and a toothpick inserted in the center comes out with a few crumbs attached, 55 to 70 minutes.

4. FOR THE SYRUP: Meanwhile, stir the granulated sugar and lemon juice together in a saucepan over medium-high heat until the sugar dissolves. Bring to a simmer, cook for 2 minutes, then remove from the heat and set aside.

5. Let the cake cool in the pan for 10 minutes, then flip it out onto a wire rack set inside a rimmed baking sheet. Turn the cake right side up, brush the top and sides of the still-warm cake with the syrup, and cool the cake completely, about 2 hours.

6. FOR THE GLAZE: Whisk the confectioners' sugar and lemon juice together in a bowl until smooth. Spread the glaze over the cake, allowing some to drip down the sides. Let the glaze set, about 15 minutes, before serving.

Cold-Oven Pound Cake

Everyone knows what pound cake is, but what's cold-oven pound cake? It is a pound cake that is baked in an oven that has not been preheated; thus the oven is stone-cold when the cake is first placed inside. Our hunt for the origin of this curious recipe took us back over 100 years. At the turn of the 20th century, gas lighting was being phased out in favor of newer electric technology. Looking to replace lost revenue, gas companies set their sights on the oven business. One of their marketing gimmicks was to push easy and "thrifty" recipes, like cold-oven pound cake, that didn't require preheating the oven. This cake became popular throughout the South and was later reported to be Elvis Presley's favorite pound cake. It is described as rising tall (it's baked in a tall tube pan rather than a loaf pan) without the aid of chemical leaveners like

> ### THE AMERICAN TABLE
> ## A THRIFTY CAKE
> --
>
> Gas ovens became widely available in the United States during the first decades of the 20th century. Because these ovens were more expensive than their wood- and coal-fired counterparts, gas companies had to get creative in marketing them. One popular tactic was to develop and promote recipes started in a cold oven, such as cold-oven pound cake, with the hook that consumers could save money on their gas ovens by not paying for "needless" preheating.

baking powder or baking soda. The cake is also purported to have a light, tender crumb with a surprisingly crisp crust. We were intrigued and set out to develop our own version.

We gathered several existing recipes and headed to the kitchen. Although most of the cakes lacked the lift and tenderness that we'd read about, one contemporary recipe showed promise; it did, however, contain a nontraditional ingredient: baking powder. Taking a cue from our Classic Lemon Pound Cake (page 112), we included ½ teaspoon of this leavener, which produced a consistently lofty, even rise. Looking into the science behind this, we learned that it worked well in our cold-oven recipe because baking powder is double-acting—it produces carbon dioxide bubbles, and thus rise, when mixed with liquid and then again in the heat of the oven. Putting the cake into a cold oven meant that the gluten did not set up as quickly, allowing the carbon dioxide more time to produce greater rise.

Though grand in stature, the cake was still too dense. To create a lighter crumb, we revisited the dairy element. Although not common in traditional pound cake, our working cold-oven recipe called for heavy cream, which we suspected was weighing down our cake, so we exchanged it for leaner whole milk. This helped a little, but swapping out all-purpose flour for cake flour yielded an even finer, more delicate crumb. Baking the cake on the lower-middle rack of an oven turned to 325 degrees ensured an evenly cooked cake with a crisp, golden crust.

COLD-OVEN POUND CAKE

SERVES 12

This cake must be started in a cold oven; the recipe will not work in a preheated oven.

3	cups cake flour
1	teaspoon salt
½	teaspoon baking powder
1	cup whole milk, room temperature
2	teaspoons vanilla extract
20	tablespoons (2½ sticks) unsalted butter, softened
2½	cups sugar
6	large eggs, room temperature

1. Grease and flour a 16-cup tube pan. Whisk the flour, salt, and baking powder together in a medium bowl. In a small bowl, whisk the milk and vanilla together.

2. In a large bowl, beat the butter and sugar together with an electric mixer on medium speed until light and fluffy, 3 to 6 minutes. Beat in the eggs, one at a time, until combined, about 1 minute.

3. Reduce the mixer speed to low and beat in one-third of the flour mixture, followed by half of the milk mixture. Repeat with half of the remaining flour mixture and the remaining milk mixture.

Beat in the remaining flour mixture until just incorporated.

4. Scrape the batter into the prepared pan and smooth the top. Wipe any drops of batter off the sides of the pan and gently tap the pan on the work surface to settle the batter. Adjust an oven rack to the lower-middle position and place the cake on the rack. Set the oven to 325 degrees and turn it on; bake the cake, without opening the oven door, until a toothpick inserted in the center comes out with a few moist crumbs attached, 70 to 80 minutes.

5. Let the cake cool in the pan for 10 minutes. Run a small knife around the edge of the cake, then flip it out onto a wire rack. Turn the cake right side up and let cool completely, about 2 hours, before serving.

7UP Pound Cake

Around the middle of the 1900s, soda companies began marketing their products as more than mere drink, urging consumers to think of soda as a pantry staple. For one such effort, an advertising campaign to "get some extra 7UP for cooking," the company distributed free promotional recipe booklets that touted dishes that used the lemon-lime concoction as an ingredient. Many of the recipes faded into obscurity, but the 7UP pound cake was one that withstood the test of time. The effervescent, slightly acidic soda gives this cake its flavor, lift, and uniquely tender texture.

Except for the soda, the recipes we found for 7UP pound cake mirrored traditional pound cake in both method and ingredients. Sugar and softened butter are beaten together until light and fluffy. Eggs are added, followed by 7UP and lemon extract or zest. The flour is mixed in until just

THE 7UP STORY

Twice, St. Louis entrepreneur Charles Grigg tried to crush the competition with his orange-flavored, jauntily named sodas "Whistle" and "Howdy." Each time, soda behemoth Orange Crush beat him back. But in October 1929, just weeks before the stock market crash that led to the Great Depression, Grigg's luck changed. He diversified into lemon and lime, launching Bib-Label Lithiated Lemon-Lime Soda, known within a few years as 7UP (the label was printed on a "bib," hence the original name). He marketed the soda to adults as "uplifting" (given the lithium in the original formula, no doubt).

Following Prohibition, 7UP was also promoted as both a hangover cure and a cocktail mixer. Many stories claim to explain the soda's mysterious name: the 7-ounce bottle, the seven ingredients in the formula, the night Grigg allegedly won big throwing sevens in a game of craps, and "up" for the jolly mood the lithium engendered. Which of these tales, if any, is true, Grigg never told, according to a company spokesman.

combined, and the batter is poured into a tube pan and baked at a moderate temperature (to prevent overbrowning) for a little over an hour. While traditional pound cakes can be dense, the 7UP version emerged with a tight yet light crumb, thanks to the soda's citric acid (which tenderizes) and carbonated water (which lifts).

Unfortunately, the flavor didn't wow us as much as the texture. The cake made with lemon extract tasted like furniture polish, and the sugar (a generous 3 cups) overwhelmed the citrus flavor of the cakes made with zest. Also, every last recipe omitted lime altogether—surprisingly, given 7UP's hallmark lemon-lime combination.

Working from a recipe in which the 7UP cake was fortified with zest, we began scaling back the sugar to bring out some citrus zing. Eventually, we achieved balanced sweetness by cutting out ½ cup of sugar. But the flavor of the cake remained flat. Unlike juice, finely grated zest can be added without affecting texture, so we added increasing amounts of both lemon and lime zest until we were at 1 tablespoon of each. The zest lent a fragrant quality, but the cake still lacked conviction. Realizing we'd need to add fresh (highly acidic) lemon and lime juice despite the troubles they might cause, we gradually added each until we'd settled on ¼ cup between the two in place of an equal amount of 7UP. Now the cake tasted great, but as we'd feared, the texture had taken a turn for the worse. A perfect pound cake hinges on a fragile emulsion of butter and eggs. The extra acid (from the juice) was causing the batter to curdle, resulting in a tough, gummy cake.

Reviewing our ingredient list, we wondered if melting the butter might help. While softened butter provides an uneven coating that exposes the batter to structure-wrecking acid, melted butter readily coats and therefore protects the gluten.

To test this, we simply melted the butter and used the food processor to ensure an even emulsification. Once the sugar and wet ingredients were combined, we slowly poured the melted butter down the feed tube. We stirred in the flour, baked and cooled the cake, then helped ourselves to a slice. This big, buttery cake had a fine, even crumb plus a bold citrusy flavor—which we amplified with a lemon-lime glaze—that warranted the 7UP name.

7UP POUND CAKE

SERVES 12

Fresh, not flat, 7UP is essential for the best texture and rise. This cake is traditionally baked in a tube pan, but a 12-cup nonstick Bundt pan will also work.

CAKE

2½	cups granulated sugar
5	large eggs, room temperature
½	cup 7UP, room temperature (see note above)
1	tablespoon grated fresh lemon zest and 2 tablespoons fresh lemon juice
1	tablespoon grated fresh lime zest and 2 tablespoons fresh lime juice (2 limes)
½	teaspoon salt
20	tablespoons (2½ sticks) unsalted butter, melted and cooled
3¼	cups cake flour

GLAZE

1	cup confectioners' sugar
1	tablespoon fresh lemon juice
1	tablespoon fresh lime juice

1. FOR THE CAKE: Adjust an oven rack to the lower-middle position and heat the oven to 300 degrees. Grease and flour a 16-cup tube pan. Process the granulated sugar, eggs, 7UP, lemon zest and juice, lime zest and juice, and salt in a food processor until smooth. With the machine running, slowly pour in the butter and process until incorporated. Transfer to a large bowl. Add the flour in three additions, whisking until combined.

2. Scrape the batter into the prepared pan and smooth the top. Wipe any drops of batter off the sides of the pan and gently tap the pan on the work surface to settle the batter. Bake the cake until a toothpick inserted in the center comes out clean, 75 to 90 minutes. Let the cake cool in the pan for 10 minutes. Run a small knife around the edge of the cake, then flip it out onto a wire rack set inside a rimmed baking sheet. Turn the cake right side up and let cool completely, about 2 hours.

3. FOR THE GLAZE: Whisk all the glaze ingredients together in a bowl until smooth. Pour the glaze over the cooled cake. Let the glaze set, about 15 minutes, before serving.

Angel Food Cake

At its heavenly best, angel food cake should be tall and perfectly shaped, have a snow-white, tender crumb, and be encased in a thin, delicate, golden crust. The recipe appears simple. The elements of the ingredient list—mostly egg whites, sugar, and flour—are combined in a straightforward manner: the egg whites are whipped with sugar and cream of tartar until soft peaks form (this gives the cake lift), flour and flavorings are folded in, and the batter is baked. Yet, in spite of the concise ingredient list and well-established method, most angel food cakes are depressingly dense, squat, and wet. Besides that, there are enough old wives' tales circulating about the nitty-gritty of making angel food cake that this dessert could be its own 101 class at culinary school. We wanted to separate the facts from fiction and develop a foolproof recipe for a perfectly cloudlike yet tender angel food cake.

We baked several angel food cakes from nearly identical recipes and weren't totally surprised by the outcome—some of the cakes were tender and statuesque with a delicate crumb, and others were misshapen and heavy. In an effort to figure out how such similar blueprints could yield very different results, we waded through—and disproved—a number of the myths that surround the making of angel food cake.

First off, the temperature of the egg whites doesn't matter; cold egg whites will whip to the same volume as room-temperature eggs (they'll just take a few minutes longer). Also, slightly under- or overbeating the whites doesn't affect texture or lift. We tried both, several times, and our cakes turned out respectably regardless. Next, the flour does need to be sifted, but not nearly as much as some old-time recipes might imply. We simply aerated the flour using a food processor. Finally, your kitchen doesn't need to be veiled in silence and stillness when the cake is in the oven; you can jump up and down in front of the oven or open the door to take a peek, and your cake won't fall.

However, there are just as many angel food cake truths that you must adhere to, the most obvious being that the key to a great angel food cake lies in voluminous, stable egg whites. The eggs must be separated carefully, as the merest speck of yolk prevents them from whipping to peaks. Cream of tartar is an absolute must, as it offers some insurance against deflated whites. It's acidic, which helps stabilize egg whites, as would lemon juice or vinegar, but it doesn't contribute any noticeable flavors.

During our tests we learned that in order to prevent deflating our whites, special care needs to be taken with the supporting ingredients—sugar and flour. While granulated or confectioners' sugar made an acceptable but somewhat heavy cake, processing the granulated sugar in a food processor until it was powdery produced an extraordinary cake. The processed sugar was fine, light, and clump-free, so it didn't deflate the egg whites. After combining the flour and sugar, we couldn't just dump it all in with the egg whites and fold; the flour-sugar mixture had to be gently sifted over the beaten egg whites in three additions to avoid putting too much weight on the whites. If we were impatient and tried to speed this process along, the egg whites were certain to deflate.

Finally, it's imperative that angel food cake cool properly; the cake must cool in the pan it is baked in, upside down. Cakes that are cooled right side up can be crushed by their own weight, leading to a flat, squat, spongy cake. (If your tube pan doesn't have feet on its rim to support it when positioned upside down, invert it over the neck of a bottle.)

While we learned that angel food cake isn't that difficult, we did find that it's exacting; the right amount of sugar and flour—down to the ounce—must be used in order to achieve that flawlessly tender texture time after time.

ANGEL FOOD CAKE

SERVES 10 TO 12

For the proper texture, it's important to use a precise amount of ingredients, so we've provided the weights for both the cake flour and sugar. Do not substitute all-purpose flour in this recipe. If your tube pan does not have a removable bottom, line the bottom of the pan with parchment paper. In either case, do not grease the pan (or the paper).

1	cup plus 2 tablespoons (4½ ounces) cake flour (see note above)
¼	teaspoon salt
1¾	cups (12¼ ounces) sugar
12	large egg whites
1½	teaspoons cream of tartar
1	teaspoon vanilla extract

1. Adjust an oven rack to the lower-middle position and heat the oven to 325 degrees. Whisk the flour and salt together in a bowl. Process the sugar in a food processor until fine and powdery, about 1 minute. Reserve half of the sugar in a small bowl.

Add the flour mixture to the food processor with the remaining sugar and process until aerated, about 1 minute.

2. With an electric mixer on medium-low speed, beat the egg whites and cream of tartar together until frothy, about 1 minute. Increase the mixer speed to medium-high. With the mixer still running, slowly add the reserved sugar and beat until soft peaks form (see page 5), about 6 minutes. Add the vanilla and mix until incorporated.

3. Sift the flour mixture over the egg whites in three additions, folding gently with a rubber spatula after each addition until incorporated. Scrape the batter into a 16-cup ungreased tube pan (see note above).

4. Bake the cake until a toothpick inserted in the center comes out clean and cracks in the cake appear dry, 40 to 45 minutes. Let the cake cool completely, inverted (see the photo below), about 3 hours. Run a knife along the edge of the pan, then flip the cake out onto a cake platter. Serve.

COOLING ANGEL FOOD CAKE

If your tube pan doesn't have feet on its rim, invert the pan over the neck of a bottle. Cool the cake, inverted, until it is completely cool, about 3 hours.

Variations
CAFÉ AU LAIT ANGEL FOOD CAKE

Add 1 tablespoon instant coffee or espresso powder to the food processor along with the flour mixture in step 1. Reduce the amount of vanilla extract to ½ teaspoon and add 1 tablespoon coffee liqueur with the vanilla in step 2.

CHOCOLATE-ALMOND ANGEL FOOD CAKE

Reduce the amount of vanilla extract to ½ teaspoon and add ½ teaspoon almond extract with the vanilla in step 2. Fold 2 ounces finely grated bittersweet chocolate into the batter along with the flour mixture in step 3.

LEMON–POPPY SEED ANGEL FOOD CAKE

Add 2 tablespoons grated fresh lemon zest and 2 tablespoons fresh lemon juice (2 lemons) along with the vanilla in step 2. Fold 1 tablespoon poppy seeds into the batter along with the flour mixture in step 3.

SHOPPING WITH THE TEST KITCHEN

Tube Pans: Tube pans are not just for looks—the tube helps very tall cakes bake faster and more evenly. After testing six brands, baking angel food and yellow sponge cakes in each, we learned that what matters most is heft, finish (we like pans that are dark and nonstick), and a removable bottom. Our favorite pan, the Chicago Metallic Professional Angel Food Cake Pan ($19.95), also has feet on its rim, handy for elevating the upturned pan as the cake cools.

Icebox Lemon Cheesecake

Icebox cheesecakes are a delicious paradox: simultaneously delicate and light, yet rich and creamy. They're especially appealing in the summer months, because there's no hot oven and no messy water bath (which many baked cheesecakes require). While plenty of them include a squeeze of lemon to perk up their flavor, we desired a no-bake cheesecake in which lemon was the main attraction. Would it be as easy as stirring in a lot more freshly squeezed lemon juice? We grabbed some lemons and headed into the test kitchen to find out.

First, we made half a dozen recipes for lemon cheesecakes we had gathered from cookbooks. As we'd suspected, most simply consisted of cheesecake batter, with varying amounts of lemon juice and zest added, poured over a graham cracker crust and chilled. The results weren't exactly shocking—in some cheesecakes, the lemon flavor was alternately fleeting or harsh, and in all of them it was one-dimensional. The zest, while fresh and bright, was chewy, which interfered with the creaminess of the cheesecakes. One recipe we tested took a different tack—lemon sauce was drizzled over slices of plain icebox cheesecake. The sauce (made from lemon juice, sugar, and cornstarch) was watery and too sweet, though, and the overall lemon flavor was nowhere near what we were aiming for. Although this last rendition was a flop, it did provide some inspiration.

But first we wanted to refine the cheesecake itself. Our working recipe called for beating together cream cheese, sugar, heavy cream, and dissolved gelatin until smooth and creamy. The batter was then poured over a baked graham cracker crust (we would revisit the crust later) in a springform pan and chilled for several hours until set. Although extra lemon juice was clearly not the

solution, it was at least a place to start. Test by test, we added increasing amounts of freshly squeezed lemon juice to the batter. We screeched to a halt at ½ cup, which tasters proclaimed was too much. The uncooked lemon juice, which would have mellowed with heat in a baked cheesecake, was aggressive and sour in an icebox cheesecake. We dialed back to ¼ cup and set out to find another way to add more lemon flavor.

We reviewed our options. Lemon zest was out, since tasters had already objected to its "chew." Not surprisingly, lemon extract tasted artificial. We needed a solution as imaginative as that sauce recipe from our initial tests but tastier and better integrated. What if we took the lemon sauce to the next level and used lemon curd, the rich, tangy spread usually smothered on scones, instead?

We stirred together eggs, sugar, and, of course, lemon juice on the stovetop, then added the butter and cream. After the cheesecake set, we spread the top with our sunny yellow curd as if we were icing a cake. It was a definite success. In our next test, we made it an even bigger success by stirring some of the curd directly into the filling. Now the filling had layered lemon flavor, and the curd topping added a bright lemon echo. And for a more refined (and pretty) finish, we made one alteration. Instead of spreading a thin layer of curd over the cake, we drizzled lines of it on the cheesecake, then swirled the lines for a marbled effect. Granted, the addition of lemon curd made our cheesecake more work than the usual icebox version, but it doubled the pleasure, too.

Finally, we tackled the crust. It occurred to us that sticking with graham crackers for the crust would be wasting an opportunity to add yet more lemon flavor to the cheesecake. We decided to substitute cream-filled lemon sandwich cookies (which would add flavor but not stringent acidity) for the graham crackers. The cookies' cream filling made

for a sturdier cheesecake crust (which now required only 2 tablespoons of butter to bind it). But the crust was too sweet. It was back in balance when we cut out the sugar and sneaked in a teaspoon of zest. That added a final glint of lemon to our icebox cheesecake without spoiling the filling's luscious, creamy texture.

ICEBOX LEMON CHEESECAKE

SERVES 12 TO 16

Any brand of lemon sandwich cookies will work well here. We prefer our fresh lemon curd, but if you're pressed for time, see page 124 for our recommended brand of store-bought lemon curd. Leftover cake should be refrigerated.

CRUST

10	lemon sandwich cookies (see note above), broken into rough pieces (about 1¼ cups)
2	tablespoons unsalted butter, melted
1	teaspoon grated fresh lemon zest

CURD

1	large egg plus 1 large egg yolk
¼	cup sugar
	Pinch salt
2	tablespoons fresh lemon juice
1	tablespoon unsalted butter
1	tablespoon heavy cream

FILLING

¼	cup fresh lemon juice (2 lemons)
1	envelope (2¾ teaspoons) unflavored gelatin
1½	pounds cream cheese, cut into 1-inch pieces and softened
¾	cup sugar
	Pinch salt
1¼	cups heavy cream, room temperature

1. FOR THE CRUST: Adjust an oven rack to the middle position and heat the oven to 350 degrees. Process the cookies in a food processor until finely ground. Add the butter and zest and pulse until combined. Sprinkle the mixture into a 9-inch springform pan and press evenly onto the bottom of the pan. Bake until lightly browned and set, about 10 minutes. Let the crust cool completely on a wire rack, about 30 minutes.

2. FOR THE CURD: Meanwhile, whisk the egg, egg yolk, sugar, and salt together in a small saucepan. Add the lemon juice and cook over medium-low heat, stirring constantly, until thick and puddinglike, about 3 minutes. Remove from the heat and stir in the butter and cream. Press the mixture through a fine-mesh strainer into a small bowl and refrigerate until needed. (The lemon curd can be refrigerated in an airtight container for up to 3 days.)

3. FOR THE FILLING: Stir the lemon juice and gelatin together in a small bowl and microwave until warm (but not bubbling), 15 to 30 seconds. Stir to dissolve the gelatin and set aside to cool.

4. In a large bowl, beat the cream cheese, sugar, and salt together with an electric mixer on medium speed until smooth and creamy, scraping down the sides of the bowl as needed, about 2 minutes. Slowly add the cream and beat until light and fluffy, about 2 minutes. Add the cooled gelatin mixture and ¼ cup of the curd, increase the mixer speed to medium-high, and beat until smooth and airy, about 3 minutes.

5. Pour the filling into the cooled crust and smooth the top. Following the photos on page 124, pour thin lines of the remaining curd on top of the cake and lightly drag a paring knife or skewer through the lines to create a marbled appearance. Refrigerate until set, at least 6 hours. To unmold the cheesecake, wrap a hot, damp kitchen towel around the cake pan and let sit for 1 minute. Remove the sides of the pan and carefully slide the cake onto a cake platter. Serve.

SHOPPING WITH THE TEST KITCHEN

Lemon Curd: Homemade lemon curd can't be beat, but sometimes convenience wins out. We found a number of brands of jarred lemon curd at the supermarket and tested them in our icebox cheesecake. We found only one that passed muster: Wilkin and Sons. This lemon curd captures the taste of real lemons and is creamy enough to use in our cheesecake (you will need ½ cup). Just know that it's a pricey purchase—it costs about $9.

MAKING SWIRLS IN ICEBOX CHEESECAKE

1. Use a measuring cup to pour the curd in four thin lines on top of the cheesecake.

2. To make the swirls, drag a paring knife or skewer perpendicularly through the lines to create a marbled design.

Icebox Oreo Cheesecake

Creamy, luscious cheesecake makes the perfect partner for the Oreo, one of the best-selling cookies of all time. Although this chocolaty, creamy combination is incredibly satisfying, when translated to a streamlined no-bake version, the texture is never quite as creamy or attractive as one would hope. Often, the filling is a spongy gray mass with random bites of cookie strewn throughout. We set out to make a rich and creamy icebox Oreo cheesecake that would deliver on both flavor and looks.

Our quest for great icebox Oreo cheesecake began with preparing several existing recipes for this popular dessert. We were disheartened to find that all of these cheesecakes were either too springy from gelatin overload or so runny that they wouldn't slice properly. And if the Oreos weren't dispersed as an unappealing gray powder, they remained distractingly chunky.

For big Oreo flavor, we started by grinding some cookies and mixing them with melted butter to make an easy press-in crust for our springform pan. We thought we could finesse the amount of gelatin in standard recipes to get the creamy-textured filling we were after, but we were wrong. After countless tests, we realized we were going to have to incorporate some eggs (not usually found in icebox cheesecakes) into our cheesecake to get the dense, velvety texture we wanted.

Thinking an eggy pudding might work, we cooked a mixture of egg yolks, milk, and cornstarch, combined it with sweetened cream cheese, poured the filling over the Oreo crust, and put the cake in the refrigerator. This cheesecake tasted pretty good and held together well, but the cornstarch had given it a slippery, glossy texture. Replacing the cornstarch with flour gave the cake stability without the slippery texture, but it still didn't exhibit the creamy density we wanted.

We tried adding sour cream and ricotta cheese, but neither was dense enough to help create that compact, baked texture. A colleague suggested that melted white chocolate might help make the cheesecake denser while adding a pleasant sweetness. We gave it a shot by stirring some chopped white chocolate into the hot pudding before cooling the pudding and combining it with the cream cheese. When set, the white chocolate firmed up the filling, and the resulting texture (and flavor) was ultra-creamy.

We were almost there, but tasters were clamoring for more Oreo flavor. Working to avoid the drab gray cheesecake of our earlier tests, we broke a dozen cookies into large pieces and added them to the cheesecake in distinct layers. At last, we had an icebox Oreo cheesecake that was a pristine black-and-white dream and tasted every bit as good as it looked.

ICEBOX OREO CHEESECAKE

SERVES 12 TO 16

Though not technically white chocolate, 2 cups of white chips can be substituted for the 8 ounces of white chocolate. Leftover cake should be refrigerated.

CRUST

| 30 | Oreo cookies, broken into rough pieces |
| 7 | tablespoons unsalted butter, softened |

FILLING

1	cup whole milk
4	large egg yolks
¼	cup all-purpose flour
8	ounces white chocolate, chopped (see note above)
4	(8-ounce) packages cream cheese, cut into chunks and softened
⅓	cup confectioners' sugar
2	teaspoons vanilla extract
⅛	teaspoon salt
12	Oreo cookies, broken into rough pieces

1. FOR THE CRUST: Process the cookies and butter together in a food processor until finely ground. Sprinkle the mixture into a 9-inch springform pan and press evenly onto the bottom and sides of the pan. Refrigerate until set, at least 1 hour or up to 2 days.

2. FOR THE FILLING: Heat ¾ cup of the milk in a medium saucepan over medium heat until simmering. Meanwhile, whisk together the egg yolks, flour, and remaining ¼ cup milk in a large bowl until smooth. Slowly whisk the hot milk into the yolk mixture to temper. Return the mixture to the saucepan and cook over medium heat, whisking constantly, until very thick and glossy, 1 to 2 minutes. Off the heat, whisk in the white chocolate until melted. Transfer the custard to a bowl, press plastic wrap directly onto the surface, and refrigerate until cold and set, at least 1 hour or up to 2 days.

3. In a large bowl, beat together the cream cheese, sugar, vanilla, and salt with an electric mixer on medium-high speed until light and fluffy, about 2 minutes. Reduce the mixer speed to medium-low and mix in the custard until just combined, about 30 seconds. Pour one-quarter of the cream cheese mixture evenly into the prepared pan and sprinkle one-third of the cookie pieces over the surface. Repeat the process twice, then top with the remaining filling. Refrigerate until set, at least 6 hours. To unmold the cheesecake, wrap a hot, damp kitchen towel around the cake pan and let sit for 1 minute. Remove the sides of the pan and carefully slide the cake onto a cake platter. Serve.

PECAN SOUR CREAM COFFEE CAKE

CHAPTER FOUR

Coffee Cakes and Morning Sweets

Blueberry Boy Bait

More than just a funny name, blueberry boy bait is a moist yellow cake topped with a layer of blueberries and crisp cinnamon sugar. This simple blueberry coffee cake made its way onto the national baking scene in 1954, when a 15-year-old girl entered her dessert—Blueberry Boy Bait—in the junior division of the Pillsbury Grand National Baking Contest. She won second place, which included a $2,000 cash prize plus a promise to print her recipe in one of Pillsbury's cookbooks. The cake was named for the effect it had on teenage boys—one bite and they were hooked. We wanted a recipe that would lure not only teenagers, but all of our tasters, too.

We prepared the 1954 boy bait recipe, along with a number of recipes we came across in our research. Several were dry and crumbly, others were cloyingly sweet, but none of them had enough blueberry flavor to please our tasting panel. We decide to refine the cake base first before considering the berries.

The recipes we had prepared all began with a basic yellow sheet cake; tasters liked the flavor and texture of the prizewinner the most, so we decided to work with this recipe. In the end, we needed to make only a few minor adjustments. For deeper flavor, we exchanged the shortening in the original recipe for butter. To tone down the sweetness of the cake, we swapped half of the granulated sugar for brown sugar; this also gave the cake a more complex flavor. The original recipe included just two eggs, but we found that adding one more egg gave the cake more structure.

Our cake was now tender yet sturdy, but we still had the blueberries to work into the equation. The original recipe just wasn't as berry-flavored as we had hoped, nor were the other recipes we uncovered in our research. Our solution was simple—we doubled the amount of berries, stirring half into the batter and sprinkling the remaining berries on top.

For the topping, just a sprinkling of sugar and cinnamon worked best, baking up into sweet, crispy flakes. Our version of blueberry boy bait, with its buttery cake and big berry flavor, reeled in everyone in the test kitchen.

BLUEBERRY BOY BAIT

SERVES 12

If using frozen blueberries, do not let them thaw, as they will turn the batter a blue-green color.

CAKE

- 2 cups plus 1 teaspoon all-purpose flour
- 1 tablespoon baking powder
- 1 teaspoon salt
- 16 tablespoons (2 sticks) unsalted butter, softened
- ¾ cup packed light brown sugar
- ½ cup granulated sugar
- 3 large eggs
- 1 cup whole milk
- ½ cup fresh or frozen blueberries (see note above)

TOPPING

- ½ cup fresh or frozen blueberries (see note above)
- ¼ cup granulated sugar
- ½ teaspoon ground cinnamon

1. FOR THE CAKE: Adjust an oven rack to the middle position and heat the oven to 350 degrees. Grease and flour a 13 by 9-inch baking pan.

2. Whisk 2 cups of the flour, baking powder, and salt together in a medium bowl. With an electric mixer on medium-high speed, beat the butter, brown sugar, and granulated sugar together until fluffy, 3 to 6 minutes. Add the eggs, one at a time, beating until just incorporated. Reduce the mixer speed to medium and beat in one-third of the flour mixture until incorporated. Beat in ½ cup of the milk. Beat in half of the remaining flour mixture, then the remaining ½ cup milk. Beat in the remaining flour mixture. Toss the blueberries with the remaining 1 teaspoon flour. Using a rubber spatula, gently fold the blueberries into the batter. Scrape the batter into the prepared pan and gently tap the pan on the work surface to settle the batter.

3. FOR THE TOPPING: Scatter the blueberries over the top of the batter. Combine the granulated sugar and cinnamon in a small bowl and sprinkle over the batter. Bake the cake until a toothpick inserted in the center comes out clean, 45 to 50 minutes, rotating the pan halfway through baking. Let the cake cool in the pan for 20 minutes, then flip it out and invert it onto a serving platter. Serve warm or at room temperature.

SHOPPING WITH THE TEST KITCHEN

Silicone Spatulas: We use a silicone spatula to stir batter, fold egg whites, and scrape the contents of a mixing bowl into a baking pan—along with numerous other cooking tasks. Whenever we're baking, we make sure to have the Rubbermaid Professional 13½-Inch High Heat Scraper ($18.99) nearby. This top-performing spatula has a long handle and a wide, stiff blade with a thin, flexible edge—perfect for both mixing thick batter and conforming to the shape of the bowl to scrape out those last bits of cookie dough.

Pecan Sour Cream Coffee Cake

Most coffee cakes are nothing more than plain old yellow cake hiding under a crumb topping. They are light and fluffy when they should be moist and rich. And even when the texture is right, often the flavor is not. When nuts are added, they're often an afterthought, with no real presence. We wanted a rich, satisfying coffee cake that had bold pecan flavor and texture.

Most coffee cake recipes follow the same technique: cream butter and sugar, beat in eggs, and alternate additions of dry ingredients and milk. This method requires 5 to 8 minutes of mixer action and whips a fair amount of air into the batter—perfect for a fluffy yellow cake but all wrong for our idea of coffee cake, which should be rich, moist, and luxurious. We tried a variety of other methods without success until we remembered a little-known cake-mixing method in which softened butter is beaten with some of the liquid ingredients directly into the flour mixture for just 2 minutes. The butter coats the flour, making the cake rich and tender. And without all of the whipping action, the batter is both denser (a good thing) and richer (an even better thing). The cake was still on the dry side, though, and the solution was as easy as replacing the milk with sour cream.

Now we moved on to the streusel layer swirled throughout the middle—arguably the best part of any coffee cake. For an overt pecan-y flavor, we tried loading on the streusel; but we could add only so much before it sank to the bottom. We tried intensifying its flavor by toasting the nuts, but the cake was still lacking in nut flavor.

Next we tried a variety of techniques, from lining the cake pan with ground pecans to adding whole and roughly chopped pecans to the batter.

The winning technique, which took this recipe from good to great, emerged when we added some of the finely ground toasted pecans we'd been including in the streusel directly to the flour mixture, making something like a "pecan flour." Now every bite—not just the streusel—was full of big pecan flavor.

PECAN SOUR CREAM COFFEE CAKE

SERVES 12

You can toast, cool, and grind the nuts for both the streusel and cake together.

STREUSEL

½	cup pecans, toasted, cooled, and ground fine (see note above)
3	tablespoons dark brown sugar
1	tablespoon all-purpose flour
1	teaspoon ground cinnamon

CAKE

6	large eggs
1¾	cups sour cream
¼	cup maple syrup
1½	tablespoons vanilla extract
3	cups all-purpose flour
1¼	cups granulated sugar
½	cup pecans, toasted, cooled, and ground fine (see note above)
4½	teaspoons baking powder
1¼	teaspoons baking soda
1	teaspoon salt
16	tablespoons (2 sticks) unsalted butter, cut into ½-inch pieces and softened

GLAZE

1	cup confectioners' sugar
2	tablespoons orange juice
1	teaspoon grated fresh orange zest

1. FOR THE STREUSEL: Combine all the streusel ingredients in a small bowl and set aside.

2. FOR THE CAKE: Adjust an oven rack to the lowest position and heat the oven to 350 degrees. Prepare a 12-cup nonstick Bundt pan following the photo on page 76. Whisk the eggs, sour cream, maple syrup, and vanilla together in a medium bowl.

3. Whisk the flour, granulated sugar, pecans, baking powder, baking soda, and salt together in a large bowl. With an electric mixer on low speed, beat the butter and half of the egg mixture into the flour mixture until the mixture starts to come together, about 15 seconds. Scrape down the sides of the bowl with a rubber spatula, add the remaining egg mixture, and continue to beat on medium speed until the batter is light and fluffy, about 2 minutes, scraping down the bowl and beaters as needed.

4. Add 5 cups of the batter to the prepared pan, smooth the top, and sprinkle the streusel evenly over the batter. Cover with the remaining batter, spreading it evenly.

5. Bake the cake until a toothpick inserted in the center comes out with a few crumbs attached,

TOASTING NUTS

Toasting nuts is well worth the extra time—it intensifies their flavor and maximizes their crunch. Here's our preferred method. Toast the nuts in a dry skillet over medium heat, shaking the pan occasionally to prevent scorching, until they are fragrant and begin to darken slightly, about 3 to 5 minutes.

about 60 minutes. Let the cake cool in the pan for 30 minutes, then flip it out onto a wire rack set inside a rimmed baking sheet. Let the cake cool completely before glazing, about 1 hour.

6. FOR THE GLAZE: Whisk all the glaze ingredients together, then drizzle over the cake before serving.

Cherry-Almond Coffee Cake

In our minds, the perfect cherry-almond coffee cake is composed of tender yellow cake paired with a bright and fresh cherry filling and topped with a crumbly almond streusel. Yet so many cherry-almond coffee cakes are closer to a nightmare than a dream, with gloppy, canned-tasting cherry filling or cake so delicate the filling falls through. As for the almond flavor, it tends to be fleeting, as most recipes rely on extract alone. We wanted a cherry-almond coffee cake as good as the ones we'd imagined, so we gathered some recipes and started baking.

One recipe we tested used a jar of cherry jam for the fruit layer, which appealed to us for simplicity's sake. Once the cake was baked, though, the jam lost its fresh pizzazz. Maybe we could develop a souped-up jam potent enough to take the heat. Fresh cherries required pitting and limited the recipe to the short harvest season. Instead, we tested frozen, canned, and dried cherries against one another, combining each with water, sugar, and cornstarch and cooking them on the stovetop until jammy, about 30 minutes. Tasters gave the thumbs up to canned sour (also called "tart") cherries, which provided a bracing counterpoint to the sweet cake. We reinforced their flavor by using the syrup they were packed in instead of water.

We tested an assortment of yellow cake recipes underneath our bright new cherry topping. All buckled under the weight of nearly 2 pounds of fruit. After a few more false starts with yellow cakes, we switched to a thicker crumb-cake batter, which contained less liquid (milk and eggs) in proportion to the flour. We also decided to replace some of the flour with ground almonds, a trick we'd used before to add nutty flavor and structure to baked goods. Now the cake had a faint nutty undertone, but to our surprise, the cherry filling once more sank. Dismayed, we dialed up our science editor, who explained that the oil from the almonds overtenderized our cake. He suggested using commercial marzipan or almond paste instead, as the manufacturers extract the oil before they produce the paste.

On the labels, we read that almond paste contains 45 percent almonds, whereas marzipan contains just 28 percent. As we expected, a marzipan cake was more sweet than nutty, while an almond-paste cake had outstanding almond flavor. Moreover, the dense paste improved the texture of the crumb. But the best news? The cherry filling stayed put.

Looking for a little tang to balance the sweetness of the paste, we replaced the milk in the batter with sour cream. Now the cake rose beautifully under the cherry topping and baked into a plush, moist crumb.

Getting the right streusel was comparatively easy—a mixture of flour, white and brown sugars, and melted butter turned into chunky, crunchy nubs. Chopped almonds made the mixture brittle, but when we reserved some almond paste for the streusel, tasters gave the results an enthusiastic endorsement. With a simple almond glaze draped over the top, the coffee cake of our dreams was at last a reality.

CHERRY-ALMOND COFFEE CAKE

SERVES 8 TO 12

Be sure to use almond paste in this recipe, not marzipan, which is much sweeter.

FILLING

2	(15-ounce) cans sour cherries
¼	cup granulated sugar
2	tablespoons cornstarch

STREUSEL AND CAKE

2½	cups all-purpose flour
½	cup granulated sugar
⅓	cup packed light brown sugar
½	teaspoon salt
7	tablespoons unsalted butter, melted, plus 8 tablespoons (1 stick) unsalted butter, softened
1	(7-ounce) tube almond paste (see note above), crumbled into small pieces (about 2½ cups)
1½	teaspoons baking powder
⅓	cup sour cream
2	large eggs
1	teaspoon vanilla extract
1	teaspoon almond extract

GLAZE

1	cup confectioners' sugar
2	tablespoons water
¼	teaspoon almond extract

1. FOR THE FILLING: Bring the cherries with their syrup, sugar, and cornstarch to a simmer in a large saucepan over medium heat. Mash the cherries with a potato masher and cook until thick and jamlike, about 25 minutes (the mixture should measure 2 cups). Refrigerate until cool, about 30 minutes.

2. FOR THE STREUSEL AND CAKE: Whisk 1¼ cups of the flour, ¼ cup of the granulated sugar, brown sugar, and ¼ teaspoon of the salt in a medium bowl. Stir in the melted butter until the mixture forms pea-size pieces. Stir in ½ cup of the almond paste; set aside.

3. Adjust an oven rack to the middle position and heat the oven to 350 degrees. Grease and flour a 13 by 9-inch baking pan. Combine the remaining 1¼ cups flour, baking powder, and remaining ¼ teaspoon salt in a medium bowl. Whisk the sour cream, eggs, vanilla, and almond extract together in a small bowl. With an electric mixer on medium-high speed, beat the remaining almond paste, remaining ¼ cup granulated sugar, and softened butter together until light and fluffy, about 2 minutes. Add the sour cream mixture and beat until incorporated. Reduce the mixer speed to low and add the flour mixture, mixing until just combined, about 1 minute. Increase the mixer speed to medium-high and beat until fluffy, about 1 minute.

4. Scrape the batter into the prepared pan. Dollop the cooled cherry mixture over the batter and spread into an even layer. Sprinkle the streusel over the cherry mixture and bake until a toothpick inserted in the center comes out clean, about 30 minutes, rotating the pan halfway through baking. Let the cake cool completely, about 2 hours.

5. FOR THE GLAZE: Combine all the glaze ingredients in a small bowl and drizzle over the cake before serving.

Almond Ring Coffee Cake

Traditional coffee cakes—with their tender crumb, rustic fruit fillings, and nutty streusels—are a coffee-break classic. But when we want something fancier, our thoughts turn to a yeasted coffee cake with buttery layers of rich dough, a sweet almond filling, and a flourish of sliced nuts and white icing. You can buy this kind of coffee cake at the supermarket (think Entenmann's), but most are made with shortening (not butter) and have an artificial flavor. Our goal was to streamline the classic recipe and make it worth doing at home.

The method for making an almond ring coffee cake is pretty standard, and we didn't expect to deviate from the formula. An almond filling is placed on a rectangle of tender yeast dough, and the whole thing is rolled up, formed into a circle, and then cut to create a floral pattern that exposes some of the filling. Although the method was well established, the ingredients required some testing. Some recipes produced rings that were too dry and others were too sweet or lacked almond flavor.

We decided to start with the filling. Most recipes use cream cheese enriched with ground almonds and sugar, but we found this combination problematic—the mixture was so soft it leaked out of the dough, and we could barely taste the almonds. We had better luck with almond paste, which had just made our Cherry-Almond Coffee Cake (page 133) a resounding success. When mixed with a little cream cheese, it gave us the nutty flavor we were looking for, and it was thick enough to stay put inside the coffee cake.

Most yeasted coffee cakes rely on brioche, a rich dough made with milk, butter, and eggs. Because our almond filling was pretty rich, we found that a lighter dough (made with one stick of butter and not two, as many recipes directed) was better.

Three egg yolks gave the dough good structure, and leaving out the whites made the dough easier to handle. (We saved the whites for gluing the garnish of sliced almonds onto the ring.)

After playing around with various amounts of granulated and brown sugar, we made the important discovery of using honey to sweeten the dough. Tasters loved its light caramel flavor; we liked the fact that honey made the dough moister and more tender.

By using a preheated and then turned-off oven as a proofing box, we were able to make our coffee cake in a couple of hours (not all day, as was the case with most recipes we tried). This was a cake we'd be making not just for special occasions, but all year long.

ALMOND RING COFFEE CAKE

MAKES 2 RINGS, EACH SERVING 6

If you don't have a stand mixer, see "Hand Mixing Yeast Doughs" on page 135. Note that you will need 3 eggs, but that the yolks and whites are used separately. Be sure to use almond paste in this recipe, not marzipan, which is much sweeter. Feel free to bake both cakes at the same time or freeze one for another time. To freeze one cake, let the cakes rise in step 7, then wrap one cake tightly with greased plastic wrap followed by aluminum foil and freeze for up to 1 month. Let the frozen cake thaw in the refrigerator for 12 hours, then return it to room temperature for about 1 hour and bake as directed. This cake also works well with Apricot-Orange Filling and Berry Filling (recipes follow). Leftover cake can be refrigerated for up to 2 days.

ALMOND FILLING

1   (7-ounce) tube almond paste
    (see note above)

4   ounces cream cheese, softened

½   cup confectioners' sugar

DOUGH

1⅓	cups whole milk, warm (110 degrees)
8	tablespoons (1 stick) unsalted butter, melted and cooled
⅓	cup honey
3	large egg yolks, lightly beaten
2	teaspoons vanilla extract
5	cups all-purpose flour
1	envelope (2¼ teaspoons) rapid-rise or instant yeast
2	teaspoons salt

TOPPING

3	large egg whites, lightly beaten
½	cup sliced almonds
1½	cups confectioners' sugar
2	ounces cream cheese, softened
2	tablespoons whole milk
½	teaspoon vanilla extract

1. FOR THE FILLING: Beat all the filling ingredients together with an electric mixer on medium speed until smooth. Cover with plastic wrap and refrigerate until ready to use.

2. FOR THE DOUGH: Adjust the oven racks to the upper-middle and lower-middle positions and heat the oven to 200 degrees. When the oven reaches 200 degrees, turn it off. Whisk the milk, melted butter, honey, egg yolks, and vanilla together in a large liquid measuring cup. Combine 4¾ cups of the flour, yeast, and salt in the bowl of a stand mixer. Using the dough hook, mix on low speed. Add the milk mixture and mix until the dough comes together, about 2 minutes.

3. Increase the mixer speed to medium and knead until the dough is smooth and shiny, 5 to 7 minutes. (If, after 5 minutes, more flour is needed, add the remaining ¼ cup flour, 1 tablespoon at a time,

HAND MIXING YEAST DOUGHS

A stand mixer makes quick work of mixing the dough in both our Almond Ring Coffee Cake and Monkey Bread (page 145), but if you don't have one, you can mix the dough by hand with equally successful results.

Whisk the liquid ingredients together in a medium bowl. In a large bowl, whisk the dry ingredients together. Stir the liquid mixture into the dry ingredients with a rubber spatula until the dough comes together and looks shaggy. Turn the dough out onto a clean work surface and knead by hand to form a smooth, round ball, 15 to 25 minutes, adding the remaining flour as indicated to prevent the dough from sticking to the work surface. Transfer to a large, lightly greased bowl, cover with greased plastic wrap, and let rise as directed.

until the dough clears the sides of the bowl but sticks to the bottom.)

4. Turn the dough out onto a lightly floured work surface and knead by hand to form a smooth, round ball. Place the dough in a large, lightly greased bowl, cover the bowl tightly with greased plastic wrap, and place in the warm oven until the dough has doubled in size, 1 to 1½ hours.

5. Line two baking sheets with parchment paper. On a lightly floured work surface, divide the dough into two equal pieces. Following the photos on page 136, and working with one piece of dough at a time, roll the dough into an 18 by 9-inch rectangle. Spread half of the filling in a 1-inch-wide strip about 1 inch above the bottom edge of the dough.

6. Loosen the dough from the work surface using a bench scraper or metal spatula, roll the dough into a tight log, and pinch the seam closed.

Transfer the log, seam side down, to one of the prepared baking sheets. Repeat with the remaining dough and filling.

7. Shape each dough log into a ring. Make about 11 cuts around the outside of the ring with scissors or a knife and twist the pieces upward. Mist both

MAKING A RING-SHAPED COFFEE CAKE

1. Working with one piece of dough at a time, roll the dough into an 18 by 9-inch rectangle. Spread a 1-inch strip of the filling about 1 inch above the bottom edge of the dough.

2. Loosen the dough from the work surface with a bench scraper or metal spatula and carefully roll the dough into an even cylinder. Pinch the seam to seal.

3. Transfer the dough log to a parchment-lined baking sheet and shape into a ring. Make about 11 cuts around the outside of the ring using a knife or scissors, spacing them 1 to 1½ inches apart.

4. Twist each piece of dough cut side up. Mist the cake with vegetable oil spray, wrap loosely in plastic wrap, and let rise in the oven until nearly doubled in size.

cakes with vegetable oil spray, wrap loosely in plastic wrap, and place in the turned-off oven until they have nearly doubled in size and spring back slowly when indented with a finger, 1 to 1½ hours.

8. FOR THE TOPPING: Heat the oven to 375 degrees. Brush the rings with the egg whites and sprinkle with the almonds. Bake the cakes until deep brown, about 25 minutes, switching and rotating the sheets halfway through baking. Let the cakes cool for 1 hour.

9. Whisk the sugar, cream cheese, milk, and vanilla together in a small bowl until smooth, then drizzle the mixture over the cakes before serving.

Variations
APRICOT-ORANGE FILLING

MAKES ENOUGH FOR 2 COFFEE-CAKE RINGS
The filling can be refrigerated in an airtight container for up to 3 days.

2	cups dried apricots
1	cup water
3	tablespoons sugar
3	tablespoons orange juice
2	tablespoons rum (optional)
1	tablespoon grated fresh orange zest

1. Bring the apricots, water, and sugar to a boil in a medium saucepan over medium-high heat. Reduce the heat to medium and simmer gently, stirring occasionally, until the apricots are soft and the water has nearly evaporated, 16 to 18 minutes.

2. Transfer the warm apricots to a food processor. Add the orange juice, rum (if using), and orange zest and process until smooth, about 1 minute. Let the mixture cool to room temperature before substituting for the Almond Filling.

BERRY FILLING

MAKES ENOUGH FOR 2 COFFEE-CAKE RINGS

The filling can be refrigerated in an airtight container for up to 3 days.

2½   cups fresh or frozen raspberries, blueberries, or blackberries
3   tablespoons sugar
2   tablespoons fresh lemon juice
2   tablespoons water
1½   tablespoons cornstarch
   Pinch salt

Stir all the ingredients together in a medium saucepan. Bring to a boil over medium heat and cook, stirring occasionally, until the mixture is thick and shiny, about 2 minutes. Let the mixture cool to room temperature before substituting for the Almond Filling.

Pecan Kringle

Wisconsin might conjure up images of cheese and beer, but in the southeast corner of the state, there's another culinary superstar: kringle. Recipes for this oval-shaped, supremely buttery Danish arrived with the many Danish immigrants who settled in Racine in the 1800s. Often eaten at Christmas, kringle combines the richness of sweet yeast dough with some of the flakiness of painstakingly made puff pastry. It's variously filled with sugared and spiced nuts, fruit, or sweetened cream cheese and is drizzled with a simple glaze. Aside from stunning amounts of butter, kringle requires one thing above all others: patience. Traditional kringle, as it is still made in Wisconsin, takes three days to make and calls for bakers to fold the dough dozens of times, stopping repeatedly to let it chill and relax. However, we did not find the thought of spending

three days folding dough relaxing. We wanted a kringle that rivaled the real McCoy in every respect, except for the hours required to make it.

We settled on a pecan filling, then mixed, rolled, and shaped nine kringle recipes that promised to cut down on time and effort. We baked them after their overnight rest. They looked impressive but tasted either heavy and cakey or lean and breadlike. Many were greasy rather than buttery, and several were encased in stiff, achingly sweet frostings.

We stepped back to get a handle on the difference between authentic and quick (comparatively speaking) kringle. Authentic kringle is made with Danish dough, a cousin of croissant and puff pastry dough, in which eggs are added to the mix of milk, flour, yeast, and sugar for an especially rich, tender texture. The dough is chilled, rolled out, wrapped around a slab of butter, rolled again, folded into thirds, and chilled again. This process forms layers of butter that melt and steam in the oven, making the dough puff and separate into thin, light-as-air pastry sheets. In the recipes that we tested, however, cubes of cold butter were cut into flour, sugar, and yeast, after which water, milk, cream, or sour cream and sometimes eggs were stirred in. The dough was simply rolled, filled, shaped into an oval, and rested.

One of the "quick" doughs that we tested stood out from the pack. It used 2 cups of sour cream as its sole wet ingredient (with 2 cups of butter, 4 cups of flour, 2 tablespoons of sugar, and 1 envelope of yeast). The recipe yielded two kringles with a tender, just-flaky crumb. Our science editor explained that the acidic sour cream weakened the dough's gluten structure, in effect mimicking the flaky texture of an authentic kringle. Unfortunately, it was greasy. We reduced the amount of butter bit by bit to 1¼ cups—the greasiness disappeared, but so did the tenderness. We experimented with using cornstarch (which has no gluten) for some of the flour, but it had little effect. Ultimately, we had to replace some of the butter with shortening, a known tenderizer. We found ¼ cup shortening and 1 cup butter to be the right combination.

With the procedure simplified, we considered the resting time. To speed our kringle along, we whittled down the overnight rest, ultimately reducing it to 4 hours with no ill effect.

Now we turned our attention to the filling and glaze. In traditional recipes a layer of brown sugar, butter, and cinnamon is topped with ground pecans. To streamline the process, we pulsed everything in a food processor (toasting the pecans first to bring out their flavor) and spread the mixture over the dough in a single layer. Our working recipe used an excessively thick glaze made from confectioners' sugar and milk. We thinned it, added vanilla extract, and applied it with a light hand.

Now we were ready to chill and relax ourselves with a big cup of coffee and an even bigger slice of our tender, buttery, flaky pecan kringle.

PECAN KRINGLE

MAKES 2 KRINGLES, EACH SERVING 8

If the dough appears shaggy and dry after adding the sour cream in step 2, add up to 2 tablespoons of ice water until the dough is smooth. If the capacity of your food processor is less than 11 cups, pulse the butter and shortening into the dry mixture in two batches in step 2. Kringle also works well with Cream Cheese Filling and Double-Berry Filling (recipes follow).

PECAN FILLING

1	cup pecans, toasted (see page 130)
¾	cup packed light brown sugar
¼	teaspoon ground cinnamon
⅛	teaspoon salt
4	tablespoons unsalted butter, cut into ½-inch pieces and chilled

DOUGH

4	cups all-purpose flour
16	tablespoons (2 sticks) unsalted butter, cut into ½-inch pieces and chilled
4	tablespoons vegetable shortening, cut into ½-inch pieces and chilled
2	tablespoons confectioners' sugar
1	envelope (2¼ teaspoons) rapid-rise or instant yeast
¾	teaspoon salt
2	cups sour cream
	Water
1	large egg, lightly beaten

GLAZE

1	cup confectioners' sugar
2	tablespoons whole or low-fat milk
½	teaspoon vanilla extract

1. FOR THE FILLING: Process the pecans, brown sugar, cinnamon, and salt in a food processor until coarsely ground. Add the butter and pulse until the mixture resembles coarse meal. Transfer to a bowl and set aside.

2. FOR THE DOUGH: Add the flour, butter, shortening, confectioners' sugar, yeast, and salt to the empty food processor and pulse until the mixture resembles coarse meal. Transfer to a bowl and stir in the sour cream until a dough forms. On a lightly floured work surface, divide the dough in half. Pat each half into a 7 by 3-inch rectangle and wrap in plastic wrap. Refrigerate the dough for 30 minutes, then freeze until firm, about 15 minutes.

3. Following the photos on page 140, roll one dough half into a 28 by 5-inch rectangle, cover the bottom half of the strip with half of the filling,

brush the edge of the uncovered dough with water, fold the dough over the filling, and pinch the seams closed. Shape into an oval, tuck one end inside of the other, and pinch to seal. Transfer to a parchment-lined baking sheet, cover with plastic wrap, and refrigerate for at least 4 hours or up to 12 hours. Repeat with the remaining dough and filling.

4. When ready to bake, adjust the oven racks to the upper-middle and lower-middle positions and heat the oven to 350 degrees. Discard the plastic wrap, brush the kringles with the egg, and bake until golden brown, 40 to 50 minutes, switching and rotating the sheets halfway through baking. Transfer the kringles to a wire rack set inside a rimmed baking sheet and let cool for 30 minutes.

5. FOR THE GLAZE: Whisk all the glaze ingredients together in a bowl until smooth. Drizzle the glaze over the kringles and let the glaze set, about 10 minutes. Serve warm or at room temperature.

MAKING PECAN KRINGLE

1. Working on a lightly floured surface, roll the dough into a 28 by 5-inch strip with one long side closest to you. The dough will be about ¼ inch thick.

2. Leaving a ½-inch border around the bottom and side edges, spread half of the filling over the bottom half of the dough.

3. Brush the edge of the uncovered dough with water and fold the dough over the filling, pinching to close the long seam.

4. Fit one end of the folded dough inside the other to make an oval and press together to seal.

Variations

CREAM CHEESE FILLING

Combine 8 ounces cream cheese, softened, ¼ cup granulated sugar, and ½ teaspoon grated fresh lemon zest in a bowl. Substitute the cream cheese mixture for the Pecan Filling.

DOUBLE-BERRY FILLING

Do not substitute raspberry jam for the preserves; it will leak out of the kringle.

Combine ½ cup raspberry preserves and ¼ cup finely chopped dried cranberries in a bowl. Substitute the preserves mixture for the Pecan Filling.

St. Louis Gooey Butter Cake

In the pantheon of classic coffee cakes, none is more quirky, or more addictive, than St. Louis gooey butter cake. There are two distinct styles of the cake. There's the chewy (and messy) version, more a bar cookie than a cake, with a cheesecake-like topping. The second style is more like an old-fashioned coffee cake, with a rich yeast dough and custardy topping. We wanted to re-create the second kind, with its combination of tender yeast cake and silky custard that literally melts in your mouth, which is substantial enough to be the perfect mate for a cup of coffee.

Our initial recipe tests were pretty far from the mark. The bases were dry and tough (more like pizza dough than coffee cake), and the toppings were runny and soupy. In the best of these early recipes the cake portion was made by mixing 1½ cups of flour, an egg, and 4 tablespoons of butter with yeast, water, sugar, and salt in a mixer; the dough was then kneaded and allowed to rise before being pressed into the pan. The topping was made by creaming butter and sugar, then mixing in corn syrup, an egg, vanilla, and flour. Once assembled, the cake was baked in a 350-degree oven.

We knew we needed to enrich, tenderize, and sweeten the cake base. Taking inspiration from rich yeasted doughs like brioche and Danish, we doubled the number of eggs. Doubling the amount of butter to a full stick made the dough a little greasy; 6 tablespoons was the right compromise. Switching from water to milk gave the cake even more substance. Doubling the amount of sugar (from 2 tablespoons to 4) lent more than the obvious sweetness; it also helped tenderize the cake.

With a richer, more tender foundation in place, we moved on to the topping. Bakers in St. Louis told us that by the time the cake base is cooked through, the topping should still jiggle slightly. As the cake cools, the topping sets up into a velvety, custardlike consistency.

Unfortunately, our experience was quite different. It was much too runny and puddled like melted ice cream when the cake was sliced. We first thought to add more flour, but the filling became pasty. We had better luck when we beat some cream cheese with the butter and sugar. The cream cheese partially firmed up the filling without making it pasty, but using any more than 2 ounces made the topping too tangy and cheesecakelike.

Cornstarch gave the filling an unpleasant slippery texture but inspired us to try instant pudding (which contains cornstarch as a thickener). Sure enough, a few tablespoons of vanilla pudding mix added flavor and provided the creamy, gooey-yet-sliceable texture that makes this cake famous.

ST. LOUIS GOOEY BUTTER CAKE

SERVES 9

Remove the cake from the oven when the perimeter is golden brown and the center is still slightly loose; the topping will continue to set as the cake cools. Leftover cake should be refrigerated.

DOUGH

¼	cup whole milk, warm (110 degrees)
1½	teaspoons rapid-rise or instant yeast
1½	cups all-purpose flour
¼	cup granulated sugar
2	large eggs, room temperature
½	teaspoon vanilla extract
½	teaspoon salt
6	tablespoons (¾ stick) unsalted butter, cut into 6 pieces and softened

TOPPING

½	cup granulated sugar
4	tablespoons (½ stick) unsalted butter, softened
2	ounces cream cheese, softened
2	tablespoons light corn syrup
1	large egg, room temperature
1	teaspoon vanilla extract
⅓	cup all-purpose flour
3	tablespoons instant vanilla pudding mix
2	tablespoons confectioners' sugar

1. FOR THE DOUGH: Adjust an oven rack to the lower-middle position and heat the oven to 200 degrees. When the oven reaches 200 degrees,

turn it off. Line an 8-inch square baking pan with an aluminum foil sling (see page 202) and grease the foil.

2. In the bowl of a stand mixer fitted with the paddle attachment, mix the milk and yeast together on low speed until the yeast dissolves. Add the flour, granulated sugar, eggs, vanilla, and salt and mix until combined, about 30 seconds. Increase the mixer speed to medium-low and add the butter, one piece at a time, until incorporated, then continue mixing for 5 minutes. Place the dough in a medium greased bowl, cover with plastic wrap, and place in the warm oven until the dough has doubled in size, about 30 minutes. Transfer the dough to the prepared baking dish. Heat the oven to 350 degrees.

3. FOR THE TOPPING: In the bowl of a stand mixer fitted with the paddle attachment, beat the granulated sugar, butter, and cream cheese together on medium speed until light and fluffy, about 2 minutes. Reduce the mixer speed to low and add the corn syrup, egg, and vanilla and mix until combined. Add the flour and pudding mix and mix until just incorporated. Drop dollops of the topping evenly over the batter, then spread into an even layer.

4. Once the oven is fully heated, bake the cake until the exterior is golden and the center of the topping is just beginning to color and jiggles slightly when the pan is gently shaken, about 25 minutes, rotating the pan halfway through baking. Let the cake cool in the pan for at least 3 hours. Remove the cake from the pan using the foil (see page 202). Dust with the confectioners' sugar and serve.

Blackberry Roly-Poly

Jam-filled roly-poly has a long history, dating back at least to the early 1800s. The humorously named dessert was regarded as a child-friendly, economical treat, especially in winter, when fresh fruit was costly. Early versions were made by brushing a simple dough with jam, rolling it into a cylinder, and boiling or steaming it wrapped in cloth. By the early 1900s, the widespread use of stoves and the invention of baking powder and baking soda had given birth to a new style of roly-poly. Made from biscuit dough and baked, this buttery, flaky, jam-filled roll soon eclipsed its precursors.

To start, we took a tour of roly-poly through the ages. Using a simple dough, we prepared three rolls and boiled one, steamed another, and baked the last. The boiled roly-poly was sodden and stodgy. The steamed dough was only marginally better. But the most modern roly-poly, the baked version, which resembled a jumbo jammy biscuit, was a hit. There were just two problems: the interior was a tad soggy and the biscuit was lean.

After experimenting with various biscuit doughs, we settled on a recipe that used chilled butter—this one tasted much richer than the earlier ones we'd prepared. Drop biscuits (made with melted butter) were too wet to roll, and cream biscuits (made with cream instead of butter) ended up dry.

To make the biscuits, we simply pulsed the butter in a food processor with flour, sugar, salt, and baking powder, then added milk to bind the dough. This dough was the richest yet, but it was still a tad lean for a dessert. Four tablespoons of butter per cup of flour is the test-kitchen standard for biscuits. One extra tablespoon per cup produced an exceptionally flaky, buttery roly-poly. Unfortunately, the added fat made the dough too soft to roll out easily. We tried freezing the dough to firm it; just 20 minutes later, it was ready to roll.

We hadn't yet solved our initial problem: the interior near the jam remained slightly wet. We'd been brushing the dough with ½ cup of store-bought jam, but it thinned while the roly-poly baked, making the inside soggy. Commercial jams are often thickened with pectin, which thins when heated. We decided to make a quick, thick homemade jam without pectin, so we cooked 2 cups of berries with ¼ cup of sugar until the berries had broken down. When the jam cooled, we brushed it on the roly-poly, rolled it, brushed the cylinder with butter, sprinkled it with sugar (two last-minute improvements), baked, and waited.

After 45 minutes, we pulled the roly-poly from the oven and waited impatiently for it to cool. When sliced, it was rustic and golden with an even swirl of fresh, bright jam. No doubt about it: our updated roly-poly would still please the kids, but now it was every bit a grown-up treat, too.

BLACKBERRY ROLY-POLY

SERVES 8

Roly-poly tastes best on the day it's made. Use a serrated knife to slice it.

2	cups fresh or frozen blackberries
⅔	cup sugar
½	teaspoon grated fresh lemon zest
3	cups all-purpose flour
1	tablespoon baking powder
1	teaspoon salt
16	tablespoons (2 sticks) unsalted butter, cut into ½-inch pieces and chilled
1	cup whole or low-fat milk

1. Cook the berries and ¼ cup of the sugar in a saucepan over medium-low heat until the berries begin to release their juice, about 3 minutes. Increase the heat to medium-high and cook, stirring frequently, until the berries break down and

the mixture is thick and jamlike, about 10 minutes (the mixture should measure ½ cup). Transfer the jam to a bowl, stir in the zest, and let cool to room temperature.

2. Pulse the flour, baking powder, salt, ⅓ cup more sugar, and all but 1 tablespoon of the butter together in a food processor until the mixture resembles coarse meal. Transfer to a large bowl and stir in the milk until combined.

3. Adjust an oven rack to the middle position and heat the oven to 375 degrees. Turn the dough out

ROLLING ROLY-POLY

1. On a lightly floured work surface, roll the chilled dough into a 12 by 10-inch rectangle.

2. Spread the jam evenly over the dough, leaving a ½-inch border around the edges.

3. Starting with the long edge, roll the dough into a cylinder. Pinch to seal the seam and ends.

4. Carefully transfer the rolled dough, seam side down, to a prepared baking sheet.

onto a lightly floured work surface and knead until smooth, 8 to 10 times. Pat the dough into a 6-inch square, wrap in plastic wrap, and freeze until just firm, about 20 minutes. Following the photos on page 144, roll the dough into a 12 by 10-inch rectangle, spread with the jam, roll into a tight cylinder, pinch the seams closed, and arrange seam side down on a parchment-lined baking sheet.

4. Microwave the remaining 1 tablespoon butter on high until melted, about 10 seconds. Brush the melted butter on the dough, sprinkle with the remaining sugar, and bake until golden brown, about 45 minutes, rotating the sheet halfway through baking. Let cool for 10 minutes on the baking sheet, then transfer to a wire rack. Serve warm or at room temperature.

Monkey Bread

Monkey bread often starts with homemade bread dough that is cut and rolled into small balls. The balls are dipped in butter, rolled in cinnamon sugar, stacked in a tube or Bundt pan, and baked. The pieces of dough appear to melt together, the sugar and butter transformed into a thick, gooey caramel that oozes into every nook and cranny. And because the balls of dough are piled one on top of another, the end result is a crowning confection of soft, sweet, sticky, and irresistibly cinnamon-y bread.

Its origins date back at least a century, but no one's sure where the name "monkey bread" came from. Some say it comes from the bread's resemblance to the prickly monkey-puzzle tree. Others think it refers to the way we eat it—that is, using our hands to pull apart the sticky clumps of bread and stuff them in our mouths, just like happy little monkeys. And for those who think monkey bread may be lacking panache, consider that former First

Lady Nancy Reagan served monkey bread at the White House.

The oldest monkey bread recipes we found in our research were two-day affairs. The dough was started the night before, refrigerated, and shaped and baked the next day. Contemporary recipes have taken the road of convenience; in most cases they use store-bought biscuit dough. We tried it, but the time saved wasn't worth it. The biscuit dough was too lean, too dry, and too bland.

We looked to the few contemporary recipes that could be made in one day and then made a few adjustments. To provide plenty of lift and yeasty flavor, we used a whole envelope of rapid-rise yeast, which also made this a same-morning operation—no need to plan ahead. Milk and melted butter went in to keep the dough rich and moist, and a little sugar made the bread sweet enough to eat on its own. To compensate for the sweetness of the dough, we changed the granulated sugar normally used to coat the dough balls to mellower light brown sugar.

Once we piled all the balls into the pan, the monkey bread went into the oven. Once it was out of the oven (after about an hour) and after a few cruel minutes of waiting, we released the bread from its pan, watching the hot caramel drip down the sides. Some recipes call for drizzling a simple confectioners' sugar glaze over the monkey bread, which may seem gratuitous, but we didn't think the glaze made the monkey bread too sweet. In fact, we thought that with the glaze the bread was now just perfect.

MONKEY BREAD

SERVES 6 TO 8

If you don't have a stand mixer, see "Hand Mixing Yeast Doughs" on page 135. After baking, don't let the bread cool in the pan for more than 5 minutes or it will stick to the pan and come out in pieces. Monkey bread is at its best when served warm.

DOUGH

    2   tablespoons unsalted butter, softened, plus
        2 tablespoons unsalted butter, melted
    1   cup milk, warm (110 degrees)
    ⅓   cup water, warm (110 degrees)
    ¼   cup granulated sugar
    1   envelope (2¼ teaspoons) rapid-rise or
        instant yeast
    3¼ cups plus 2 tablespoons all-purpose flour
    2   teaspoons salt

COATING

    1   cup packed light brown sugar
    2   teaspoons ground cinnamon
    8   tablespoons (1 stick) unsalted butter,
        melted

GLAZE

    1   cup confectioners' sugar
    2   tablespoons milk

1. FOR THE DOUGH: Adjust an oven rack to the lower-middle position and heat the oven to 200 degrees. When the oven reaches 200 degrees, turn it off. Grease a 12-cup nonstick Bundt pan with the softened butter. Set aside.

2. In a large liquid measuring cup, mix together the milk, water, melted butter, granulated sugar, and yeast. Mix 3¼ cups of the flour and salt together in a stand mixer fitted with the dough hook. Turn the machine to low and slowly add the milk mixture. (If the dough does not come together or it's too wet, add the remaining 2 tablespoons flour and mix until the dough forms a cohesive mass.) After the dough comes together, increase the mixer speed to medium and mix until the dough is shiny and smooth, 6 to 7 minutes. Turn the dough out onto a lightly floured work surface and knead briefly to form a smooth, round ball. Place the dough in a large, lightly greased bowl and cover the bowl with greased plastic wrap. Place in the warm oven until the dough doubles in size, 50 to 60 minutes.

3. FOR THE COATING: While the dough is rising, mix the brown sugar and cinnamon together in a bowl. Place the melted butter in a second bowl. Set aside.

4. Gently remove the dough from the bowl and, following the photos, pat into a rough 8-inch square. Using a bench scraper or knife, cut the dough into 64 pieces. Roll each piece of dough into a ball.

MAKING MONKEY BREAD

1. After patting the dough into an 8-inch square, cut the square into quarters.

2. Cut each quarter into 16 pieces, for a total of 64 pieces of dough.

3. Roll each piece of dough into a rough ball, then coat the balls with melted butter and sugar.

4. Layer the buttered and sugared dough balls in the buttered pan.

Working with one at a time, dip the balls in the melted butter, allowing the excess butter to drip back into the bowl. Roll in the brown sugar mixture, then layer the dough balls in the prepared pan, staggering the seams where the dough balls meet as you build layers.

5. Cover the pan tightly with plastic wrap and place in the turned-off oven until the dough balls are puffy and have risen 1 to 2 inches from the top of the pan, 50 to 70 minutes.

6. Remove the pan from the oven and heat the oven to 350 degrees. Unwrap the pan and bake until the top is deep brown and the caramel begins to bubble around the edges, 30 to 35 minutes. Let the monkey bread cool in the pan for 5 minutes, then turn out onto a platter and let cool slightly, about 10 minutes.

7. FOR THE GLAZE: Meanwhile, whisk the confectioners' sugar and milk together in a small bowl until smooth. Drizzle the glaze over the warm monkey bread and serve warm.

SHOPPING WITH THE TEST KITCHEN

Bench Scrapers: A bench scraper is a rectangular blade with a wood or plastic handle affixed to one side. Bench scrapers are ideal for countless baking tasks, like dividing dough into smaller pieces or cleaning up a messy countertop. Our favorite is the OXO Good Grips Stainless Steel Multi-Purpose Scraper and Chopper ($8.95), which has a sturdy blade and comfortable handle. We also like the ruler marked along the blade, which is helpful for accurate measuring when patting or rolling out dough to a specific size.

Tick Tock Orange Sticky Rolls

While the entertainment industry immortalizes its stars in celluloid and cement handprints, Hollywood residents fondly recall another local legend—the Tick Tock Tea Room. From 1930 through 1988, the Tick Tock served up countless platters of meatloaf, roast turkey, and fried chicken to its working-class clientele. The restaurant's defining touch was the complimentary basket of hot sticky rolls that preceded each meal. When the Tick Tock closed its doors over twenty years ago, it also closed the book on those incredible orange rolls.

We found two recipes for these rolls, one from a 1977 *Los Angeles Times* article and one from a 1994 cookbook called *Hollywood du Jour*. The recipes are very similar: dough made from packaged biscuit mix is rolled out, covered with cinnamon sugar and orange zest, and then rolled into a log. Individual pieces are cut, then set in a baking dish (spiral side up, like cinnamon rolls or sticky buns) atop a glaze made with orange juice concentrate, sugar, and butter. When the rolls come out of the oven, they are turned out with the gooey glaze on top. Unfortunately, both recipes produced sloppy, soggy rolls soaked through with glaze.

The fluffy boxed-mix biscuits had soaked up too much liquid. Homemade cream biscuits were sturdier but didn't have much flavor. Biscuits made with buttermilk and melted butter (instead of cream) tasted great and stood up to the glaze better—especially when we defied convention and kneaded the dough before rolling and cutting. After 5 minutes of kneading, the biscuits were still plenty tender, but now they offered some resistance to the glaze.

The candy-sweet original orange glaze started with ¾ cup of orange juice concentrate. We tried fresh and store-bought orange juice, but neither packed as much orange flavor. To temper its sweetness, we reduced the concentrate by ¼ cup and cut the cloying granulated sugar with an equal amount of brown sugar. The glaze was still too thin and easily absorbed into the biscuits, so for our next test, we simmered the ingredients in a saucepan until they formed a thick glaze.

A happy kitchen accident brought this recipe home. We had made the glaze and then gotten distracted before we had a chance to start the dough; by the time the dough was ready, the glaze had hardened in the cake pan. We went ahead and threw the rolls in anyway. Starting with a hardened glaze kept the rolls from soaking up too much liquid, and the rolls now browned much better than when they'd been saturated with the orange syrup.

With their orange-cinnamon filling and caramel-y, sticky orange glaze, these Tick Tock Orange Sticky Rolls are simply irresistible.

THE AMERICAN TABLE

IN REMEMBRANCE OF A TEA ROOM PAST

The Tick Tock Tea Room opened in 1930, when Norwegian immigrants Arthur and Helen Johnson bought a run-down home on North Cahuenga Boulevard in Los Angeles and converted it into a restaurant. They hung their most prized possession, an antique clock, on the wall and the rest was history; soon there were 48 clocks decorating the restaurant. For those without movie studio expense accounts, the Tick Tock Tea Room offered three courses of good, humble cooking at affordable prices. The Johnsons would serve more than 2,000 three-course meals on busy days. The Tick Tock was such a success, thanks in part to the sweet sticky rolls that came with every meal, that the family opened two more locations in the Los Angeles area. The last Tick Tock closed for good in 1988.

TICK TOCK ORANGE STICKY ROLLS

SERVES 8

Don't let the rolls sit in the pan for more than 5 minutes after baking. The glaze will begin to harden and the buns will stick.

GLAZE

- ½ **cup frozen orange juice concentrate, thawed**
- ¼ **cup packed light brown sugar**
- ¼ **cup granulated sugar**
- 3 **tablespoons unsalted butter**

FILLING

- ½ **cup packed light brown sugar**
- ¼ **cup granulated sugar**
- 2 **teaspoons ground cinnamon**
- 1 **teaspoon grated fresh orange zest**
- ⅛ **teaspoon ground cloves**
- ⅛ **teaspoon salt**
- 1 **tablespoon unsalted butter, melted**

DOUGH

- 2¾ **cups all-purpose flour**
- 2 **tablespoons granulated sugar**
- 2 **teaspoons baking powder**
- ½ **teaspoon baking soda**
- ½ **teaspoon salt**
- 1¼ **cups buttermilk**
- 6 **tablespoons (¾ stick) unsalted butter, melted**

1. FOR THE GLAZE: Grease a 9-inch cake pan. Bring all of the glaze ingredients to a simmer in a small saucepan over medium heat. Cook until the mixture thickens and clings to the back of a spoon, about 5 minutes. Pour the mixture into the prepared pan. Let cool until the glaze hardens, at least 20 minutes.

2. FOR THE FILLING: Adjust an oven rack to the lower-middle position and heat the oven to 350 degrees. Combine all of the filling ingredients except the butter in a bowl. Using a fork, stir in the butter until the mixture resembles wet sand.

3. FOR THE DOUGH: Whisk the flour, granulated sugar, baking powder, baking soda, and salt together in a medium bowl. Whisk the buttermilk and butter together in a small bowl (the mixture will clump), then stir into the flour mixture until combined. Knead the dough on a lightly floured work surface until smooth, about 5 minutes.

4. Roll the dough into a 12 by 9-inch rectangle. Pat the filling onto the dough, leaving a ½-inch border around the edges. Starting at one long edge, roll the dough into a tight cylinder and pinch the seam together. Cut the log into eight pieces and arrange the pieces, cut side down, on the cooled glaze, placing one roll in the center and the remaining rolls around the edge of the pan.

5. Bake until the rolls are golden and the glaze is darkened and bubbling, 18 to 25 minutes, rotating the pan halfway through baking. Let cool in the pan for 5 minutes, then turn out onto a serving platter. Let the rolls sit for 10 minutes before serving.

Orange Drop Doughnuts

Cake doughnuts (a relative of batter-dropped doughnuts) are an all-American phenomenon that started in the late 1800s, thanks to the availability of baking powder. Many 19th-century cookbooks show these quicker doughnuts being rolled and stamped out (like their yeasted brethren). Eventually, doughnut makers realized that dropping spoonfuls of cake batter into hot oil meant that fresh doughnuts could be on the table in minutes, so they could satisfy their cravings sooner.

Drop doughnuts caught on like wildfire, and soon there were flavors of every kind—spiced, chocolate, and orange. In the late 1940s and into the 1950s, the name "orange drop doughnuts" started to appear in Betty Crocker cookbooks and magazines. We tried these recipes, and, truth be told, they were pretty good. With a little more work, we hoped to make a super-orangey doughnut worthy of breakfast in bed.

Some recipes use nearly 3 cups of flour for two dozen doughnuts, but these heavy (yet tasty) lead balls fell to the bottom of our bellies. Two cups of flour—paired with 2 teaspoons of baking powder—worked much better. Two eggs and a little melted butter made these doughnuts properly rich.

For liquid ingredients, some recipes call for milk as well as orange juice. But diluting the orange flavor just seemed wrong, so we added only juice. For even more orange flavor, we added a whopping tablespoon of grated zest to the batter—far more than the teaspoon or so found in older recipes.

Finally, we took a cue from a few recipes and rolled the hot doughnuts in a batch of homemade orange-flavored sugar. The pleasant aroma of citrus wafted through the test kitchen, and soon our fellow doughnut hounds lined up to enjoy a fresh, hot orange doughnut.

ORANGE DROP DOUGHNUTS

MAKES 24 TO 30 DOUGHNUTS

These doughnuts are best eaten right away.

- 1   cup sugar
- 1   tablespoon plus 1 teaspoon grated fresh orange zest (3 oranges)
      About 2 quarts vegetable oil
- 2   cups all-purpose flour
- 2   teaspoons baking powder
- ¼   teaspoon salt
- 2   large eggs
- ½   cup orange juice
- 2   tablespoons unsalted butter, melted and cooled
- ½   teaspoon vanilla extract

1. Pulse ½ cup of the sugar and 1 teaspoon of the zest in a food processor until blended, about five pulses. Transfer to a medium bowl.

2. Heat 3 inches of oil in a large Dutch oven over medium-high heat until the temperature reaches 350 degrees on a candy thermometer or instant-read thermometer that registers high temperatures. Whisk the flour, baking powder, and salt together in a medium bowl. Whisk the eggs, remaining ½ cup sugar, and remaining 1 tablespoon orange zest together in a large bowl. Whisk in the orange juice, butter, and vanilla until well combined. Stir in the flour mixture until evenly moistened.

3. Following the photo, and using two spoons, scoop out a Ping-Pong ball–size portion of batter and carefully scrape the batter into the hot oil. Repeat five more times and fry the doughnuts until they are crisp and deeply browned on all sides, 3 to 6 minutes, adjusting the heat as necessary to maintain the oil at 350 degrees. Using a slotted spoon,

transfer the doughnuts to a paper towel–lined plate and let drain for 5 minutes.

4. Add the doughnuts to the bowl with the orange sugar and toss until well coated. Transfer to a serving platter and repeat with the remaining batter, adjusting the oil temperature as necessary. Serve warm.

Variations
SPICE DROP DOUGHNUTS
Substitute 1 tablespoon cinnamon, ¾ teaspoon ground nutmeg, and ½ teaspoon allspice for the orange zest in step 1. Substitute ½ cup whole milk for the orange juice and add 1½ teaspoons ground cinnamon, 1 teaspoon ground nutmeg, and ¼ teaspoon ground allspice to the doughnut batter. Roll the fried, drained doughnuts in the spice sugar before serving.

BANANA DROP DOUGHNUTS
Substitute 1 tablespoon ground cinnamon for the orange zest in step 1. Substitute ½ cup whole milk for the orange juice and add 1 mashed ripe banana and 1 teaspoon ground cinnamon to the batter. Roll the fried, drained doughnuts in the cinnamon sugar before serving.

FRYING ORANGE DROP DOUGHNUTS

Scoop out a Ping-Pong ball–size portion of batter using a spoon. Using a second spoon, gently scrape the batter into the hot oil, frying until deeply browned, 3 to 6 minutes.

Old-Fashioned Buttermilk Doughnuts

With no rising required, buttermilk doughnuts are what you want if you don't want to spend hours at the stove but crave a tasty, home-style accompaniment to your morning coffee. We wanted a recipe that would provide us with a pile of robust country doughnuts with great crunch and flavor—in less than an hour.

We proceeded to test half a dozen different recipes for non-yeast fried doughnuts, choosing methods that seemed as different as possible so that we could judge a wide range of outcomes. And this is exactly what we got: everything from flat, greasy rounds of dough to high-rise cakey rings. Our final recipe, therefore, needed to give us a doughnut with good crunch and a minimum of grease, a true country doughnut, rather than an airy Dunkin' Donuts confection.

As a starting point, we cobbled together a master recipe using buttermilk, eggs, flour, sugar, baking powder, baking soda, melted butter, salt, and nutmeg. We made up a batch of dough and fried it in vegetable oil. The resulting doughnuts were good but needed improvement.

We tried increasing the amount of butter in the recipe, but it did not improve the flavor. We did, however, have some luck when we added one extra egg yolk. This made a moister dough, and the extra fat also created a more tender doughnut. Additionally, we tried boosting the flour by ¼ cup and determined that this drier dough does make a less crisp, but also less greasy, product. It is also a bit firmer and more chewy inside, but the lack of crackle on the outside placed this variation in second place.

With the recipe set, we were ready to begin our most important set of tests, involving frying the doughnuts. In terms of cooking temperature, we found that with the oil at 350 degrees the dough absorbed too much of it, whereas at 385 degrees the outside started to burn before the inside could cook through. A temperature of 360 degrees seemed the ideal. We discovered, though, that it works best to start out with the oil at 375 degrees because the temperature will fall back to between 360 and 365 degrees as soon as the doughnuts are put in. Also, we found it essential to bring the oil back up to temperature between batches; otherwise the fried doughnuts were greasy.

Many recipes call for cooking doughnuts for 1½ minutes per side, a time that we found to be much too long. Once the doughnuts had been placed in the hot oil and flipped, we tested 40 seconds, 50 seconds, 60 seconds, and 70 seconds and found that 50 seconds was ideal. The center was just cooked, and the doughnut did not take on that dry, catch-in-your-throat texture. The big surprise, however, was that doughnuts cooked longer were

MAKING BUTTERMILK DOUGHNUTS

1. Roll out the dough on a heavily floured work surface, then stamp out the rounds as close together as possible. Gather the scraps, press into a disk, and repeat.

2. Carefully slip the dough rings into the hot oil, a few at a time. As the doughnuts rise to the surface of the hot oil, flip them over with tongs or a slotted spoon.

also greasier. The shorter the frying time, the less chance the oil had to penetrate the dough.

We didn't allow our doughnuts much time to cool—not because we were impatient, but because they're actually better while still toasty. With a pile of old-fashioned doughnuts ready in record time, we vowed to spend the rest of the day on our coffee break.

OLD-FASHIONED BUTTERMILK DOUGHNUTS

MAKES 15 TO 17 DOUGHNUTS

You can add ¼ cup of flour to the recipe for a chewier doughnut with a less crisp exterior. These doughnuts are best eaten very warm, as soon out of the pot as possible. The dough can be made by hand, using a large bowl with a wooden spoon, or in a mixer as directed.

3½	cups all-purpose flour (see note above)
1	cup sugar
2	teaspoons baking powder
1½	teaspoons ground nutmeg
1	teaspoon salt
½	teaspoon baking soda
¾	cup buttermilk
4	tablespoons unsalted butter, melted
2	large eggs plus 1 large egg yolk
	About 2 quarts vegetable oil

1. Mix 1 cup of the flour, sugar, baking powder, nutmeg, salt, and baking soda in the bowl of a stand mixer fitted with the paddle attachment.

2. Mix the buttermilk, butter, eggs, and egg yolk in a liquid measuring cup. Add the buttermilk mixture to the flour mixture and beat on medium speed until smooth, about 30 seconds. Reduce the mixer speed to low, add the remaining 2½ cups flour, and mix until just combined, about 30 seconds. Stir the batter once or twice with a wooden spoon or rubber spatula to ensure that all the liquid is incorporated. (The dough will be moist and tacky.)

3. Heat 3 inches of oil in a large Dutch oven over medium-high heat until the temperature reaches 375 degrees on a candy thermometer or instant-read thermometer that registers high temperatures. Turn the dough out onto a heavily floured work surface and, using a floured rolling pin, roll out to a ½-inch thickness. Following the photos on page 152, stamp out the dough rings using a floured doughnut cutter, reflouring between cuts. Transfer the dough rounds to a baking sheet or wire rack. Gather the scraps and gently press them into a disk; repeat the rolling and stamping process until all the dough is used. (The cut doughnuts can be covered with plastic wrap and stored at room temperature for up to 2 hours.)

4. Carefully drop the dough rings into the hot oil, four or five at a time. (Do not overcrowd.) When they rise to the surface, turn the doughnuts with tongs or a slotted spoon. Fry the doughnuts until golden brown, about 50 seconds per side, adjusting the heat to maintain the oil at 375 degrees. Drain on a paper towel–lined baking sheet or wire rack. Repeat frying with the remaining dough rings, adjusting the oil temperature as necessary. Serve immediately.

Variation
CINNAMON-SUGAR BUTTERMILK DOUGHNUTS

Combine 1 cup granulated sugar and 1 tablespoon ground cinnamon in a medium bowl. Let the fried doughnuts cool for 1 minute, then toss them in the cinnamon sugar.

CARROT CUPCAKES

Cupcake Heaven

Yellow Cupcakes

The cupcakes we remember from childhood birthday parties were rich, dense, and moist yellow cakes lavishly topped with mounds of fluffy, lush, sweet frosting. Unfortunately, times have changed. Nowadays, busy parents pick up a box of cupcakes from the supermarket bakery. Often, these cupcakes are dry and crumbly or cloyingly sweet, rubbery, and leaden. We wanted to make the best yellow cupcake ever, one so delicious that kids would savor the cake itself instead of just licking off the frosting. We also wanted a cupcake good enough to satisfy the grown-ups, too.

In our quest, we tried almost every yellow cupcake recipe we could find and discovered no clear winners. The major ingredients (flour, sugar, eggs, butter, and some sort of dairy product) were consistent, but their proportions were up for grabs. For a dozen cupcakes, we started with 1½ cups of all-purpose flour, an amount that appeared in a number of recipes. When it came to the eggs, quantities ranged from three yolks to three whole eggs, with varying combinations of yolks and whole eggs appearing in a handful of recipes. The version we liked best included one whole egg and two yolks; these little cakes were a lovely golden hue and tasted incredibly rich.

Next, it was time to consider the dairy element. We found that a single stick of butter, softened, proved ample. Any more than that, and the cakes were greasy; any less, and they tasted lean. Then we had to nail down the supporting dairy ingredient. We made cupcakes using whole milk, buttermilk, yogurt (low-fat and full-fat), heavy cream, and sour cream. The slightly tangy, rich sour cream won out.

As for the sugar, we tried a range of amounts. More than a cup resulted in the cloyingly sweet cupcakes we were trying to avoid; less than a cup produced flavorless cupcakes that were closer to muffins. A single cup was perfect; these cakes had the right level of sweetness and still boasted a rich, complex flavor.

For cupcakes with a fine, velvety crumb, we had to find the right mixing method. We tested a number of procedures, from the classic creaming method, which starts with creaming the butter and sugar together, adding eggs, and then alternately adding dry and wet ingredients, to the reverse creaming method in which the butter is cut into the flour and other dry ingredients before the eggs and liquid are added. While all the cupcakes were good, we found that the best-textured cakes came about when we used the simplest method—throwing all the ingredients into a bowl and mixing. Tasters raved about these tender yellow cakes, and we were thrilled that they were a snap to make.

At last, we had tender, lightly sweetened yellow cupcakes that were so good, and so easy, we suspected they'd start showing up a little more often—and not just at birthday parties.

TENDER YELLOW CUPCAKES

MAKES 12 CUPCAKES

To double the recipe, use 3 whole eggs and 2 yolks and double the remaining ingredients. Any Easy Frosting (pages 160–161) tastes great on these cupcakes.

1½	cups all-purpose flour
1	cup sugar
1½	teaspoons baking powder
½	teaspoon salt
8	tablespoons (1 stick) unsalted butter, softened
½	cup sour cream
1	large egg plus 2 large egg yolks, room temperature
1½	teaspoons vanilla extract
1	recipe Easy Frosting (pages 160–161)

1. Adjust an oven rack to the middle position and heat the oven to 350 degrees. Line a 12-cup muffin tin with cupcake liners.

2. Whisk the flour, sugar, baking powder, and salt together in a large bowl. Beat in the butter, sour cream, egg, egg yolks, and vanilla with an electric mixer on medium speed until smooth and satiny, about 30 seconds. Give the batter a final stir with a rubber spatula to make sure it is thoroughly combined.

3. Using a greased ¼-cup measure, portion the batter into each muffin cup. Bake the cupcakes until the tops are pale gold and a toothpick inserted in the center comes out clean, 20 to 25 minutes, rotating the tin halfway through baking. Let the cupcakes cool in the tin for 10 minutes, then transfer them to a wire rack to cool completely, about 30 minutes, before frosting.

SHOPPING WITH THE TEST KITCHEN

Muffin Tins: The best muffin tins brown cupcakes and muffins evenly and release them easily, and the worst brown them on the top but leave them pallid and underbaked on the bottom, plus they leave some of the crust behind. We found that even though some muffin tins were labeled nonstick, they definitely didn't perform as such. The top performing tin in our tests was the Wilton Avanti Everglide Non-Stick 12-Cup Muffin Pan ($13.99), which turned out well-browned muffins and cupcakes and boasted wide extended rims and a raised lip, making it easy to retrieve baked goods from the oven.

Chocolate Cupcakes

It doesn't matter if they're out of a box or the family cookbook; most chocolate cupcakes offer little in the way of rich, chocolaty flavor. One bite, and you'll wonder if the cocoa powder was added for its dark hue only. And in the few cupcakes that do offer a modicum of cocoa flavor, the texture seems to be lacking, with a crumb that's either too crumbly or too fluffy. We wanted a light, moist, cakey cupcake that didn't fall apart after one bite. Most important, it had to taste unabashedly of chocolate.

Our foray into chocolate cupcakes began with a search for chocolate cupcake recipes. What followed was a cupcake-baking marathon. We made all manner of chocolate cupcakes: chocolate mayonnaise cupcakes, cocoa-only cupcakes, cupcakes with vegetable oil, cupcakes with buttermilk, and so on.

While some were OK, none were great. Solid chocolate flavor and moist, tender texture seemed not to coincide. Well-textured cupcakes used a light hand with the chocolate, but those that truly tasted of chocolate seemed weighed down by it. It would take more than a few tries to create the best chocolate cupcake, with ideal texture and flavor.

Given the "either-or" scenario from our early tests, it made sense to first determine the best mixing method, as this would probably influence the amounts of ingredients. First we tried the method that we used for our Tender Yellow Cupcakes (throwing everything in a bowl and mixing), but the results, perhaps because of the addition of chocolate, failed to impress us. Next, we backtracked to trying the typical cake-making method of creaming the butter and sugar in a stand mixer until light and fluffy, adding the eggs, and then finally the wet and dry ingredients. The batter, fluffy with air, was so voluminous that the muffin cups were nearly filled to overflowing; when baked, the cupcakes' caps spread too far and wide.

Then we decided to try our luck with the melted-butter method, a simple mixer-free method that we often use to make brownies. These cupcakes had a light, cakey texture with a tender, fine crumb. That they were incredibly easy and quick to make was a bonus. The procedure entailed whisking together the eggs and sugar, adding the melted butter and chocolate, and then stirring in the dry ingredients in two additions, with buttermilk (deemed the best liquid in early tests) added in between. It couldn't be easier.

Next up: the chocolate. Cocoa powder, unsweetened chocolate, bittersweet or semisweet chocolate, and combinations thereof were the candidates. We found that the cocoa and unsweetened chocolate alone could each provide blunt flavor (because of their high percentages of cocoa solids), but both came up short in the nuance department. Bittersweet and semisweet chocolate could supply nuance and complexity but not assertive chocolate flavor. Obviously, it was going to take two forms of chocolate to achieve the bold, balanced flavor we sought. Ultimately, ½ cup of cocoa (Dutch-processed was preferred over natural for its fuller, deeper flavor) and 2 ounces of bittersweet chocolate were the winning combination. The cupcakes were now deep, dark, and terrifically chocolaty. Also, we found that instead of treating the cocoa as a dry ingredient and combining it with the flour, it was better to mix it with the butter and chocolate as they melted, a technique known as "blooming" that made the chocolate flavor stronger and richer.

While our preliminary tests showed that buttermilk added a nice, light, tangy flavor, we wondered if sour cream might add more richness. Tasters were on board and found the cupcakes made with sour cream to be richer and moister (but not at all greasy).

Then came the tricky part: the leavening. Baking soda, which reacts with the acidic sour cream, was the obvious choice, but we could add only so much before the cupcakes took on a soapy flavor. A half-teaspoon was the limit, but this amount didn't provide adequate lift, so we enlisted the aid of some baking powder. These cupcakes domed ever so slightly, for picture-perfect cupcakes.

Now our chocolate cupcakes were rich, moist, and super-chocolaty—and they weren't that much more difficult to assemble and bake than a boxed cake mix. Finally, we could have our cake and eat it, too.

RICH CHOCOLATE CUPCAKES

MAKES 12 CUPCAKES

This recipe can be doubled. Any Easy Frosting (pages 160–161) tastes great on these cupcakes.

8	tablespoons (1 stick) unsalted butter, cut into 4 pieces
2	ounces bittersweet chocolate, chopped
½	cup Dutch-processed cocoa powder
¾	cup all-purpose flour
¾	teaspoon baking powder
½	teaspoon baking soda
2	large eggs, room temperature
¾	cup sugar
1	teaspoon vanilla extract
½	teaspoon salt
½	cup sour cream
1	recipe Easy Frosting (pages 160–161)

1. Adjust an oven rack to the lower-middle position and heat the oven to 350 degrees. Line a 12-cup muffin tin with cupcake liners.

2. Combine the butter, chocolate, and cocoa in a medium heatproof bowl set over a saucepan filled with ½ inch of barely simmering water (don't let the bowl touch the water). Heat the mixture until

the butter and chocolate are melted; whisk until smooth and fully combined. Set aside and let cool until just warm to the touch.

3. Whisk the flour, baking powder, and baking soda together in a small bowl. Whisk the eggs in a second medium bowl; add the sugar, vanilla, and salt and whisk until fully incorporated. Add the cooled chocolate mixture and whisk until combined. Sift one-third of the flour mixture over the chocolate mixture and whisk until combined. Whisk in the sour cream until combined, then sift the remaining flour mixture over the top and whisk until the batter is homogeneous and thick.

4. Using a greased ¼-cup measure, portion the batter into each muffin cup. Bake the cupcakes until a toothpick inserted in the center comes out clean, 18 to 20 minutes, rotating the tin halfway through baking. Let the cupcakes cool in the tin for 10 minutes, then transfer them to a wire rack to cool completely, about 30 minutes, before frosting.

Easy Frosting

Sure, frosting out of a can is an easy solution when it comes to dressing cupcakes. But, like many other commercial products, these frostings rely on lots of shortening and sugar and, as a result, often set up into a stale-tasting, crystalline layer. We wanted frosting that tasted of real butter and stayed creamy long after being spread on our cakes.

We tried a number of frostings, but tasters were won over by a simple buttercream frosting. In this type of frosting, butter and confectioners' sugar are whipped together until light and fluffy. Sometimes a little egg yolk or milk is added for a silkier texture, but we found that a bit of heavy cream was even better.

In just minutes, we had a simple frosting that provided the ideal canvas for an array of flavors. Vanilla and chocolate were a given, but we also developed coffee and peppermint variations.

EASY VANILLA FROSTING
MAKES ABOUT 1½ CUPS, ENOUGH TO FROST 12 CUPCAKES

This frosting and the variations work well with both our Tender Yellow Cupcakes (page 156) and Rich Chocolate Cupcakes (page 158). This recipe can be doubled.

10	tablespoons (1¼ sticks) unsalted butter, softened
1¼	cups confectioners' sugar
	Pinch salt
1	tablespoon heavy cream
1½	teaspoons vanilla extract

In a large bowl, beat the butter with an electric mixer on medium-high speed until smooth, about 30 seconds. Decrease the mixer speed to medium-low and beat in the sugar and salt until the mixture is fully combined, 1 to 2 minutes. Add the cream and vanilla and continue to beat until incorporated, about 10 seconds. Increase the mixer speed to medium-high and beat until light and fluffy, 4 to 6 minutes. (The frosting can be refrigerated in an airtight container for up to 3 days. Bring the frosting to room temperature before using.)

Variations
EASY CHOCOLATE FROSTING
Omit the heavy cream and reduce the amount of confectioners' sugar to 1 cup and the vanilla extract to ½ teaspoon. After beating in the cream and vanilla, reduce the mixer speed to low and gradually beat in 4 ounces melted and cooled semisweet or bittersweet chocolate.

EASY COFFEE FROSTING

Reduce the amount of vanilla extract to ½ teaspoon. Add 1½ teaspoons instant espresso powder to the cream and vanilla and stir to dissolve before adding to the butter and sugar mixture.

EASY PEPPERMINT FROSTING

Reduce the amount of vanilla extract to ¼ teaspoon. Add ¾ teaspoon peppermint extract to the butter and sugar mixture along with the vanilla.

Carrot Cupcakes

Moist and dense, carrot cake went from 1970s health food fad to decadent dessert almost overnight. But we wanted to know if the carrot cake could make another transition—from layer cake to cupcake. Our goal: richly spiced carrot cupcakes with a sweet cream cheese frosting.

We started by preparing some published recipes, but these were panned as excessively oily and overpoweringly spiced. The very ingredients that give carrot cake its moist, dense texture—large amounts of carrots and oil—were making our cupcakes seem more like muffins.

For a less greasy texture, we turned to the obvious culprit and cut the amount of oil. This worked, but not completely; there was still an oily residue left behind, and the texture was still dense. For a lighter, more cakelike texture, we tried swapping out the oil for butter, and the results were dramatic: the cupcakes were significantly more cakey and fluffy. There were two issues at play. First, butter contains water, and oil does not; when cooked, the water evaporates, releasing some of the excess moisture. Second, once the cupcakes return to room temperature, the butter solidifies, whereas the oil stays liquid; that difference translates into a cakey, rather than dense, texture.

We found that the namesake ingredient was also playing a role in the texture of the cakes. Cutting back from a pound of carrots to a half-pound helped to lighten the cupcakes, while still keeping a significant amount of carrot-y presence.

Next, we played around with the spice amounts until we had the right combination of cinnamon, nutmeg, and cloves. Now our cakes were perfectly spiced. Some tasters liked the addition of raisins or chopped walnuts, but others preferred their cupcakes without, so we leave the choice up to you.

Once we had the perfect cupcake, we turned to the frosting. Tasters wanted something light and fluffy to match the delicate texture of the cupcakes. We combined butter and confectioners' sugar, then beat in half a bar of cream cheese and some vanilla. This creamy yet fluffy frosting was the perfect accent to our moist, tender carrot cupcakes.

CARROT CUPCAKES

MAKES 12 CUPCAKES

If you prefer, you can grind the carrots in a food processor rather than grate them by hand. If you add the optional currants and walnuts, the cupcakes will need to bake an additional 7 to 10 minutes. This recipe is easily doubled. Do not use low-fat or nonfat cream cheese or the frosting will turn out soupy.

CUPCAKES

8	tablespoons (1 stick) unsalted butter, melted and cooled
¾	cup granulated sugar
¼	cup packed dark brown sugar
2	large eggs, room temperature
1¼	cups all-purpose flour
¾	teaspoon baking powder
½	teaspoon baking soda
½	teaspoon salt
½	teaspoon ground cinnamon
¼	teaspoon ground nutmeg

_⅛ teaspoon ground cloves

8 ounces carrots, peeled and grated on small holes of box grater (see note above)

½ cup currants or chopped raisins (optional; see note above)

½ cup chopped walnuts (optional; see note above), toasted (see page 130)

FROSTING

4 tablespoons (½ stick) unsalted butter, softened

1 cup confectioners' sugar

4 ounces cream cheese, cut into 4 pieces and softened (see note above)

¾ teaspoon vanilla extract

1. FOR THE CUPCAKES: Adjust an oven rack to the middle position and heat the oven to 350 degrees. Line a 12-cup muffin tin with cupcake liners.

2. Whisk the melted butter, granulated sugar, brown sugar, and eggs together in a large bowl. Mix in the remaining ingredients until thoroughly combined.

3. Using a greased ¼-cup measure, portion the batter into each muffin cup. Bake the cupcakes until a toothpick inserted in the center comes out clean, 15 to 18 minutes (about 25 minutes if using currants and walnuts), rotating the tin halfway through baking. Let the cupcakes cool in the tin for 10 minutes, then transfer them to a wire rack to cool completely, about 30 minutes.

4. FOR THE FROSTING: In a large bowl, beat the butter and confectioners' sugar together with an electric mixer on medium-high speed until light and fluffy, 3 to 6 minutes. Add the cream cheese, one piece at a time, beating thoroughly after each addition. Add the vanilla and beat until no lumps

remain. (The frosting can be refrigerated in an airtight container for up to 5 days. Bring the frosting to room temperature before using.)

5. Spread the frosting evenly over the cupcakes and serve.

Red Velvet Cupcakes

Traditional red velvet cake is a velvety, tender, brilliant red cake, swathed in sweet but tangy cream cheese frosting. Since this cake is as delicious as it is eye-catching, we thought it would be great miniaturized into cupcakes, a pile of which would make the perfect dessert-table centerpiece.

A bit of research revealed that red cakes aren't new on the dessert circuit; they've been around for years. The red color is the by-product of a chemical reaction between vinegar and/or buttermilk and cocoa powder. Red cakes—with names like Red Devil Cake and Oxblood Cake—date back to the late 19th century. Over time, the naturally occurring red hue was augmented first by beets (a common ingredient during the sugar rations of World War II) and then by red food coloring (the standard choice in most recipes published since the 1950s).

Although the exact origins of red velvet cake itself are muddled, most sources mention the Waldorf-Astoria Hotel and the 1950s, but this history is most definitely false—the recipe did not start there. During the 1960s recipes appeared in countless newspapers, which sourced this classic in the Deep South, the Pacific Northwest, and even Canada. The best-known version of the recipe appeared in James Beard's 1972 classic *American Cookery.*

Although we weren't able to figure out the precise origins of red velvet cake, we had accumulated enough research to start developing our cupcakes.

We tried a few recipes with beets, but no one liked their vegetal flavor. After several tests, we realized food coloring was a must and there was no use trying to skimp on it; any less than 1 tablespoon yielded cupcakes that were more pink than red.

Despite the addition of cocoa powder, these are not meant to be dense, rich chocolate cakes—the cocoa is there for color. Some recipes include as little as 1 teaspoon of cocoa. We found that 1 tablespoon produced the best color and gave the cakes a pleasant (but mild) cocoa flavor.

Now the cupcakes were definitely red, but they were also speckled with brown at the edges. We had been mixing the cocoa powder with the dry ingredients, yet it didn't seem to be evenly distributed in the cupcakes. A few recipes suggested combining the cocoa powder with the red food coloring to make a paste before adding it to the batter, a step that had seemed fussy. It turns out that it was necessary; mixing the paste made the cakes uniformly red, even at the edges.

Now that we had the red part down, we turned to the velvet. After fiddling with the basic formula, we realized that a super-acidic batter (with both buttermilk and vinegar) was needed to react with the baking soda and create a fine, tender crumb. Thoroughly creaming the butter also helped.

To top off our little red cakes, a sweet, tangy, white cream cheese frosting provided contrast in both color and flavor. We now had cupcakes that were both red and velvety—and delicious, too.

RED VELVET CUPCAKES

MAKES 12 CUPCAKES

For the cake to have the proper rise and color, you must use natural cocoa powder; do not substitute Dutch-processed cocoa powder. Do not use low-fat or nonfat cream cheese or the frosting will turn out soupy.

CUPCAKES

1	cup plus 2 tablespoons all-purpose flour
1	teaspoon baking soda
	Pinch salt
1	large egg, room temperature
½	cup buttermilk, room temperature
1½	teaspoons white vinegar
½	teaspoon vanilla extract
1	tablespoon natural cocoa powder (see note above)
1	tablespoon red food coloring
6	tablespoons (¾ stick) unsalted butter, softened
¾	cup granulated sugar

FROSTING

8	ounces cream cheese, softened (see note above)
5	tablespoons unsalted butter, cut into chunks and softened
1	tablespoon sour cream
¾	teaspoon vanilla extract
⅛	teaspoon salt
1	cup confectioners' sugar

1. FOR THE CUPCAKES: Adjust an oven rack to the middle position and heat the oven to 350 degrees. Line a 12-cup muffin tin with cupcake liners.

2. Whisk the flour, baking soda, and salt together in a medium bowl. In a second medium bowl, whisk the egg, buttermilk, vinegar, and vanilla together. In a small bowl, mix the cocoa and red food coloring together to form a smooth paste.

3. In a large bowl, beat the butter and granulated sugar together with an electric mixer on medium-high speed until light and fluffy, 3 to 6 minutes. Reduce the mixer speed to low and beat in one-third of the flour mixture, followed by half of the buttermilk mixture. Repeat with half of the remaining flour mixture and the remaining buttermilk mixture. Beat in the remaining flour mixture until just combined. Beat in the cocoa mixture until the batter is uniform.

4. Give the batter a final stir with a rubber spatula to make sure it is thoroughly combined. Using a greased 1/4-cup measure, portion the batter into each muffin cup. Bake the cupcakes until a toothpick inserted in the center comes out with a few crumbs attached, 15 to 20 minutes, rotating the tin halfway through baking. Let the cupcakes cool in the tin for 10 minutes, then transfer them to a wire rack to cool completely, about 30 minutes.

5. FOR THE FROSTING: Meanwhile, beat the cream cheese, butter, sour cream, vanilla, and salt together in a large bowl with an electric mixer on medium-high speed until smooth, 2 to 4 minutes. Reduce the mixer speed to medium-low, slowly add the confectioners' sugar, and beat until smooth, 2 to 4 minutes. Increase the mixer speed to medium-high and beat until the frosting

is light and fluffy, 2 to 4 minutes. (The frosting can be refrigerated in an airtight container for up to 3 days. Bring the frosting to room temperature before using, then rewhip with an electric mixer on medium speed until smooth, about 2 minutes.)

6. Spread the frosting evenly over the cupcakes and serve.

Boston Cream Cupcakes

Boston cream pie is composed of two layers of sponge cake, a custard filling, and a rich chocolate glaze. This popular dessert (which, of course, is not a pie but a cake) was invented in 1855 at Boston's Parker House Hotel and is the official dessert of Massachusetts. Tradition is all well and good, but we wanted to put a modern-day twist on this old-fashioned cake—and thus we set our sights on transforming this venerable cake into a cupcake.

We found more recipes for the cupcake version of this dessert than you might expect; unfortunately, most of them called for just three ingredients: a box of cake mix, a packet of pudding, and a can of frosting. What we had in mind was something with more homemade flavor, so we turned instead to recipes for the original dessert, which is made with sponge cake. But these recipes weren't quite right either; tasters disliked sponge cupcakes, finding their light, airy texture too insubstantial in small form.

Considering the cakes first, we knew they would have to be tender but also sturdy enough to support the traditional "cream" that is the hallmark of Boston cream pie. We started with our Tender Yellow Cupcakes (page 156), but these sank slightly under the weight of a simple custard we

whipped up, so we made some adjustments to the recipe. Trading in the sour cream for milk, upping the amount of flour, and adding two egg whites (three whole eggs instead of just one egg and two yolks) gave our cupcakes more structure. To keep the tenderness intact amid all these ingredient changes, we reviewed various mixing methods and eventually settled on the reverse creaming method. Reverse creaming calls for cutting the butter into the dry ingredients; this method kept our cupcakes tender and moist.

Moving on to the other components of our Boston cream cupcakes, we considered the custard first. We decided that we would fill the cupcakes with the custard, rather than slicing uber-thin cupcake layers and spreading the custard in between. Thus, we wanted a rich, creamy custard that was stiff enough to hold its shape inside the cupcake but still gooey enough to ooze slightly when we bit into it. Heavy cream (rather than milk or half-and-half), three egg yolks, and a good amount of cornstarch gave our pastry cream the perfect consistency. For the glaze, tasters preferred the strong flavor of bittersweet chocolate to semisweet or milk chocolate, and they loved the sheen provided by a few tablespoons of corn syrup.

Now that we had assembled all of the components, we had to get the pastry cream inside the cupcake. In most recipes the cupcake is filled by inserting the tip of a loaded pastry bag into the cake's top, bottom, or side. Yet with every squirt, the cupcakes cracked. After sacrificing a couple of dozen, we knew we had to find a better way. To make room for the filling, we cut small "cones" off the tops of our cupcakes, scooped out some of the cake, filled the hole with the pastry cream, and then replaced the tops of the cones. Once the glaze was applied, the incision became invisible.

Our updated Boston cream cupcakes were now ready for the next generation of dessert lovers.

BOSTON CREAM CUPCAKES

MAKES 12 CUPCAKES

It's important to bake these cupcakes in a greased and floured muffin tin rather than paper cupcake liners, so the chocolate glaze can run down the sides of the cupcakes.

PASTRY CREAM

1⅓	cups heavy cream
3	large egg yolks
⅓	cup sugar
	Pinch salt
4	teaspoons cornstarch
2	tablespoons unsalted butter, cut into 2 pieces
1½	teaspoons vanilla extract

CUPCAKES

1¾	cups all-purpose flour
1	cup sugar
1½	teaspoons baking powder
¾	teaspoon salt
12	tablespoons (1½ sticks) unsalted butter, cut into 12 pieces and softened
3	large eggs, room temperature
¾	cup whole milk, room temperature
1½	teaspoons vanilla extract

GLAZE

8	ounces bittersweet chocolate, chopped
⅔	cup heavy cream
¼	cup light corn syrup
½	teaspoon vanilla extract

1. FOR THE PASTRY CREAM: Bring the cream to a simmer in a medium saucepan over medium heat. Meanwhile, whisk the egg yolks, sugar, and salt together in a medium bowl, then whisk in the cornstarch until pale yellow and thick, about 30 seconds.

2. Slowly whisk the hot cream into the egg mixture to temper, then return the mixture to the saucepan and cook over medium heat, whisking constantly, until thick and glossy, about 1½ minutes. Off the heat, whisk in the butter and vanilla. Transfer the mixture to a small bowl, press plastic wrap directly on the surface, and refrigerate until chilled and set, about 2 hours.

3. FOR THE CUPCAKES: Adjust an oven rack to the middle position and heat the oven to 350 degrees. Grease and flour a 12-cup muffin tin.

4. Whisk the flour, sugar, baking powder, and salt together in a large bowl. Using an electric mixer on medium-low speed, beat the butter into the flour mixture, one piece at a time, about 30 seconds. Continue to beat the mixture until it resembles moist crumbs, 1 to 3 minutes. Beat in the eggs, one at a time, until combined, about 30 seconds. Beat in the milk and vanilla, then increase the mixer speed to medium and beat the batter until smooth, light, and fluffy, 1 to 3 minutes.

5. Using a greased ⅓-cup measure, portion the batter into each muffin cup. Bake the cupcakes until a toothpick inserted in the center comes out with a few moist crumbs attached, 18 to 20 minutes, rotating the tin halfway through baking. Let the cupcakes cool in the tin for 10 minutes, then transfer them to a wire rack to cool completely, about 30 minutes.

6. FOR THE GLAZE: Microwave all the glaze ingredients together, whisking often, until melted and smooth, 1 to 2 minutes. Let the glaze cool, uncovered, until it is thickened but still pourable, about 20 minutes.

7. Following the photos, cut around the inside edge of the top of each cupcake, removing a cone-shaped piece of cake, and cut off the pointed end. Fill the cupcake with 2 tablespoons of the pastry cream, replace the top, and set each cupcake on a wire rack set over a parchment-lined baking sheet. Spoon the glaze over the cupcakes, letting it run down the sides. Refrigerate the cupcakes until the glaze has set, about 10 minutes, before serving.

FILLING CREAM CUPCAKES

1. Insert the tip of a small knife at a 45-degree angle about ⅛ inch from the edge of the cupcake and cut all the way around, removing a cone of cake.

2. Cut off (and discard) the pointed end of each cone, so that the remaining cake disk measures about ¼ inch thick.

3. Using a spoon, fill each cupcake with 2 tablespoons of pastry cream, then cover each with a cupcake top. Press lightly to adhere.

4. Spoon 2 tablespoons of the glaze over each filled cupcake, allowing it to drip down the sides.

Chocolate Cream Cupcakes

While Ho Hos, Ding Dongs, and Ring Dings bring back fond childhood memories for many, none are quite as iconic as Hostess CupCakes, which have been a snack-time staple for both kids and adults since the early 1900s. But when we caved in to our cravings recently, we were disappointed by the wan, dull chocolate shell and salty, sugary shortening inside. Then and there, we vowed to make a chocolate cream cupcake that tasted as good as it looked. We wanted a moist, tender cake with deep chocolate flavor, a buttery filling that wouldn't dribble out, and a shiny, fudgy glaze. Given that this cupcake has three components—batter, filling, and frosting—we knew that some work was inevitable. Still, we hoped to develop as simple a recipe as possible.

A check of baking books and the Internet revealed that we weren't the first to attempt a Hostess-style cupcake. Some recipes were incredibly time-consuming, creating fillings and frostings that were over-the-top involved. One recipe, however, stood out for its dump-and-stir ease, moist texture, and decently chocolaty crumb. The recipe began with dissolving or "blooming" cocoa in boiling water to deepen its flavor. The cocoa solution was combined with oil, sour cream, sugar, and eggs, which in turn was then combined with the flour, baking soda, and salt. Tasters liked the texture of this cupcake but thought the chocolate flavor needed a boost. To enhance it, we added chocolate chips, which conveniently melted in the boiling water. In a subsequent test, we discovered that a tablespoon of espresso powder gave the cupcakes even more chocolate depth.

Moving on to the filling, we tried the simplest trick we could think of: we divvied up the batter among the muffin tins and pushed a marshmallow into each. While baking, however, the marshmallow floated to the surface, melted, and created a moonlike crater. We considered seven-minute frosting, made by cooking egg whites, sugar, and water over simmering water and then whipping the mixture until thick and fluffy (about seven minutes, hence the name). But we quickly reconsidered—our cupcakes were enough trouble as it was, so we didn't want the filling to be too much work. Some recipes used marshmallow crème, confectioners' sugar, and softened butter beaten together—a promising approach on ease alone. But these fillings were so soft they dripped out of the cupcakes.

We wondered if mixing the marshmallow crème with some gelatin would help to stabilize it. We dissolved an envelope of gelatin (about 2 teaspoons) in water; combined it with the marshmallow crème, butter for richness, and vanilla for flavor; and refrigerated the mixture. This filling was so rubbery we could have bounced it off the floor. Cutting back by more than half (to ¾ teaspoon gelatin) worked well—now we had a set but creamy filling.

To fill the cupcakes, we followed the protocol we'd used for our Boston Cream Cupcakes (page 166). We removed a small portion of cake from the top of the cupcakes, filled the space with our marshmallow crème mixture, and replaced only the top part of the cake cutout.

For the finishing touch, we created a quick glaze by melting ½ cup of semisweet chocolate chips with 3 tablespoons of heavy cream. The glaze was appropriately fudgy but a bit soft. When we replaced the cream with butter, it firmed right up. We couldn't resist piping a flourish of swirls across each cupcake (extra filling piped out beautifully, saving us the trouble of making a separate icing). Finally, we put our homemade cupcakes to the test against the originals. Tasters agreed: there was no contest.

CHOCOLATE CREAM CUPCAKES

MAKES 12 CUPCAKES

To ensure an appropriately thick filling, be sure to use marshmallow crème (such as Fluff or Kraft Jet-Puffed Marshmallow Creme), not marshmallow sauce.

CUPCAKES

1	cup all-purpose flour
½	teaspoon baking soda
¼	teaspoon salt
½	cup boiling water
⅓	cup Dutch-processed cocoa powder
⅓	cup semisweet chocolate chips
1	tablespoon instant espresso powder
2	large eggs
¾	cup sugar
½	cup sour cream
½	cup vegetable oil
1	teaspoon vanilla extract

FILLING

3	tablespoons water
¾	teaspoon unflavored gelatin
4	tablespoons (½ stick) unsalted butter, softened
1	teaspoon vanilla extract
	Pinch salt
1¼	cups marshmallow crème (see note above)

DECORATING CREAM CUPCAKES

After letting the glaze set on the cupcakes, pipe on a curlicue using the reserved marshmallow filling.

GLAZE

½	cup semisweet chocolate chips
3	tablespoons unsalted butter

1. FOR THE CUPCAKES: Adjust an oven rack to the middle position and heat the oven to 325 degrees. Grease and flour a 12-cup muffin tin. Combine the flour, baking soda, and salt in a bowl.

2. Whisk the water, cocoa, chocolate chips, and espresso together in a large bowl until smooth. Add the eggs, sugar, sour cream, oil, and vanilla and mix until combined. Whisk in the flour mixture until incorporated. Using a greased ¼-cup measure, portion the batter into each muffin cup. Bake the cupcakes until a toothpick inserted in the center comes out with a few dry crumbs attached, 18 to 22 minutes, rotating the tin halfway through baking. Let the cupcakes cool in the tin for 10 minutes, then transfer them to a wire rack to cool completely, about 30 minutes.

3. FOR THE FILLING: Combine the water and gelatin in a large bowl and let sit until the gelatin softens, about 5 minutes. Microwave the mixture until bubbling around the edges and the gelatin dissolves, about 30 seconds. Stir in the butter, vanilla, and salt until combined. Let the mixture cool until just warm to the touch, about 5 minutes, then whisk in the marshmallow crème until smooth; refrigerate until set, about 30 minutes. Transfer ⅓ cup of the marshmallow mixture to a pastry bag fitted with a small plain tip; reserve the remaining mixture for filling the cupcakes.

4. FOR THE GLAZE: Microwave the chocolate chips and butter together in small bowl, stirring occasionally, until smooth, about 30 seconds. Let the glaze cool to room temperature, about 10 minutes.

5. Following the photos on page 167, cut around the inside edge of the top of each cupcake, removing a cone-shaped piece of cake, and cut off the pointed end. Fill the cupcake with 1 tablespoon of the filling and replace the top. Frost each cupcake with 2 teaspoons of the cooled glaze and let sit for 10 minutes. Following the photo on page 170, using the pastry bag, pipe curlicues across the glazed cupcakes. Serve.

Black-Bottom Cupcakes

Black-bottom cupcakes are moist, fudgy, nearly black cupcakes containing a creamy center of tangy cheesecake filling studded with mini chocolate chips—what's not to love? Determined to make our own version, we gathered a stack of printed recipes and headed into the test kitchen with high hopes.

Our confidence quickly faltered as soon as we lined up our cupcakes for tasters. Most of them were greasy, slumped, and devoid of rich chocolate flavor. As for the cheesecake centers, they baked up dry, chalky, or completely separated from the cake in sunken craters. We were looking for a cake that had big chocolate flavor and was sturdy enough to support the cheesecake filling.

The cake portion of black-bottom cupcakes traditionally gets its dark color and chocolate flavor from cocoa powder. Tasters preferred the rounded flavor of Dutch-processed cocoa to natural cocoa. Adding a little sour cream to the batter accentuated the chocolate and added richness. Although the cake was now tasting good, we were frustrated that the cheesecake center was still pulling away. It turns out the problem was with the cake, not with the filling.

Black-bottom cupcakes are usually made with oil, which contributes to the soft, fudgy texture.

But oil also makes the cake leaden and greasy—so greasy that the filling can't adhere to it. However, when we used butter (creaming it with the sugar) instead of oil, the aerated batter baked up too tender to support the filling. As a last resort, we tried melting the butter. The batter looked dense and sticky (just like the batter made with oil), but as the cupcakes cooled we saw a big difference. The butter had resolidified and the cake was no longer greasy. Best of all, it was sturdy enough to support the cheesecake filling.

But we still weren't happy with the filling's flavor. In most recipes the filling consists of cream cheese, sugar, and a whole egg, but the yolk lent an unappealing yellow hue and mealy texture when baked. Using two whites added moisture and helped the filling look better, but it also dulled the tang of the cream cheese. Since we were already using sour cream in the cake batter, we added some to the cheesecake filling, and it restored a needed tang. The inclusion of mini chocolate chips made the filling complete and reinforced the chocolate flavor of the fudgy cupcakes.

BLACK-BOTTOM CUPCAKES

MAKES 12 CUPCAKES

Do not substitute regular chocolate chips for the miniature chips; regular chips are much heavier and will sink to the bottom of the cupcakes.

FILLING

1	(8-ounce) package cream cheese, softened
¼	cup sugar
⅛	teaspoon salt
1	large egg white
1	tablespoon sour cream
¼	cup semisweet mini chocolate chips (see note above)

CUPCAKES

¾	cup all-purpose flour
⅔	cup sugar
¼	cup Dutch-processed cocoa powder
½	teaspoon baking soda
¼	teaspoon salt
¾	cup water, room temperature
6	tablespoons sour cream, room temperature
4	tablespoons (½ stick) unsalted butter, melted and cooled
½	teaspoon vanilla extract

1. Adjust an oven rack to the lower-middle position and heat the oven to 400 degrees. Line a 12-cup muffin tin with cupcake liners.

2. FOR THE FILLING: In a medium bowl, beat the cream cheese, sugar, and salt together with an electric mixer on medium speed until smooth, about 30 seconds. Beat in the egg white and sour cream until combined, about 30 seconds. Stir in the chocolate chips.

3. FOR THE CUPCAKES: Whisk the flour, sugar, cocoa, baking soda, and salt together in a large bowl. Whisk in the water, sour cream, melted butter, and vanilla until just incorporated.

4. Using a greased ⅓-cup measure, portion the batter into each muffin cup. Spoon a rounded tablespoon of the cream cheese mixture onto the center of each cupcake.

5. Bake the cupcakes until the tops just begin to crack, 18 to 22 minutes, rotating the tin halfway through baking. Let the cupcakes cool in the tin for 10 minutes, then transfer them to a wire rack to cool completely before serving.

SHOPPING WITH THE TEST KITCHEN

Cooling Racks: A wire cooling rack is an essential piece of equipment when making many baked goods. Traditional row-style racks can gouge delicate cupcakes or cakes. The problem is the parallel metal bars, which are so thin and flimsy that they dig into baked goods and leave permanent marks. We prefer grid-style cooling racks with crisscrossing bars; when tightly woven, they can support even the heaviest cake or biggest cookie without marring the exterior. We especially like cooling racks that can fit inside a standard 18 by 13-inch sheet pan. Our favorite is the CIA Bakeware 17 by 12-inch Cooling Rack ($15.95). We also recommend the Libertyware Cross Wire Cooling Rack, Half-Sheet Pan Size, which is our best buy at $5.25.

Raspberry Mini Cheesecakes

Just like cupcakes, mini cheesecakes are a classic—no matter the season, no matter the event, they always seem to occupy a space on the dessert tray or buffet table. But take a bite of one and you'll wonder why. Most of the time, they're dry and crumbly, with barely a hint of bright cream cheese flavor. We wanted mini cheesecakes that tasted rich, tangy, luscious, and creamy. Dressed up with raspberries, these miniature cheesecakes would be pretty enough to display but easy to assemble and delicious enough that you'd want to make them for any occasion.

We started our testing with a test-kitchen recipe for classic cheesecake, which included the usual ingredients—cream cheese, sugar, eggs, sour cream, vanilla extract, salt, and lemon juice. For the crust, we gathered butter, graham crackers, and sugar, along with our muffin tin for baking. However, this seemed like a long roster for what we hoped would be a simple and speedy dessert, so we looked for ways to cut corners.

As we were mulling over ways to streamline our cheesecakes, we remembered a back-of-the-can recipe from years ago that used sweetened condensed milk. Plugging it into our recipe let us eliminate the sugar and sour cream; the duo of cream cheese and sweetened condensed milk was enough to create a rich and creamy filling. In a subsequent test, tasters decided the sweetened condensed milk lent enough flavor to the filling that we could also eject the vanilla and lemon juice.

Building the crusts next, we went through the tedious steps of making a graham cracker–butter mixture, packing it into each tin, baking until crisp, topping with cheesecake batter, and baking again. But this was a hassle. Since we essentially needed mini cookie crusts for our mini cheesecakes, what if we just used a small cookie? We found that 2-inch-wide shortbread cookies fit into our muffin cups perfectly.

Recipes for mini cheesecakes often call for greased muffin tins, but prying our cheesecakes out of the individual cups was messy and difficult. Using cupcake liners made things far easier and sped the cleanup; the wrapper peeled off neatly, too, and added presentation points.

Traditional cheesecakes often are topped with fruit or glazed; we opted for the latter. To glaze the cheesecakes, we heated some raspberry jam in the microwave to thin it slightly; now we were able to spread the jam easily and evenly over our cooled cheesecakes. After sampling one (OK, maybe a few), we got the idea of adding even more raspberry flavor by dolloping a layer of jam over the cookie as well. After the cheesecakes baked, there was just enough room for a fresh raspberry on top—the perfect garnish for the perfect little cheesecake.

RASPBERRY MINI CHEESECAKES

MAKES 12 MINI CHEESECAKES

Sandies, made by Keebler, are the test kitchen's favorite brand of shortbread cookies for making the crusts since they fit perfectly in a muffin tin. If you use a thinner cookie, your mini cheesecakes will be slightly smaller. Do not use low-fat or nonfat cream cheese or the filling will turn out soupy.

12	round shortbread cookies, 2 inches wide and ½ inch thick (see note above)
½	cup seedless raspberry jam
1	(8-ounce) package cream cheese, softened (see note above)
½	cup sweetened condensed milk
2	large eggs
12	fresh raspberries, for garnish (optional)

1. Adjust an oven rack to the middle position and heat the oven to 300 degrees. Line a 12-cup muffin tin with cupcake liners. Place one cookie in each muffin cup and top each with 1 teaspoon jam.

2. With an electric mixer on medium-high speed, beat the cream cheese in a medium bowl until light and fluffy, about 2 minutes. Gradually beat in the condensed milk, scraping down the sides of the bowl as necessary, until incorporated. Add the eggs, one at a time; beat until smooth, 2 to 3 minutes.

3. Divide the batter evenly among the muffin cups. Bake until set, about 20 minutes. Transfer the tin to a wire rack; let cool to room temperature, about 20 minutes. Refrigerate until set, about 1 hour.

4. Remove the cheesecakes from the muffin tin. Microwave the remaining ¼ cup jam until thinned slightly, about 15 seconds, and glaze each cheesecake with about 1 teaspoon jam. Top each cheesecake with a fresh raspberry, if using, and serve.

ULTIMATE CHOCOLATE CHIP COOKIES

CHAPTER SIX

Bake Sale Cookies, Brownies, and Bars

Ultimate Chocolate Chip Cookies

Nestlé first printed the recipe for Toll House cookies on the back of chocolate chip bags in 1939. And ever since, generations of bakers have packed them into lunches, taken them to bake sales, and kept them on hand for afternoon snacks. But while the Toll House cookie's cakey texture and buttery, one-note flavor might have their appeal, are these really the best that chocolate chip cookies can be? We wanted a truly great chocolate chip cookie—it had to be moist and chewy on the inside and crisp at the edges, with complex flavors to balance the sweetness.

Reviewing recipes, we saw a number of unusual techniques for creating a better chocolate chip cookie—from resting the dough for up to three days (to create a drier dough that caramelizes more quickly in the oven and achieves richer flavor) to portioning and freezing the dough before baking (to prevent the dough from spreading, thereby keeping the center moist and chewy). Granted, we were after the best cookie possible. But cookies, by nature, are easy—they shouldn't take days to make. We wanted a simple, straightforward path to cookie heaven.

We decided to start by tackling texture. The Toll House recipe calls for creaming the butter with sugar to create tiny air bubbles that bring a cakey lift to cookies. But we suspected that using melted butter would contribute a noticeable chewiness to the cookies (when butter melts, the water separates from the fat and can interact with the flour to create more chewiness). One test told us we were on the right track.

Since we were already melting the butter, we hit on the idea of browning it. Browned butter has a rich, nutty flavor, and we suspected it would contribute these complex notes to our cookies—we

were right. Because browning can burn off the butter's moisture, we browned just a portion of it.

Up next: sugar. Besides adding sweetness, sugar affects texture. White sugar granules lend crispness, and brown sugar enhances chewiness. The Toll House recipe calls for equal amounts of white and brown sugar; we got the best results when we skewed the ratio slightly. We simply upped the brown sugar (tasters preferred dark for its deeper flavor) to 60 percent and knocked the white down to 40 percent.

Now we tested various types of flour. Cake flour, with its low protein content, yielded a crunchy, crumbly cookie, and bread flour, with its higher protein content, gave us cookies that were so dense and chewy that they were closer to chocolate chip bread than chocolate chip cookies. In the end, just cutting back on the all-purpose flour by ½ cup increased moistness in the cookies and allowed the chewiness contributed by the brown sugar to come to the forefront. The only problem: with less flour, the cookies were a little greasy. To resolve the issue, we cut back on the butter by 2 tablespoons.

Finally, we were ready to evaluate the role of eggs in our dough. Because egg whites tend to create a cakey texture in baked goods, we decided to cut back on them and started by eliminating one white. Now our cookies were incredibly moist and chewy.

We had achieved our chewiness, but the complex flavor wasn't quite there yet. Browning the butter had helped, but now we were stumped on how to create richer cookies. That's when things came together.

In the middle of stirring the butter, sugar, and eggs together, we paused to regroup and consider our options. Ten minutes later, we found that the sugars had dissolved and the mixture had turned thick and shiny, like frosting. We didn't think much of it until we pulled the finished cookies from the oven. Instead of the smooth, matte surface of the previous batches, these cookies emerged with a slightly glossy sheen and a craggy surface. Also, they boasted a deep, toffeelike flavor. Mysteriously, these cookies finally had just the texture we were after: crisp on the outside and chewy within.

Our science editor explained that allowing the sugar to rest in the liquids enabled more of it to dissolve in the moisture before baking. Dissolved sugar caramelizes more easily, creating rich, toffeelike flavors and a chewy texture. When sugar dissolved in water is heated, the moisture burns off and the sugar breaks apart, creating a brittle, amorphous structure—hence, the crispier texture. But that effect occurs mainly at the cookie's outer edges; the remaining moisture becomes concentrated in the center.

For our next batch, we had this caramelization in mind and kept the oven temperature hot, 375 degrees—the same as for Toll House cookies. Watching carefully, we left the cookies in the oven until they were golden brown, just set at the edges, and soft in the center.

With a tall glass of milk at the ready, we sat down to sample our efforts. These were the ultimate chocolate chip cookies: crisp and chewy, gooey with chocolate, and flavored with a medley of sweet, buttery, caramel, and toffee notes.

ULTIMATE CHOCOLATE CHIP COOKIES

MAKES ABOUT 16 LARGE COOKIES

Avoid using a nonstick skillet to brown the butter; the dark color of the nonstick coating makes it difficult to gauge when the butter is browned. Use fresh, moist brown sugar instead of hardened brown sugar, which will make the cookies dry. This recipe works with light brown sugar, but the cookies will be less full-flavored. For the best results, bake only one sheet of cookies at a time. The unbaked dough can be shaped into balls and frozen on a large plate; when they are frozen solid, transfer them to a large zipper-lock bag. To bake, arrange the frozen cookies on the baking sheets—do not thaw—and bake as directed, increasing the baking time to 19 to 24 minutes.

1 ¾	cups all-purpose flour
½	teaspoon baking soda
14	tablespoons (1 ¾ sticks) unsalted butter
¾	cup packed dark brown sugar (see note above)
½	cup granulated sugar
2	teaspoons vanilla extract
1	teaspoon salt
1	large egg plus 1 large egg yolk
1 ¼	cups semisweet chocolate chips or chunks
¾	cup chopped pecans or walnuts (optional), toasted (see page 130)

1. Adjust an oven rack to the middle position and heat the oven to 375 degrees. Line two large baking sheets with parchment paper. Whisk the flour and baking soda together in a medium bowl and set aside.

2. Melt 10 tablespoons of the butter in a medium skillet over medium-high heat, about 2 minutes. Continue cooking, swirling the pan constantly, until the butter is dark golden brown and has a nutty aroma, 1 to 3 minutes longer. Using a heatproof spatula, transfer the browned butter to a large heatproof bowl. Stir the remaining 4 tablespoons butter into the hot butter until completely melted.

3. Add the brown sugar, granulated sugar, vanilla, and salt and whisk until fully incorporated. Add the egg and egg yolk and whisk until the mixture is smooth with no lumps remaining, about 30 seconds. Let the mixture sit for 3 minutes, then whisk for 30 seconds. Repeat the process of resting and whisking two more times until the mixture is thick, smooth, and shiny. Using a rubber spatula or wooden spoon, stir in the flour mixture until just combined, about 1 minute. Stir in the chocolate chips and nuts (if using), giving the dough a final stir to make sure no flour pockets remain.

4. Working with 3 tablespoons of dough at a time, roll the dough into balls and lay them on the prepared baking sheets, spaced about 2 inches apart.

5. Bake the cookies, one sheet at a time, until golden brown and still puffy and the edges have begun to set but the centers are still soft, 10 to 14 minutes, rotating the baking sheet halfway through baking. Transfer the baking sheet to a wire rack and let the cookies cool completely on the sheet before serving.

SHOPPING WITH THE TEST KITCHEN

Dark Chocolate Chips: Chocolate has just three basic ingredients—cocoa butter, cocoa solids, and sugar. So does it really matter which brand of chocolate chips you buy? After sampling eight brands, we found that it does. The higher the cacao percentage (the total amount of cocoa butter and cocoa solids), the darker the chocolate and the more intense the flavor. Our favorite, Ghirardelli 60% Cacao Bittersweet Chocolate Chips, had the highest percentage of cacao in our lineup—comparable to bar chocolate—and by far the most cocoa butter; in addition, its low sugar content allowed the chocolate flavor to shine. A wider, flatter shape and high percentage of fat helped the chips melt into thin layers in our chocolate chip cookies for a pleasing balance of cookie and chocolate in every bite.

Thick and Chewy Chocolate Cookies

All too often, chewy chocolate cookies fall short of what they promise. Although there might be a ton of chocolate in the ingredient list, the flavor is fleeting and dull, and the cookie's texture is cakey and dry. We wanted a chewy, dense cookie that was also rich and intense in flavor. We set our sights on a triple-chocolate cookie (with bittersweet, semisweet, and unsweetened chocolates) that was decadent and rich and full of chocolaty flavor from the first bite to the last.

Most cookies are made by creaming butter and sugar, then adding eggs and the dry ingredients. This method simply won't work with triple-chocolate cookies—there's no place to add all of that melted chocolate. The brownie method—melt chocolate and butter, add sugar, eggs, and flour—was the most common choice in the recipes we found, but we had trouble getting the cookies to hold their shape.

We had better luck beating the eggs and sugar together until fluffy, then adding the melted chocolate along with the melted butter, and adding the dry ingredients last. Beating the eggs and sugar for a few minutes gave the dough more structure. When baked, these cookies had an appealingly crisp shell, almost like a meringue cookie.

As for the kind of chocolate, tasters liked a relatively small amount of unsweetened chocolate (too much was overpowering) balanced by equal amounts of bittersweet and semisweet chocolate. We found that premium bittersweet bar chocolates were actually too rich (and too greasy) for this recipe. We had better luck with bittersweet chocolate chips, which contain less fat than bittersweet chocolate bars. The melted chips improved the dough by making it less fluid, yet they also added the same grown-up, not-too-sweet flavor as the bittersweet bar chocolates. A small amount of instant coffee amplified the flavors nicely.

The semisweet chocolate is the buffer that rounds out the harsh edges of the bittersweet and unsweetened chocolates. But when we added even a small amount of melted semisweet chocolate, the cookies became gooey and cloying. After much trial and error, we hit upon a novel idea. We added the semisweet chocolate in chip form once the dough was assembled. Because the chips softened but did not melt in the oven, they added chocolate flavor without increasing the fluidity of the batter or harming the texture of the cookies.

At last, we had a cookie that delivered: it was both rich and soft, with an incredibly satisfying chewy texture and an intense chocolaty center.

THICK AND CHEWY TRIPLE-CHOCOLATE COOKIES

MAKES ABOUT 26 COOKIES

The key to the fudgy texture of these cookies is letting them cool directly on the baking sheets. Avoid using bittersweet bar chocolate—the cookies will be too rich and won't hold their shape.

3	ounces unsweetened chocolate, chopped
1½	cups bittersweet chocolate chips
7	tablespoons unsalted butter, cut into chunks
2	teaspoons instant coffee
2	teaspoons vanilla extract
3	large eggs, room temperature
1	cup sugar
½	cup all-purpose flour
½	teaspoon baking powder
½	teaspoon salt
1½	cups semisweet chocolate chips

1. Melt the unsweetened chocolate, bittersweet chocolate chips, and butter in a large heatproof

ARRANGING CHOCOLATE COOKIES

Staggering the rows of cookie dough ensures that 13 cookies will fit on a single large baking sheet.

bowl set over a medium saucepan filled with 1 inch barely simmering water (don't let the bowl touch the water), stirring frequently, until completely smooth and glossy. Remove the bowl from the heat and set aside to cool slightly.

2. Stir the coffee and vanilla together in a small bowl until the coffee is dissolved. Beat the eggs and sugar in a large bowl with an electric mixer on medium-high speed until very thick and pale, about 4 minutes. Beat in the vanilla-coffee mixture until incorporated, 20 seconds. Reduce the mixer speed to low, add the cooled chocolate mixture, and mix until thoroughly combined, about 30 seconds.

3. Whisk the flour, baking powder, and salt together in a medium bowl. Using a rubber spatula, fold the flour mixture and semisweet chocolate chips into the dough. Give the dough a final stir to make sure no flour pockets remain. Cover the bowl with plastic wrap and let sit at room temperature until the dough firms to the consistency of thick brownie batter, about 30 minutes.

4. Meanwhile, adjust the oven racks to the upper-middle and lower-middle positions and heat the oven to 350 degrees. Line two large baking sheets with parchment paper. Following the photo and working with 1 heaping tablespoon of dough at a time, place the dough on the prepared baking sheets, spaced about 2 inches apart. Bake the cookies until shiny and cracked on top, 11 to 14 minutes, switching and rotating the baking sheets halfway through baking. Transfer the baking sheets to wire racks and let the cookies cool completely on the sheets before serving.

Peanut Blossom Cookies

When Freda Smith entered her peanut blossoms in the 1957 Pillsbury Bake-Off, little did she know that she had created a cookie sensation that would withstand the test of time. This Gibsonburg, Ohio, native may not have won the $25,000 first prize (although as a runner-up she won a General Electric stove, among other things), but her peanut blossoms—chocolate-kissed peanut butter cookies—quickly eclipsed that year's winner, a recipe for walnut-flavored butter cookies called accordion treats.

Since Freda's recipe is where it all began, we used it as a starting point to create our own version. Although her recipe produced a good cookie, tasters wanted more peanut flavor. Freda's recipe calls for creamy peanut butter, so we went with chunky peanut butter in our next test. These cookies received praise for their strong peanut flavor, but tasters disliked their craggy texture and appearance. We decided to stick with creamy peanut butter and try replacing some of the flour with ground peanuts. Sure enough, finely ground peanuts added a deep peanut flavor to the cookies without compromising their texture.

The cookies were almost perfect, but we were frustrated by one thing: the Hershey's Chocolate Kiss. Every recipe that we found called for the Kisses to be pressed into the cookies immediately after baking. But we found that the residual heat in the cookies softened the Kisses so much that they took at least 4 hours to firm up again. If we took a bite any sooner, chocolate would squirt out of the cookie.

After a bit of tinkering, we found an unlikely solution to the problem of gushing Kisses. Strangely enough, placing the chocolates on the cookies during the last 2 minutes of baking helped them to firm up more quickly. Why? It turns out that a little direct heat stabilizes and sets the exterior of the chocolate; the Kisses handled this way were firm enough to eat in half the time (after just 2 hours on a wire rack), which pleased all of our tasters.

PEANUT BLOSSOM COOKIES

MAKES ABOUT 48 COOKIES

Any Hershey's Chocolate Kiss works in this recipe; you will need one 1-pound bag of Kisses. For the best results, bake only one sheet of cookies at a time. Note that although the cookies will be cool enough to eat after about 30 minutes, the Kisses will take 2 hours to set completely.

1⅓	cups all-purpose flour
½	cup salted dry-roasted peanuts
¼	teaspoon baking soda
¼	teaspoon baking powder
¼	teaspoon salt
8	tablespoons (1 stick) unsalted butter, softened
⅓	cup packed dark brown sugar
⅓	cup granulated sugar
½	cup creamy peanut butter
1	large egg
1	teaspoon vanilla extract
48	Hershey's Chocolate Kisses, unwrapped (see note above)

1. Adjust an oven rack to the middle position and heat the oven to 350 degrees. Line two large baking sheets with parchment paper. Process ⅔ cup of the flour and peanuts together in a food processor until the mixture resembles coarse meal, about 15 seconds. Transfer the mixture to a medium bowl and stir in the remaining ⅔ cup flour, baking soda, baking powder, and salt.

2. In a large bowl, beat the butter, brown sugar, and granulated sugar together with an electric mixer on medium-high speed until light and fluffy, 3 to 6 minutes. Beat in the peanut butter, egg, and vanilla until combined, about 30 seconds, scraping down the bowl as necessary.

3. Reduce the mixer speed to low and slowly add the flour mixture, mixing until combined, about 30 seconds. Cover the bowl with plastic wrap and refrigerate until the dough is stiff, about 30 minutes.

4. Working with 1½ teaspoons of dough at a time, roll the dough into balls and lay them on the prepared baking sheets, spaced about 1½ inches apart, 12 dough balls per sheet. Bake the cookies, one sheet at a time, until just set and beginning to crack, 9 to 11 minutes, rotating the baking sheet halfway through baking. Working quickly, remove the baking sheet from the oven and firmly press one Kiss into the center of each cookie. Continue to bake the cookies until lightly golden, about 2 minutes longer.

5. Let the cookies cool on the baking sheet for 10 minutes, then transfer to a wire rack and let cool completely before serving. Repeat with the remaining dough using cooled, freshly lined baking sheets.

Thin and Crispy Oatmeal Cookies

Some people like a big, hearty, and chewy oatmeal cookie, with raisins and nuts in every bite. A lesser known, but just as beloved version of oatmeal cookies is thin, crisp, and delicate. This style allows the simple flavor of buttery oats to really stand out. We wanted to develop just such an oatmeal cookie that combined the refinement of a lace cookie with the ease of a drop cookie.

We began our testing with the choice of fat. Because we wanted rich, buttery flavor, we rejected the idea of shortening from the get-go (even though it typically provides a crispier texture) and settled on butter.

As for sugar, most recipes use a combination of brown and granulated sugars, and we saw no reason to depart from this duo. Brown sugar lends rich flavor and moisture, and granulated sugar provides crispness and encourages browning.

To contribute better structure and richer flavor to the cookies, an egg or two is beaten in next. One egg held the cookies together nicely, but two gave them a cakey texture. Along with the single egg, we added a teaspoon of vanilla to round out the flavor. Now that the wet ingredients were all set, we were ready to tackle the dry stuff.

A fairly standard amount of 1½ cups of flour gave the cookies a thicker texture. We slowly cut down the amount until we ended up with 1 cup of flour. Though these cookies emerged from the oven with enough structure and were more crisp than their predecessors, they still weren't on the mark. Because they didn't spread enough, they lacked the thinness we were looking for, and the dry edges and slightly chewy centers were obviously wrong. We tried reducing the amount of oats as well, but that still didn't solve the problem.

Could the leavener be the issue? Here are the basic principles of leavener: Use too little and there won't be enough bubbles to help the dough rise; use too much and you end up with excess carbon dioxide, which causes the bubbles to get too big. These big bubbles eventually combine with one another, rise to the top of the dough, and burst, resulting in a flat product. But since what we wanted was a thin, flat cookie, perhaps we could make this "mistake" work to our advantage. After testing varying amounts and combinations of baking powder and baking soda, we found that ¾ teaspoon of baking powder coupled with ½ teaspoon of baking soda gave us exactly what we wanted. This time, the cookies puffed up in the oven, collapsed, and spread out, becoming a much thinner version of their former selves.

One last issue remained. To guard against the tough, dry cookies that can result from overbaking, most recipes for thick and chewy cookies say to remove them from the oven when they still look slightly raw. Suspecting this was a precaution we didn't need to heed, we tried baking the cookies all the way through until they were fully set and evenly browned. Since the cookies were now thin, they didn't become tough. Instead, they were crisp throughout. And rather than transferring them warm from the baking sheet to a wire rack, we accidentally discovered that the cookies got crispier when left to cool completely on the baking sheet—less work, with even better results! We'd finally achieved our goal: a thin, delicate oatmeal cookie with buttery flavor and just the right amount of crunch.

THIN AND CRISPY OATMEAL COOKIES

MAKES ABOUT 24 COOKIES

For the best results, bake only one sheet of cookies at a time. Place them on the baking sheet in three rows, with three cookies in the outer rows and two cookies in the center row. If you reuse a baking sheet, allow the cookies on it to cool for at least 10 minutes before transferring them to a wire rack, then reline the sheet with fresh parchment paper before baking more cookies. We developed this recipe using Old Fashioned Quaker Oats. Other brands of old-fashioned oats can be substituted but may cause the cookies to spread more. Do not use instant or quick-cooking oats.

1	cup all-purpose flour
¾	teaspoon baking powder
½	teaspoon baking soda
½	teaspoon salt
14	tablespoons (1¾ sticks) unsalted butter, softened
1	cup granulated sugar
¼	cup packed light brown sugar
1	large egg
1	teaspoon vanilla extract
2½	cups old-fashioned rolled oats (see note above)

1. Adjust an oven rack to the middle position and heat the oven to 350 degrees. Line three large baking sheets with parchment paper. Whisk the flour, baking powder, baking soda, and salt together in a medium bowl.

2. In a large bowl, beat the butter, granulated sugar, and brown sugar together with an electric mixer on medium-low speed until just combined, about 20 seconds. Increase the mixer speed to medium and continue to beat until light and fluffy, about 1 minute longer. Add the egg and vanilla and beat on medium-low speed until fully incorporated, about 30 seconds, scraping down the sides of the bowl as necessary. With the mixer speed on low, slowly add the flour mixture and mix until just incorporated and smooth, about 10 seconds. With the mixer still running, gradually add the oats and mix until well incorporated, about 20 seconds. Give the dough a final stir to make sure no flour pockets remain.

3. Working with 2 tablespoons of dough at a time, roll the dough into balls and lay them on the prepared baking sheets, spaced about 2½ inches apart, eight dough balls per sheet (see note above). With the bottom of a measuring cup or a flat-bottomed glass, gently press the balls into ¾-inch-thick disks.

REFRESHING STORED COOKIES

Leftover cookies should be stored in an airtight container at room temperature. To restore that just-baked freshness, recrisp the cookies in a 425-degree oven for 4 to 5 minutes. Let the cookies cool on the baking sheet for a couple of minutes before removing them and serve them while they're warm. (Note that this method doesn't work for Peanut Blossom Cookies, Black-and-White Cookies, Whoopie Pies, or Hermits.)

---

4. Bake the cookies, one sheet at a time, until the cookies are a deep golden brown, the edges are crisp, and the centers yield to a slight pressure when pressed, 13 to 16 minutes, rotating the baking sheet halfway through baking. Let the cookies cool on the baking sheet for 10 minutes, then serve warm or transfer to a wire rack and let cool completely.

Sand Tarts

Thin, crisp, buttery, and dusted with a "sandy" coating of cinnamon sugar, sand tarts were once one of America's favorite cookies. We found recipes in *The Presbyterian Cookbook* and *Buckeye Cookery*, both from the 1870s, and in Fannie Merritt Farmer's *The Boston Cooking-School Cook Book* (1896). It is believed that these cookies were brought to American shores by German immigrants in the 19th century, and they became especially popular in Maryland, Pennsylvania, and Ohio.

Twentieth-century recipes aim for flat, crisp cookies dusted with cinnamon sugar and decorated with a ring of sliced almonds (which makes the cookies look a bit like sand dollars). Almost every recipe we uncovered gave similar instructions: cream copious amounts of butter and sugar; add two whole eggs and flour; refrigerate the dough to make it more workable; then roll it thin, stamp out the cookies, adorn them with cinnamon sugar and almonds, and bake until crisp. But when we prepared these recipes, we began to see why this cookie has fallen out of favor. Even when chilled overnight, the rich, sticky dough was almost impossible to roll out to the desired thickness without tearing.

Considering other shaping options, we tried a trick the test kitchen often employs for sugar cookies—rolling the dough into balls, rolling the

balls in sugar (or cinnamon sugar), and then flattening them with the bottom of a measuring cup before baking. This was easy and worked great, provided we flattened the cookies in two steps, with more cinnamon sugar added between pressings to minimize sticking and add even more flavor.

But the cookies were still doming, and we wanted them to be flat and crisp. Eliminating one of the egg whites reduced the doming slightly, but not enough. Turning to our mixing method, we realized we were beating a lot of air into the dough as we creamed the butter and sugar—air that was giving the cookies extra height. Switching from an electric mixer to a food processor helped minimize air in the dough, but our real breakthrough happened when we switched the order in which we added ingredients to the processor. Cutting the butter into the sugar and flour (a technique known as reverse creaming) incorporated almost no air and finally produced the flat, crisp cookies we were after. In the end, a modern appliance helped make this recipe relevant for a new generation of American bakers.

SAND TARTS

MAKES ABOUT 36 COOKIES

We prefer the look of sliced natural almonds for this recipe, but blanched sliced almonds will work fine.

2	cups all-purpose flour
1¾	cups sugar
¾	teaspoon salt
16	tablespoons (2 sticks) unsalted butter, cut into 16 pieces and softened
1	large egg plus 1 large egg yolk
1½	teaspoons ground cinnamon
¼	cup sliced almonds (see note above)

1. Adjust the oven racks to the upper-middle and lower-middle positions and heat the oven to

SHAPING SAND TARTS

1. Using your hands, roll the dough into 1½-inch balls, then roll each ball in cinnamon sugar. Place the balls 3 inches apart on the baking sheets, nine dough balls per sheet.

2. Press each dough ball into a 2-inch disk with the bottom of a measuring cup or a flat-bottomed glass.

3. Sprinkle each disk with more cinnamon sugar, then flatten further into a 2½-inch round.

4. Lightly press 5 almond slices into each round of dough in a circular pattern.

350 degrees. Line two large baking sheets with parchment paper. Process the flour, 1½ cups of the sugar, and salt together in a food processor until combined. Add the butter, one piece at a time, and pulse until just incorporated. Add the egg and egg yolk and pulse until a soft dough forms.

2. Wrap the dough in plastic wrap, flatten into a 1-inch-thick disk, and freeze until firm, about 15 minutes. Combine the remaining ¼ cup sugar and cinnamon in a shallow baking dish or pie plate. Break the disk of chilled dough in half; return one half to the freezer. Working with 1½ tablespoons of chilled dough at a time, roll the dough into 1½-inch balls with floured hands. Following the photos on page 186, roll the balls in the cinnamon sugar to coat. Lay the balls on the prepared baking sheets, spaced about 3 inches apart, nine dough balls per sheet. With the bottom of a measuring cup or a flat-bottomed glass, gently press the balls into 2-inch disks, sprinkle with more cinnamon sugar, flatten into 2½-inch disks, and garnish with the almonds.

3. Bake the cookies until the edges are lightly browned, 10 to 12 minutes, switching and rotating the sheets halfway through baking. Let the cookies cool on the baking sheets for 5 minutes, then transfer to a wire rack and let cool completely before serving. Repeat with the remaining dough using cooled, freshly lined baking sheets.

Snickerdoodles

A true cookie-jar classic, snickerdoodles are simple, chewy, cinnamon-flavored cookies with a uniquely crinkly top. In fact, these cookies were named for their looks; their moniker is a corruption of a German word that translates as "crinkly noodles." We tried a number of traditional recipes, but none were as chewy or as crinkly as we expected. We decided to get to the bottom of what makes a great snickerdoodle—in terms of both flavor and looks.

Traditionally, a snickerdoodle has a subtle tang or sour undertone that contrasts with the cinnamon-sugar coating. Many recipes rely on both baking soda and cream of tartar as the leavening agents for two reasons. First, the cream of tartar provides the characteristic tang. Second, the cream of tartar and baking soda cause the cookie to rise very quickly and then collapse somewhat, resulting in the characteristic crinkly top.

We tested both baking powder and the baking soda and cream of tartar combination. As we expected, the latter is essential to this cookie. To make the cookies especially tangy, we found it helpful not to add vanilla. The vanilla can take away from the sourness, which is fairly subtle.

Most of the recipes we tested resulted in cookies that were not nearly chewy enough. We found that increasing the amount of sugar helped, but we wondered why some traditional snickerdoodle recipes included vegetable shortening. Although we usually prefer butter in cookies for the rich flavor it contributes, we thought it might be worth trying shortening in this case. Unlike butter, which contains about 18 percent water, shortening is 100 percent fat. The water in butter evaporates in the oven and helps the cookies to spread. Since shortening does not contain water, in theory it should help reduce spread in the oven and keep the cookies thick and chewy.

Our tests revealed that using both butter and shortening did in fact guarantee the dense, chewy texture we wanted. When we used equal parts shortening and butter, the cookies still tasted richly of butter, but now they were also deliciously chewy. A roll in cinnamon sugar before baking gave the finished cookies a nice crust that made them irresistible.

SNICKERDOODLES
MAKES ABOUT 24 COOKIES
Cream of tartar is essential to the flavor of these cookies, and it works in combination with the baking soda to give the cookies lift; do not substitute baking powder. For the best results, bake only one sheet of cookies at a time.

1 ¾ **cups sugar**

1 **tablespoon ground cinnamon**

2 ½ **cups all-purpose flour**

2 **teaspoons cream of tartar**

1 **teaspoon baking soda**

½ **teaspoon salt**

8 **tablespoons (1 stick) unsalted butter, softened**

½ **cup vegetable shortening**

2 **large eggs**

1. Adjust an oven rack to the middle position and heat the oven to 375 degrees. Line two large baking sheets with parchment paper. Combine ¼ cup of the sugar and cinnamon in a shallow baking dish or pie plate and set aside. In a medium bowl, whisk the flour, cream of tartar, baking soda, and salt together.

2. In a large bowl, beat the butter, shortening, and remaining 1 ½ cups sugar together with an electric mixer on medium speed until light and fluffy, 3 to 6 minutes. Beat in the eggs, one at a time, until incorporated, about 30 seconds, scraping down the sides of the bowl as necessary.

3. Reduce the mixer speed to low and slowly add the flour mixture, mixing until combined, about 30 seconds. Give the dough a final stir to make sure no flour pockets remain.

4. Working with 2 tablespoons of dough at a time, roll the dough into balls with wet hands, then roll in the cinnamon sugar to coat. Lay the balls on the prepared baking sheets, spaced about 2 inches apart.

5. Bake the cookies, one sheet at a time, until the edges are set and just beginning to brown but the centers are still soft and puffy, 10 to 12 minutes, rotating the baking sheet halfway through baking.

(The cookies will look raw between the cracks and seem underdone.)

6. Let the cookies cool on the baking sheet for 10 minutes, then serve warm or transfer to a wire rack and let cool completely.

Classic Sugar Cookies

Sugar cookies should be a snap to make: cream butter with sugar; mix in egg, vanilla, flour, salt, and a leavener; roll the balls of dough in sugar; and bake. But more often than not, the resulting cookies range from humpbacked, cakey mounds to flat, brittle disks, with a smooth rather than crackly top and a one-note sweetness. We were determined to develop a recipe that would produce a sugar cookie that was crisp at the edges, soft and chewy in the center, crackly-crisp on top—and, most important of all, richly flavored.

We tried a number of recipes and found we could eliminate most of them right off the bat. The bulk of recipes were for all-butter cookies, which didn't have ample chewy texture. As with our Snickerdoodles (page 187), we suspected we'd need a combination of fats to get the optimal chew we were after. One recipe used both butter and vegetable oil; this one produced what seemed to be the closest to the soft, chewy sugar cookie we wanted, so we started there and began by finessing the amounts of fat. We eventually settled on just 6 tablespoons of butter and 5 ounces of vegetable oil for a somewhat chewy texture and rich, buttery flavor. For more chewiness, we decided to skip the creaming step and melt the butter instead. As a bonus, we wouldn't need to pull out the stand mixer: we could mix all the ingredients by hand.

But there was a downside to using oil and melting the butter. The two doses of liquid fat made the dough so soft that it practically poured onto the baking sheet. Plus, now that we were no longer creaming the butter, as most cookie recipes specify, there wasn't enough air in the dough, and the cookies were baking up too flat. We spent the next several tests readjusting the other ingredients to compensate. More flour helped build up structure, and more baking powder added lift. To keep the cookies from being a bit too dry and biscuitlike, we ramped up the sugar, salt, and vanilla and added a tiny bit of milk.

With this new formula, the chewiness of our cookies was spot on. But we still had a few problems. The cookies had gone from too flat to a bit humped, and they didn't have much of that appealingly crackly top that makes a sugar cookie so tempting. But most important, trading more than half of the rich butter for neutral-tasting vegetable oil had rendered the cookies very sweet—and only sweet—especially once we rolled the dough in sugar before baking.

Looking for something to take the edge off all that sugariness, we automatically ruled out lemon zest or juice; such strong citrus flavor dropped our cookies squarely into the lemon family. In the past, we've had luck adding a cultured dairy product like buttermilk, sour cream, or yogurt to baked goods to round out their flavors. But when we tried each of these, the dough was once again too soft to hold its shape.

Scanning the supermarket dairy aisle, we zeroed in on cream cheese, wondering if it would enrich the dough's flavor without adding much liquid. To keep the chew level up, we'd have to trade some of the oil for the cream cheese. Ultimately, adding 2 ounces of cream cheese and going down to ⅓ cup of vegetable oil gave us cookies with the same texture but much-improved flavor. As a bonus, now that we had added acidic cream cheese to the mix, we could add baking soda to the dough (baking

soda requires the presence of an acid to work properly), fixing the problem of slightly humped cookies with not enough crackle. Just a half teaspoon produced cookies with the rustic crispy, crackly top that made this dessert perfect.

CLASSIC SUGAR COOKIES
MAKES ABOUT 24 COOKIES

For the best results, bake only one sheet of cookies at a time. The mixed dough will be slightly soft. Be sure to handle the dough as briefly and gently as possible when shaping the cookies; overworking the dough will result in flatter cookies.

2¼	cups all-purpose flour
1	teaspoon baking powder
½	teaspoon baking soda
½	teaspoon salt
1½	cups sugar, plus ⅓ cup for rolling
2	ounces cream cheese, cut into 8 pieces
6	tablespoons (¾ stick) unsalted butter, melted
⅓	cup vegetable oil
1	large egg
1	tablespoon milk
2	teaspoons vanilla extract

1. Adjust an oven rack to the middle position and heat the oven to 350 degrees. Line two large baking sheets with parchment paper. Whisk the flour, baking powder, baking soda, and salt together in a medium bowl. Set aside.

2. Place 1½ cups of the sugar and cream cheese in a large bowl. Place the remaining ⅓ cup sugar in a shallow baking dish or pie plate and set aside. Pour the melted butter over the sugar and cream cheese and whisk to combine (some small lumps of cream cheese will remain). Whisk in the oil until incorporated. Add the egg, milk, and vanilla and whisk until smooth. Add the flour mixture and mix with a rubber spatula until a soft, uniform dough forms.

3. Working with 2 tablespoons of dough at a time, roll the dough into balls. Working in batches, roll the balls in the reserved sugar to coat and lay on the prepared baking sheet, spaced about 1½ inches apart, 12 dough balls per sheet. With the bottom of a measuring cup or a flat-bottomed glass, press the balls into 2-inch disks. Sprinkle the tops evenly with the remaining sugar, using 2 teaspoons per sheet. (Discard the remaining sugar.)

4. Bake the cookies, one sheet at a time, until the edges are set and just beginning to brown, 11 to 13 minutes, rotating the sheet halfway through baking. Let the cookies cool on the baking sheet for 5 minutes, then transfer to a wire rack and let cool completely before serving.

Variation
CHAI-SPICE SUGAR COOKIES
Add ¼ teaspoon ground cinnamon, ¼ teaspoon ground ginger, ¼ teaspoon ground cardamom, ¼ teaspoon ground cloves, and a pinch finely ground black pepper to the sugar and cream cheese mixture in step 2 and reduce the amount of vanilla extract to 1 teaspoon.

Brown Sugar Cookies

Having perfected our sugar cookies (see page 188) using an unexpected dairy product (cream cheese), we wondered if another ingredient change-up would take a new batch of sugar cookies to the next level. We decided to swap out the granulated sugar in favor of brown sugar, for a cookie rife with butterscotch and caramel notes. We wanted

our cookie to have a crackling-crisp exterior and a chewy interior. And, like Mick Jagger, it had to scream "brown sugar."

Given our extensive cookie-making experience, we knew that the standard technique of creaming softened butter with sugar (or, in this case, brown sugar) until fluffy, before adding the remaining ingredients, would beat in tiny air bubbles and give us cookies that were cakey and tender—not what we had in mind. Melted butter is what we wanted to use for cookies with structure and chew, so we began our cookie-making marathon there.

Cookies made with 2 sticks of melted butter and an entire 1-pound box of brown sugar had plenty of flavor, but these taffylike confections were greasy and threatened to pull out our dental work. Using dark brown sugar rather than light brown sugar allowed us to get more flavor from less sugar. Cookies made with 1¾ cups of dark brown sugar had the best texture and decent flavor. To prevent the greasiness, we cut back to 1¾ sticks of butter.

To amp up the flavor of our cookies even further, we decided to brown the butter. However, since browning burns off some of the butter's moisture, we decided to brown only a portion of it. The complex nuttiness added by the browned butter made a substantial difference in the flavor of the finished cookies.

Looking at the rest of the ingredient list, we found that a single egg didn't provide enough structure. Thinking that two eggs would solve the problem, we were surprised when a test batch turned out dry and cakey. Splitting the difference, we added one whole egg plus a yolk and were pleased with the results.

Too much flour gave the cookies a homogeneous texture; too little, and a candylike chew reemerged. Two cups of flour, plus a couple of extra tablespoons, was the perfect match for the amounts of butter, sugar, and egg we'd settled on.

The choice of leavener still remained. Many baked goods with brown sugar (which can be slightly acidic) call for baking soda, so we tried that first. When we used baking soda by itself, the cookies had an open, coarse crumb and craggy top. Tasters loved the craggy top but not the coarse crumb. When we used baking powder by itself, the cookies had a finer, tighter crumb but the craggy top disappeared. After a dozen rounds of testing, we found that ¼ teaspoon of baking powder mixed with ½ teaspoon of baking soda moderated the coarseness of the crumb without compromising the craggy tops.

We had developed a good cookie, but we thought of one more thing that would put it over the top. Before baking, we rolled the dough balls in brown sugar. The brown sugar clumped in some spots, but overall the crackling sugar exterior added good crunch and flavor. Cutting the brown sugar with granulated sugar solved the clumping problem and ensured that our cookies were evenly (and attractively) coated.

BROWN SUGAR COOKIES

MAKES ABOUT 24 COOKIES

Avoid using a nonstick skillet to brown the butter; the dark color of the nonstick coating makes it difficult to gauge when the butter is browned. Use fresh, moist brown sugar instead of hardened brown sugar, which will make the cookies dry. For the best results, bake only one sheet of cookies at a time.

14	tablespoons (1¾ sticks) unsalted butter
¼	cup granulated sugar
2	cups packed dark brown sugar
2	cups plus 2 tablespoons all-purpose flour
½	teaspoon baking soda
¼	teaspoon baking powder
½	teaspoon salt
1	large egg plus 1 large egg yolk
1	tablespoon vanilla extract

1. Melt 10 tablespoons of the butter in a medium skillet over medium-high heat, about 2 minutes. Continue cooking, swirling the pan constantly, until the butter is dark golden brown and has a nutty aroma, 1 to 3 minutes longer. Using a heatproof spatula, transfer the browned butter to a large heatproof bowl. Stir the remaining 4 tablespoons butter into the hot butter until completely melted; set aside to cool, about 15 minutes.

2. Meanwhile, adjust an oven rack to the middle position and heat the oven to 350 degrees. Line two large baking sheets with parchment paper. In a shallow baking dish or pie plate, combine the granulated sugar and ¼ cup of the brown sugar, using your fingers, until well combined; set aside. Whisk the flour, baking soda, and baking powder together in a medium bowl.

3. Add the remaining 1¾ cups brown sugar and salt to the melted butter; mix until no sugar lumps remain, about 30 seconds. Add the egg, egg yolk, and vanilla and mix until fully incorporated, about 30 seconds, scraping down the sides of the bowl as necessary. Add the flour mixture and mix until just combined, about 1 minute. Give the dough a final stir to make sure no flour pockets remain.

CHECKING BROWN SUGAR COOKIES

To tell when the cookies are done, gently press halfway between the edge and center of the cookie. When it's done, it will form an indentation with slight resistance. Check early and err on the side of underdone.

4. Working with 2 tablespoons of dough at a time, roll the dough into balls. Roll the balls in the reserved sugar mixture to coat and lay on the prepared baking sheets, spaced about 2 inches apart.

5. Bake the cookies, one sheet at a time, until browned and still puffy and the edges have begun to set but the centers are still soft (the cookies will look raw between the cracks and seem underdone), 12 to 14 minutes, rotating the baking sheet halfway through baking. Do not overbake.

6. Let the cookies cool on the baking sheet for 5 minutes, then transfer to a wire rack and let cool completely before serving.

Hermits

The hermit is a cookie certainly worthy of its eccentric name. Depending on whom you ask, it can be soft and cakey or dry and biscuitlike; packed with dried fruit and nuts or free of both; and heavily seasoned with warm spices like ginger, cloves, and nutmeg or flavored only with molasses.

After a taste test that included cookies we baked in-house and commercially produced hermits from local and national bakeries, tasters agreed that an ideal hermit should have a texture in between a cake and a brownie—that is, it should be soft, moist, and dense. We decided that hermits should be studded with raisins and taste predominantly of molasses, but with warm spices lingering in the background.

From the outset we knew that attaining the right texture would be tricky. Most hermit recipes we tried relied on two eggs as well as some baking soda for their rise. The result is a puffy cookie that is dry and too cakey for our taste. Leaving out one of the eggs made them too dense, but we realized we were

THE AMERICAN TABLE
HERMIT HISTORY

Recipes for hermits began appearing in late 19th-century New England cookbooks, such as Maria Parloa's *Miss Parloa's New Cook Book* (1880) and Fannie Merritt Farmer's *The Boston Cooking-School Cook Book* (1896). Most historic explanations for the unusual name are murky at best. One version claims that the dark brown cookies resemble a reclusive monk's robe, and another has it that these cookies are best if stashed away for several days, like a hermit. The most likely explanation is etymological: the German and Dutch word for the Moravians (a Czech Republic people famous for their spice cookies), *hernhutter*, is thought to have been corrupted into "hermit" in English.

on the right track. In the next batch we omitted the white of one of the eggs, and the resulting cookies were everything we wanted—soft and rich but with a slightly cakey crumb. The cakey crumb is the secret to their longevity; we enjoyed these cookies up to a week after baking them. And, as the story of how they got their name suggests, the flavors were better after a couple of days of storage.

For both sweetening and flavor, hermits depend on molasses. Most tasters favored mild, although some liked the stronger-flavored dark molasses. Molasses alone was not enough to fully sweeten the cookies, so we included ½ cup of light brown sugar.

A healthy amount of raisins contributed more sweetness and rounded out the flavors. They also contrasted nicely with the crisp crust and soft crumb.

As for the spices, cinnamon, cloves, allspice, and ginger were essential, and an unlikely spice, pepper, contributed a kick that heightened the piquancy of the other spices.

Our cookies were sweet and spicy, and soft and homey. They were also appropriately named—almost all disappeared long before we could get our hands on them.

HERMITS

MAKES ABOUT 16 COOKIES

The dusting of confectioners' sugar is optional, but it does improve the cookies' appearance. Be sure to use finely ground black pepper here.

2	cups all-purpose flour
½	teaspoon baking soda
½	teaspoon ground cinnamon
½	teaspoon ground cloves
¼	teaspoon ground allspice
¼	teaspoon ground ginger
⅛	teaspoon pepper (see note above)
½	teaspoon salt
8	tablespoons (1 stick) unsalted butter, melted and cooled
½	cup packed light brown sugar
2	large eggs, 1 whole and 1 separated, white lightly beaten
½	cup light or dark molasses
1½	cups raisins
2	tablespoons confectioners' sugar (optional) (see note above)

1. Whisk the flour, baking soda, spices, and salt together in a medium bowl. Set aside.

2. Whisk the melted butter and brown sugar together in a second medium bowl until just combined. Add the whole egg, egg yolk, and molasses and whisk thoroughly. Using a rubber spatula, fold the flour mixture into the molasses mixture until combined. Stir in the raisins. Cover the bowl with plastic wrap and refrigerate for at least 1 hour.

3. Adjust an oven rack to the middle position and heat the oven to 350 degrees. Line a baking sheet with parchment paper.

4. Following the photos, divide the dough in half and shape each half into a 14-inch log on the prepared baking sheet. Brush the logs with the egg white.

5. Bake until the tops of the logs have browned and spring back when touched, 20 to 25 minutes, rotating the baking sheet halfway through baking. Let the logs cool on the baking sheet on a wire rack for 15 minutes. Using two metal spatulas, transfer the logs to a cutting board and slice them crosswise into cookies about 2 inches thick. Let the cookies cool to room temperature and dust with confectioners' sugar (if using) before serving.

MAKING HERMITS

1. Divide the dough in half and shape each half on a parchment-lined baking sheet into a log that measures 14 inches long and 2 inches across.

2. Using two metal spatulas, transfer the baked logs to a cutting board. With a sharp chef's knife or serrated knife, cut the logs crosswise into cookies about 2 inches thick.

Black-and-White Cookies

A treat found in nearly every New York City deli, the black-and-white cookie is made from butter, sugar, eggs, milk, flour, and a touch of lemon and painted with side-by-side coats of chocolate and vanilla icing. We set out to develop a cakey, tender cookie with a low, even rise and smooth, flavorful chocolate and vanilla icings.

Our testing began with a range of black-and-white cookie recipes. We didn't want a dense, rich butter cookie or a sweet, crunchy sugar cookie, so recipes that fell into these camps were rejected. We decided to focus our testing on a recipe claiming to be the original black-and-white cookie recipe.

Neither crisp like sugar cookies nor rich like shortbread, these cookies did approximate the distinctive cakelike texture of a black-and-white cookie. But they needed a lot of work. Doughy and thick, the cookies had a texture that lay somewhere between a scone and an eggy cake. The cookies had thin edges but mottled and bumpy centers, not the smooth-surfaced, perfectly round cookies we had imagined. Although it fell short, we sensed that this recipe had the very rough-hewn makings of an ideal New York black-and-white cookie.

We followed the traditional creaming method, using 2 sticks of butter and 1¾ cups of sugar. Then we turned to the eggs and flour. We knew we wanted to reduce the amounts of both. The original recipe called for 2½ cups of all-purpose flour and 2½ cups of cake flour. We tried reducing the total amount of flour to 4 cups, 2 cups of each type. The reduction of flour improved the texture of the cookies dramatically, but we still found them on the tough side. We then experimented with different combinations of all-purpose and cake flour and finally settled on using only cake flour, which has less protein than all-purpose flour and yields a more delicate crumb. The resulting cookies had a tender, cakelike texture and very fine crumb.

As for the eggs, we tried using two eggs and two egg yolks, three whole eggs, and four yolks, among other variations, and found that two whole eggs worked perfectly. One cup of milk added to the batter in stages, alternating with the flour, was just right. In addressing the leavener, we discovered that just ½ teaspoon of baking powder gave our cookies a thin, even rise. They were almost perfect.

To give the cookies their subtle lemon flavor, we found that ½ teaspoon of lemon extract did the job. Although 1 tablespoon of lemon juice is an acceptable substitute if lemon extract is unavailable, tasters preferred the cookies made with lemon extract. They also liked vanilla extract in the cookies; a single teaspoon gave the subtle, higher lemon notes some depth and rounded out the flavor.

Black-and-white cookies derive their name from their characteristic icing: half of the cookie is covered in chocolate icing and the other half in vanilla. We came up with numerous versions of the icing recipe, all calling for confectioners' sugar, some with milk or cream, some with water, boiling water, or corn syrup. In most recipes some of the vanilla icing is combined with melted chocolate; others used melted chocolate and cream alone for the chocolate icing. We wanted an icing that would be easy to spread and would coat the cookie in a smooth, even layer. We also wanted the icing to have a bit of a shine and to harden so that our fingers wouldn't be covered in a sticky mess. The vanilla icing had to have a subtle vanilla flavor and our chocolate icing had to taste of chocolate, not of brown-colored confectioners' sugar. After numerous tests, we discovered that confectioners' sugar in combination with corn syrup produced the best consistency and appearance. Unsweetened chocolate worked better than bittersweet, semisweet, or milk chocolate, giving the other half of the cookies a rich, dark shine.

BLACK-AND-WHITE COOKIES

MAKES ABOUT 24 LARGE COOKIES

Don't substitute "lemon flavor" or lemon oil for the lemon extract. In a pinch, however, you can substitute 1 tablespoon fresh lemon juice. If the chocolate icing cools so that it is no longer spreadable, microwave it for 30 seconds to resoften.

COOKIES

4	cups cake flour
½	teaspoon baking powder
½	teaspoon salt
16	tablespoons (2 sticks) unsalted butter, softened
1¾	cups granulated sugar
2	large eggs
1	teaspoon vanilla extract
½	teaspoon lemon extract (see note above)
1	cup whole milk

ICINGS

¼	cup light corn syrup
⅓	cup plus 2–4 teaspoons water
5	cups confectioners' sugar
1	teaspoon vanilla extract
2	ounces unsweetened chocolate, chopped

1. FOR THE COOKIES: Adjust the oven racks to the upper-middle and lower-middle positions and heat the oven to 350 degrees. Line two large baking sheets with parchment paper. Whisk the flour, baking powder, and salt together in a medium bowl.

2. In a large bowl, beat the butter and granulated sugar together with an electric mixer on medium speed until light and fluffy, 3 to 6 minutes. Beat in the eggs, vanilla, and lemon extract until combined, about 30 seconds, scraping down the bowl as necessary. Reduce the mixer speed to low and beat in one-third of the flour mixture, followed by

half of the milk. Repeat with half of the remaining flour mixture and the remaining milk. Beat in the remaining flour mixture until combined.

3. Scoop ¼-cup mounds of batter onto the prepared baking sheets, spaced about 2 inches apart, 6 mounds per sheet. Use the back of a spoon or a finger dipped in water to smooth the tops of the cookies. Bake the cookies until the edges are just beginning to turn light golden brown, about 15 minutes, switching and rotating the baking sheets halfway through baking.

4. Let the cookies cool on the baking sheets for 10 minutes, then transfer to a wire rack. Repeat with the remaining batter, using cooled, freshly lined baking sheets.

5. FOR THE ICINGS: Bring the corn syrup and ⅓ cup of the water to a boil in a medium saucepan over medium-high heat. Remove the pan from the heat and whisk in the confectioners' sugar and

ICING BLACK-AND-WHITE COOKIES

 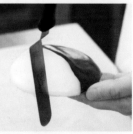

1. Spread half of each cookie with the chocolate icing. Tilt the cookie and run the spatula around the edge to scrape off the excess icing.

2. Once the chocolate icing is set, spread the other half of each cookie with the vanilla icing. Tilt the cookie and run the spatula around the edge to scrape off the excess.

vanilla until smooth. Microwave the chocolate in a small bowl, stirring occasionally, until smooth, about 1 minute. Measure half of the icing into a bowl and whisk in the melted chocolate and the remaining 2 to 4 teaspoons water as needed until the mixture is smooth and spreadable.

6. Place two large wire racks over parchment paper for easy cleanup. Following the photos on page 197, spread about 2 tablespoons of the chocolate icing over half of each cookie with a small spatula, then let sit on the wire rack until the icing has just set, about 15 minutes. Spread the vanilla icing over the other half of each cookie and let sit until the icings have hardened, about 1 hour, before serving.

Whoopie Pies

Lately, it seems that whoopie pies—two chocolate cookielike cakes stuffed to the gills with a fluffy marshmallow filling—are everywhere we look, from fancy bakeries to county fairs. But where did these treats originally come from, and why the funny name? And, most important, how could we make them at home?

It turns out that Maine and Pennsylvania—the Pennsylvania Dutch of Lancaster County, to be specific—both claim whoopie pies as their own. After weeks of reading through old newspapers and talking to librarians and bakery owners, here's what we learned.

Maine's earliest claim dates back to 1925, when Labadie's Bakery in Lewiston first sold whoopie pies to the public. As we continued our research, we ran across an advertisement for a whoopie pie wrapper contest in the *Portland* (ME) *Press Herald*: "Collect the most wrappers and a brand new 1950 Plymouth Sedan could be yours!" In small letters underneath we saw the words "Berwick Cake Co.—Boston." Some research showed that the Berwick Cake Company began manufacturing Whoopie! Pies (the exclamation point was part of the name) in 1927. These sources claim that whoopie pies were named after the musical *Whoopie* (from which came the well-known song "Makin' Whoopie"); *Whoopie* had its debut in Boston in 1927. In addition, Marshmallow Fluff, a key ingredient in many whoopie pie recipes, was invented in nearby Somerville ten years earlier.

What about Pennsylvania's claim on whoopie pies? We found an article in a copy of the *Gettysburg Times* from 1982 that spoke of a chocolate cake sandwich with a fluffy cream center. These sandwiches were called "gobs" and were sold by the Dutch Maid Bakery of Geistown, Pennsylvania. The name was different, but the description (and a huge picture) showed that these were no doubt whoopie pies by another name. In 1980 Dutch Maid Bakery purchased the rights to the gob from the Harris-Boyer Baking Company, which had started manufacturing gobs in 1927.

We weren't able to resolve the conflicting claims about the origins of the whoopie pie (although we're pretty confident that they date back to the 1920s), but we figured we could bake some up ourselves. Whoopie pie recipes haven't changed much over the years. Original recipes used a devil's food cake base, with "soda" and "soured milk" to lift the cakes. In today's vernacular, baking soda and buttermilk work well in their place. The original cakes contained lard, but many recipes have switched to shortening or vegetable oil, both of which extend the cakes' shelf life. Although it's considered heresy in the whoopie world, we used butter instead of shortening. Moist and tender, these cakes were snatched up as fast as we could bake them, so we had no concern about shelf life.

Originally, the filling was a whipped frosting made of sugar and lard, but recipes soon switched to marshmallow crème, which was easily purchased under the name of Marshmallow Fluff. Instead of mixing the marshmallow with lard or vegetable shortening, we turned once more to butter. We slathered this fluffy filling between two chocolate cookie-cakes and our whoopie pies were done. And as soon as we put them on a plate, they were history, too.

WHOOPIE PIES

MAKES 6 PIES

Marshmallow crème with a thicker consistency (like Marshmallow Fluff) yields the best results in this recipe. If the filling is too soft to work with, chill it briefly; alternatively, if the filling seems stiff, microwave it for about 15 seconds, stirring occasionally.

CAKES

2	cups all-purpose flour
½	cup Dutch-processed cocoa powder
1	teaspoon baking soda
½	teaspoon salt
8	tablespoons (1 stick) unsalted butter, softened
1	cup packed light brown sugar
1	large egg, room temperature
1	teaspoon vanilla extract
1	cup buttermilk

FILLING

12	tablespoons (1½ sticks) unsalted butter, softened
1¼	cups confectioners' sugar
1½	teaspoons vanilla extract
⅛	teaspoon salt
2½	cups marshmallow crème (see note above)

MAKING WHOOPIE PIES

1. Scoop generous ⅓-cup mounds of batter onto each prepared baking sheet.

2. Spread the filling evenly over the bottoms of half of the cooled cakes. Press the bottoms of the remaining cakes on top to make sandwiches.

1. FOR THE CAKES: Adjust the oven racks to the upper-middle and lower-middle positions and heat the oven to 350 degrees. Line two large baking sheets with parchment paper. Whisk the flour, cocoa, baking soda, and salt together in a medium bowl.

2. In a large bowl, beat the butter and brown sugar together with an electric mixer on medium speed until light and fluffy, 3 to 6 minutes. Beat in the egg and vanilla until combined, about 30 seconds, scraping down the bowl as necessary.

3. Reduce the mixer speed to low and slowly beat in half of the flour mixture, followed by half of the buttermilk. Repeat with half of the remaining flour mixture and the remaining buttermilk. Add the remaining flour mixture until combined.

4. Scoop six generous ⅓-cup mounds of batter onto each baking sheet, spaced about 3 inches apart. Bake the cakes until they spring back when pressed,

15 to 18 minutes, switching and rotating the baking sheets halfway through baking. Let the cakes cool completely on the baking sheets, about 1 hour.

5. FOR THE FILLING: Beat the butter and confectioners' sugar together in a medium bowl with an electric mixer on medium speed until light and fluffy, about 2 minutes. Beat in the vanilla and salt. Beat in the marshmallow crème until incorporated, about 2 minutes.

6. Spread ⅓ cup of the filling evenly over the bottom of a cake, then make a sandwich by pressing the bottom of another cake onto the filling; repeat with the remaining cakes and filling. Serve.

Raspberry–Cream Cheese Brownies

Scan any bake sale table, and you're guaranteed to see piles of brownies. Sadly, they're usually boring, dry specimens that hardly taste of chocolate. We wanted a rich, dense brownie, but we also wanted to liven it up with a swirl of cream cheese and a bit of raspberry flavor. Because both chocolate and cream cheese are used to taking center stage in baked goods, they would need to learn to play together nicely in our brownies. We set out to make a raspberry–cream cheese brownie so that all the flavors were in balance, with bold berry flavor and a moist, creamy layer of cream cheese.

Our testing began with the test kitchen's recipe for moist, fudgy brownies. As is usual for brownies, the chocolate and butter are melted together, then the sugar and eggs are mixed in, followed by the flour, baking powder, and salt. We quickly realized that to balance the extra sugar that would come from the raspberry and cream cheese elements,

MAKING CREAM CHEESE BROWNIES

1. Top half of the brownie batter with dollops of cream cheese filling and spread into an even layer.

2. Dollop jam over the cream cheese filling, then use the tip of a knife to swirl it into the filling.

3. Spread the remaining brownie batter evenly over the filling.

we needed to use unsweetened chocolate; a test of brownie batters made with unsweetened versus semisweet chocolate proved us right.

Next, we added a standard-issue creamy layer made from cream cheese, sugar, vanilla, and an egg yolk. When spread over the top of the brownies, the cream cheese layer dried up and became flaky; sandwiching the cream cheese mixture between two layers of brownie batter worked much better and kept the cream cheese moist.

We then turned to the raspberry part of the equation. Most recipes for raspberry–cream cheese

brownies have you swirl a little jam into the cream cheese layer and call it a day. That's good if what you're looking for is just a hint of flavor. For bold berry flavor, we swirled in some jam and also scattered the cream cheese layer with fresh berries before adding more brownie batter on top and baking. But instead of the bright flavor we'd envisioned, we got a pan full of soggy, seedy brownies.

What if we added raspberry jam to the brownie batter, too? We tried it, keeping the swirl in place, and these brownies baked up with a winning raspberry depth. On the downside, the jam made them somewhat wet. Knowing that sugar adds moisture as well as sweetness, we wondered if reducing the amount of sugar would reduce the sogginess. We cut the sugar by ¼ cup (exactly the amount of jam we had added to the batter) and baked a new batch. We were thrilled to find that we'd not only repaired the brownies' texture but also boosted the raspberry flavor—with less sugar, the flavor popped and more than held its own against the chocolate.

Now we had decadent, dense brownies, full of raspberry flavor and enriched with cream cheese, that would put the average bake sale brownie to shame.

RASPBERRY–CREAM CHEESE BROWNIES

MAKES 25 SMALL BROWNIES

For the jam, we used Smucker's, which is the test kitchen's top-rated seedless jam; preserves will also work. Because the brownies are so rich, almost like truffles, we cut them into small squares. Leftover brownies should be refrigerated.

FILLING

1	(8-ounce) package cream cheese, softened
¼	cup sugar
1	large egg yolk
¾	teaspoon vanilla extract

BROWNIES

⅔	cup all-purpose flour
½	teaspoon baking powder
½	teaspoon salt
8	tablespoons (1 stick) unsalted butter, cut into ¼-inch pieces
4	ounces unsweetened chocolate, chopped
½	cup raspberry jam (see note above)
1¼	cups sugar
3	large eggs
1½	teaspoons vanilla extract

1. FOR THE FILLING: Adjust an oven rack to the middle position and heat the oven to 350 degrees. Following the photo, line an 8-inch square baking pan with an aluminum foil sling and grease the foil. Process all the filling ingredients together in a food processor until smooth, about 20 seconds.

MAKING A FOIL SLING

1. Lay two sheets of foil in the pan, perpendicular to each other, so that extra foil is hanging over the edges. (If the dish is rectangular, the sheets will be different sizes.) Push the foil into the corners and grease the foil.

2. After the brownies or bars have baked and cooled, use the foil sling to transfer them to a cutting board before peeling away the foil and cutting them into tidy squares.

2. FOR THE BROWNIES: Combine the flour, baking powder, and salt in a small bowl. Microwave the butter and chocolate together in a large bowl, stirring occasionally, until smooth, about 1 minute. Whisk in ¼ cup of the jam and let cool slightly. Add the sugar, eggs, and vanilla to the chocolate mixture, stirring until combined. Whisk in the flour mixture until no streaks of flour remain.

3. Microwave the remaining ¼ cup jam until warm, about 30 seconds; stir until smooth. Scrape half of the batter evenly into the prepared pan. Following the photos on page 200, dollop the filling over the batter and spread into an even layer. Dollop the warm jam over the filling and, using the tip of a knife, swirl the jam into the filling. Spread the remaining brownie batter evenly over the filling.

4. Bake until a toothpick inserted in the center comes out with a few dry crumbs attached, 50 to 60 minutes, rotating the pan halfway through. Transfer the pan to a wire rack and let the brownies cool completely, about 2 hours. Remove the brownies from the pan using the foil, cut into 25 squares, and serve.

Turtle Brownies

Dark chocolate brownies, rich and chewy caramel, and sweet pecans—it's hard to go wrong with turtle brownies. But it's even harder to make them right. Too often, turtle brownie recipes call for boxed brownie mixes and jarred caramel sauce, yielding cakey, dry brownies slathered in painfully sweet caramel. We wanted something reminiscent of the candy: rich, nutty, and chocolaty, with enough bittersweet caramel to sink our teeth into.

We began by choosing the type and amount of chocolate, starting with unsweetened chocolate on its own. But we found the flavor of these brownies too potent and one-note, lacking in any complexity. Adding semisweet chocolate to the mix made the brownies too sweet, especially when we included the caramel. Bittersweet chocolate worked better and made for a more complex chocolate flavor overall.

We now had to get the texture right by adjusting the quantities of eggs, flour, and leavener. The light, open texture of classic cakey brownies was easily overwhelmed by the caramel. On the other hand, a dense, fudgy brownie was more confectionery than baked good once paired with the caramel. We wanted something in between. Two whole eggs worked nicely to give the brownies structure without too much lift. Three-quarters of a cup of all-purpose flour was ideal for producing a moist, chewy brownie. The leavener of choice was baking powder; ½ teaspoon gave the brownies the slightest amount of lift, for a distinct crumb without too much cakiness.

The final additions to the brownies were a generous amount of chopped pecans and—for yet another dimension of chocolate—a handful of chocolate chips. (Some tasters found the chocolate chips superfluous, so we made them an optional ingredient.)

With the brownie component complete, it was onward to the caramel. A common technique is to layer the caramel with the brownie batter (and sometimes swirl it in) before baking. With this method, though, the caramel is practically lost in the dark color of the chocolate, and the turtle brownie simply doesn't look the part.

We tried several tactics, including prebaking the bottom brownie layer and adding flour to the caramel to produce a distinct middle layer. It was all to no avail. We returned to layering and swirling, this time drizzling the baked brownies with additional caramel. Better, but they still didn't read as "turtle" brownies. Undaunted, we blanketed the entire surface of the cooled, baked brownies with caramel, then garnished each square with a toasted pecan half. Finally, tasters were appeased.

Still, this turtle had not crossed the finish line: the caramel sauce didn't have enough chew—or enough textural contrast with the brownie. We knew from trial and error that a typical caramel sauce was too fluid for a turtle brownie. Because the brownies would likely be eaten at room temperature—or slightly chilled—the caramel had to be viscous enough to hold its form. For the 1¼ cups of sugar needed to yield the right amount of caramel, we experimented with 1 cup of cream and eventually worked our way down to a mere 6 tablespoons, which produced a caramel that was pleasantly chewy and gooey. Adding some corn syrup to the mix prevented the caramel from becoming gritty, and butter made the sauce smooth and silky.

Finally, our turtle brownies had come out of their shell.

TURTLE BROWNIES

MAKES 25 SMALL BROWNIES

To drizzle the caramel in step 4, use a ¼-cup dry measuring cup that has been sprayed with vegetable oil spray. If the caramel is too cool to pour easily, reheat it in the microwave.

CARAMEL

¼	cup water
2	tablespoons light corn syrup
1¼	cups sugar
6	tablespoons heavy cream
2	tablespoons unsalted butter
1	teaspoon vanilla extract
¼	teaspoon salt

BROWNIES

8	tablespoons (1 stick) unsalted butter, cut into 8 pieces
4	ounces bittersweet chocolate, chopped coarse
2	ounces unsweetened chocolate, chopped coarse

MAKING CARAMEL FOR TURTLE BROWNIES

1. Stir the water, corn syrup, and sugar together with a spatula. Cover the mixture until it boils and the sugar dissolves, then uncover.

2. Cook until the bubbles show a faint golden color, then lower the heat and swirl gently. (The mixture should not be a deep golden color.)

3. Cook for 1 to 3 minutes longer, until the mixture is light amber (the color of honey). Remove the pan from the heat.

4. Whisk in the cream, then add the butter, salt, and vanilla, which will cause the caramel to turn a darker shade of amber.

¾	cup all-purpose flour
½	teaspoon baking powder
2	large eggs, room temperature
1	cup sugar
2	teaspoons vanilla extract
¼	teaspoon salt
⅔	cup pecans, chopped
⅓	cup semisweet chocolate chips (optional)
25	pecan halves (see note above), toasted (see page 130)

1. FOR THE CARAMEL: Combine the water and corn syrup in a medium saucepan. Pour the sugar into the center of the saucepan, taking care not to let it hit the sides of the pan. Gently stir with a clean spatula to moisten the sugar thoroughly. Cover and bring to a boil over medium-high heat; cook, covered and without stirring, until the sugar is completely dissolved and the liquid is clear, 3 to 5 minutes. Uncover and continue to cook, without stirring, until the liquid has a faint golden color, 3 to 5 minutes longer. Reduce the heat to medium-low and continue to cook, swirling occasionally, until the caramel is light amber and the temperature reaches 360 degrees on a candy thermometer or instant-read thermometer that registers high temperatures, 1 to 3 minutes longer. Off the heat, carefully and slowly whisk in the cream until combined (the mixture will bubble and steam vigorously). Stir in the butter, vanilla, and salt. Transfer the caramel to a microwave-safe bowl and set aside.

2. FOR THE BROWNIES: Adjust an oven rack to the lower-middle position and heat the oven to 325 degrees. Following the photo on page 202, line an 8-inch square baking pan with an aluminum foil sling and grease the foil.

3. Melt the butter and bittersweet and unsweetened chocolates together in a medium bowl in the

MAKING TURTLE BROWNIES

1. Spread half of the brownie batter evenly in the prepared baking pan, then drizzle with a scant ¼ cup warm caramel.

2. Repeat with the remaining brownie batter and a scant ¼ cup more of the caramel. Using the tip of a knife, swirl the caramel and brownie batter together.

3. After the brownies have baked and cooled, reheat the remaining caramel in the microwave, then pour over the brownies and spread into an even layer.

4. After removing the brownies from the pan and cutting them, press a pecan half into each brownie.

microwave, stirring often, 1 to 3 minutes. Let the mixture cool slightly. In a small bowl, whisk the flour and baking powder together. In a large bowl, whisk the eggs, sugar, vanilla, and salt together. Whisk in the cooled chocolate mixture until combined. Stir in the flour mixture until just incorporated. Add the pecans and chocolate chips (if using), giving the batter a final stir to make sure no flour pockets remain.

4. Scrape half of the brownie batter evenly into the prepared pan. Drizzle a scant ¼ cup of the caramel over the batter. Drop the remaining brownie batter in large mounds over the caramel layer and spread it into an even layer. Drizzle a scant ¼ cup more caramel over the top. Using the tip of a knife, swirl the caramel and brownie batter together. Bake the brownies until a toothpick inserted in the center comes out with only a few moist crumbs attached, 35 to 40 minutes, rotating the pan halfway through baking. Transfer the pan to a wire rack and let the brownies cool completely, about 2 hours.

5. Heat the remaining caramel (you should have about ¾ cup) in the microwave until warm and pourable but still thick (do not boil), 45 to 60 seconds, stirring once or twice; pour the caramel over the brownies and spread into an even layer. Refrigerate the brownies, uncovered, until the caramel has set, about 2 hours.

6. Remove the brownies from the pan using the foil, cut into 25 squares, and press a pecan half onto the surface of each brownie. Serve chilled or at room temperature.

Mississippi Mud Brownies

Mississippi mud brownies are über-fudgy brownies that boast a dense gooeyness similar to the texture of the silt that settles in the Mississippi River delta. This pecan-laced brownie is topped with mini marshmallows when the base is set but still moist, briefly returned to the oven, and then covered with chocolate frosting once cooled. But the frosting, marshmallows, and brownie can all add up

to a toothache. We wanted a dense, rich brownie with a balanced sweetness.

We prepared brownies using several existing recipes, but they were more like candy than brownies, and their chocolate flavor was lost under the marshmallows and cloying frosting. All these great ingredients were not living up to their potential.

We started with the most promising brownie recipe from our initial testing, which had a decent fudgy texture but little chocolate flavor. A combination of upping the amount of unsweetened chocolate (there were already 3 cups of sugar in the ingredient list) and adding ⅓ cup of cocoa powder lent deeper chocolate flavor and had no adverse effect on the brownies' texture. Plus, unlike semisweet or bittersweet chocolate, cocoa powder didn't contribute any sugar to our brownies, which were about to be topped with marshmallows. Only the nuts remained; ¾ cup of chopped pecans added plenty of textural interest without being distracting.

Next, rather than using mini marshmallows, we found that a thin layer of marshmallow crème evenly coated the brownies and kept the sugar quotient in check. We initially heated the marshmallow crème in the microwave to make it easy to spread, but after a few tests, we realized we simply needed to dollop it on the hot brownies and let it sit for a minute; the heat from the brownies softened the crème so that all we had to do was grab a spatula to spread it out in an even layer.

We moved on to the chocolate frosting, which tasters thought was overkill. Maybe since the brownie layer was so chocolaty, the frosting could now be minimized to just a melted drizzle. We melted a few chocolate chips and added a little oil to keep the chocolate flowing from the spoon as we waved it over the brownies. With just a small quantity of chocolate, we were able to give our rich and fudgy brownies an impressive, dressed-up look.

MISSISSIPPI MUD BROWNIES

MAKES 24 BROWNIES

Be careful not to overbake these brownies; they should be moist and fudgy.

BROWNIES

6	ounces unsweetened chocolate, chopped
16	tablespoons (2 sticks) unsalted butter, cut into 16 pieces
1½	cups all-purpose flour
⅓	cup Dutch-processed cocoa powder
½	teaspoon salt
3	cups sugar
5	large eggs
¾	cup chopped pecans

TOPPING

¾	cup marshmallow crème
¼	cup semisweet chocolate chips
2	teaspoons vegetable oil

1. FOR THE BROWNIES: Adjust an oven rack to the middle position and heat the oven to 325 degrees. Following the photo on page 202, line a 13 by 9-inch baking pan with an aluminum foil sling and grease the foil.

2. Microwave the chocolate and butter together in a large bowl, stirring occasionally, until smooth, 1 to 2 minutes; let cool slightly. Combine the flour, cocoa, and salt in a second bowl. Whisk the sugar and eggs together in a third bowl, then whisk in the melted chocolate mixture. Stir the flour mixture into the chocolate mixture until no streaks of flour remain. Fold in the pecans and scrape the batter evenly into the prepared pan. Bake until a toothpick inserted in the center comes out with a few moist crumbs attached, about 35 minutes, rotating the pan halfway through baking. Transfer the pan to a wire rack.

MAKING MISSISSIPPI MUD BROWNIES

1. Use a spatula to spread the marshmallow crème evenly over the hot brownies.

2. Drizzle the melted chocolate from a spoon to create a decorative pattern.

3. FOR THE TOPPING: Dollop the marshmallow crème over the hot brownies and let sit until softened, about 1 minute. Meanwhile, microwave the chocolate chips and oil in a small bowl until smooth, stirring occasionally, about 30 seconds. Following the photos, spread the marshmallow crème evenly over the brownies, then drizzle with the melted chocolate. Transfer the pan to a wire rack and let the brownies cool completely, about 2 hours. Remove the brownies from the pan using the foil, cut into 24 squares, and serve.

Oatmeal-Butterscotch Bars

"Oatmeal scotchies," oat bars studded with sweet, orange-hued butterscotch chips, are a fond childhood favorite for many of us in the test kitchen. The simplest recipes consist of oatmeal cookie dough with a bag of butterscotch morsels stirred in. But when we tasted bars made from a recipe on a bag of butterscotch chips—the recipe our mothers would have used—they were awfully sweet, and the tasters felt that the chips gave the bars an "unnatural taste." Instead of melting into the dough like chocolate chips, these chips turned hard and waxy. The cakey texture of the bars was OK, but we wanted a chewier, moister version.

We hit the grocery store in search of better-tasting butterscotch products. We tried jarred butterscotch sauce, but it was too mild and the bars turned tough and taffylike. Crushed butterscotch candies were even more artificial-tasting than the chips. Having nowhere else to turn, we grudgingly reconsidered the butterscotch chips.

First, we found that melting the chips eliminated their textural shortcoming. Reducing the amount of sugar solved the sweetness issue, and melting the butter rather than creaming it gave the bars the chewy texture we wanted. Only one problem remained: several tasters still thought the butterscotch flavor could be better.

Toasting the oats didn't make much of a difference, but browning the butter (rather than just melting it) improved the bars tremendously, deepening the butterscotch flavor. Substituting assertive dark brown sugar for light brown sugar created even more depth of flavor—and "scotchies" far better than the ones from the recipe on the bag.

OATMEAL-BUTTERSCOTCH BARS

MAKES 24 BARS

For chewier bars, substitute old-fashioned rolled oats.

BARS

2	cups quick-cooking oats (see note above)
1¼	cups all-purpose flour
½	teaspoon baking soda
½	teaspoon salt
¾	cup butterscotch chips
16	tablespoons (2 sticks) unsalted butter
1	cup packed dark brown sugar

1	large egg
2	teaspoons vanilla extract

GLAZE

¼	cup butterscotch chips
2	tablespoons dark brown sugar
1	tablespoon water
⅛	teaspoon salt

1. FOR THE BARS: Adjust an oven rack to the lower-middle position and heat the oven to 350 degrees. Following the photo on page 202, line a 13 by 9-inch baking pan with an aluminum foil sling and grease the foil. Whisk the oats, flour, baking soda, and salt together in a medium bowl.

2. Place the butterscotch chips in a large heatproof bowl. Melt the butter in a small saucepan over medium-low heat and continue to cook until golden brown in color, about 12 minutes. Using a heatproof spatula, transfer the browned butter to the bowl with the butterscotch chips and whisk until melted and smooth. Whisk in the brown sugar until dissolved. Whisk in the egg and vanilla until combined. Stir in the flour mixture, in two additions, until just incorporated. Give the batter a final stir to make sure no flour pockets remain.

3. Scrape the batter into the prepared pan and smooth the top. Bake the bars until a toothpick inserted in the center comes out with just a few moist crumbs attached, 16 to 20 minutes, rotating the pan halfway through baking.

4. FOR THE GLAZE: Meanwhile, place the butterscotch chips in a medium heatproof bowl. Bring the brown sugar, water, and salt to a simmer in a small saucepan over medium-high heat. Pour the hot sugar mixture over the butterscotch chips and whisk until melted and smooth.

5. Drizzle the glaze over the warm bars. Transfer the pan to a wire rack and let the bars cool completely, about 2 hours. Remove the bars from the pan using the foil, cut into 24 squares, and serve.

Seven-Layer Bars

With layers of chocolate chips, coconut, and nuts piled high over a buttery graham cracker crust, seven-layer bars sound appealing. There's no batter or dough to make—just layer pantry staples into a baking dish and wait for the oven to transform a jumble of ingredients into a chewy, crispy, sweet bar cookie. But after testing the original recipe (first published on a can of Eagle brand sweetened condensed milk), we weren't very impressed. Yes, the recipe was easy, but the crust was bland and soggy, the coconut and nuts tasted raw, and the bars were dry. We decided to give this 1950s classic a makeover.

We started with the crust. Prebaking produced the crisp texture we were looking for. We experimented with ingredients to boost flavor in the crust and finally hit upon the solution: toffee bits. Their buttery, salty flavor gave the crust real personality.

To improve their flavor and texture, we toasted the coconut and nuts. Rice Krispies (not part of the original recipe) lent welcome crunch and lightness. To emphasize the chocolate flavor, we added a layer of milk chocolate, melted right over the hot crust, in addition to the usual chocolate chips.

Arguably, the best part of a seven-layer bar is the rich butterscotch flavor and chewy texture added by the sweetened condensed milk. To remedy the sandy, dry texture of the original recipe, why not add more of it? We found that two full cans created a rich, moist, candylike bar cookie with plenty of chew and great caramel flavor.

SEVEN-LAYER BARS
MAKES 24 BARS

Two kinds of Heath Toffee Bits are sold at the supermarket; be sure to buy the ones with chocolate. Don't substitute store-bought graham cracker crumbs here because they will taste too sandy in the bars. Any brand of toasted rice cereal will work in this recipe.

1	cup chocolate-covered toffee bits (see note above)
12	whole graham crackers, broken into rough pieces (see note above)
8	tablespoons (1 stick) unsalted butter, melted and cooled
8	ounces milk chocolate, chopped fine
1	cup Rice Krispies cereal (see note above)
1	cup pecans, toasted (see page 130) and chopped coarse
1	cup semisweet chocolate chips
1	cup sweetened shredded coconut, toasted (see page 212)
2	(14-ounce) cans sweetened condensed milk
1	tablespoon vanilla extract

1. Adjust an oven rack to the middle position and heat the oven to 350 degrees. Following the photo on page 202, line a 13 by 9-inch baking pan with an aluminum foil sling and grease the foil.

MAKING AN EVEN CRUST

Sprinkle the crumb mixture over the pan bottom and press down firmly, using the flat bottom of a measuring cup to form an even layer.

2. Process the toffee bits to a fine powder in a food processor, about 10 seconds. Add the graham cracker pieces and process the mixture to fine crumbs, about 30 seconds. Add the melted butter and pulse to incorporate. Sprinkle the mixture into the prepared pan and, following the photo on page 210, press into an even layer with the bottom of a measuring cup. Bake the crust until fragrant and beginning to brown, about 10 minutes.

3. Remove the crust from the oven, sprinkle with the milk chocolate, and let sit until the chocolate is softened but not melted, about 5 minutes. Smooth the softened chocolate into an even layer.

4. Layer the Rice Krispies, pecans, chocolate chips, then coconut into the pan, in that order, pressing on each layer to adhere. Whisk the condensed milk and vanilla together and pour the mixture evenly over the top. Bake the bars until golden brown, 25 to 30 minutes, rotating the pan halfway through baking.

5. Transfer the pan to a wire rack and let the bars cool completely, about 2 hours. Remove the bars from the pan using the foil, cut into 24 squares, and serve.

TOASTING COCONUT

To toast coconut, spread it on a rimmed baking sheet and place it in a 350-degree oven, stirring often, until lightly golden, 7 to 10 minutes. As the toasted coconut cools, it will turn crisp.

Rice Krispies Treats

Rice Krispies Treats have been around for what seems like forever—at least since the 1930s. But even though they're a distinctly American sweet with a long history, they can be a little ho-hum. We wanted to doll up this kids' classic for a more adult (but still kid-friendly) dessert.

We first reviewed the back-of-the-cereal-box recipe and discovered that—with some minor adjustments—it held up to the test of time just fine. We found that using 5 cups of Rice Krispies cereal (as opposed to the 6 cups called for in the traditional recipe) to one 10-ounce bag of marshmallows produced creamier, richer treats, and a little vanilla extract and salt (both missing from the original recipe) added lots of flavor. Our tasters wanted thicker, more substantial squares, so we patted the mixture into an 8-inch square pan instead of the usual 13 by 9-inch pan.

We decided that the bold and tempting flavors of chocolate and cherries would collaborate nicely in a Rice Krispies treat, so we stirred in 1 cup of chopped dried cherries with the cereal (maraschino cherries were wet and messy and fresh cherries made the treats soggy).

In many recipes the cooled treats are smothered with a layer of melted chocolate, but we wanted flavor in, not just on, the treats. We decided to employ a combination of dark and white chocolate to punch up the flavor. White chocolate chips, melted with the butter and marshmallows, added a richer flavor to the treats, and melted semisweet chocolate chips, drizzled over the top, gave them a dressed-up look.

For two equally exciting variations, we added chocolate, pecans, and caramel to our base recipe for a decadent turtle treat, and peanuts and peanut butter chips for our homage to another American favorite, the fluffernutter.

CRISPY CHOCOLATE-CHERRY TREATS

MAKES 16 SQUARES

Any brand of toasted rice cereal will work in this recipe.

3	tablespoons unsalted butter
1	(10-ounce) bag marshmallows
½	cup white chocolate chips
½	teaspoon salt
¼	teaspoon vanilla extract
5	cups Rice Krispies cereal (see note above)
1	cup dried cherries, chopped
½	cup semisweet chocolate chips

1. Following the photo on page 202, line an 8-inch square baking pan with an aluminum foil sling and grease the foil. Melt the butter in a large saucepan or Dutch oven over low heat. Add the marshmallows, white chocolate chips, and salt and cook, stirring constantly, until melted and smooth, about 8 minutes. Stir in the vanilla.

2. Off the heat, stir in the Rice Krispies and cherries until incorporated. Scrape the mixture into the prepared pan and press into the bottom and corners with a greased spatula. Let the mixture cool completely, about 1 hour.

3. Microwave the semisweet chocolate chips in a small bowl until smooth, 30 to 60 seconds, stirring occasionally. Drizzle the melted chocolate over the cooled treats. Let the drizzled chocolate cool, about 15 minutes. Remove the treats from the pan using the foil, cut into 16 squares, and serve.

Variations
CRISPY TURTLE TREATS

Substitute ½ cup semisweet chocolate chips for the white chocolate chips in step 1. Omit the cherries and stir in 15 soft caramel candies, quartered, and 1 cup chopped toasted pecans with the cereal in step 2.

CRISPY FLUFFERNUTTER TREATS

Substitute ½ cup peanut butter chips for the white chocolate chips in step 1, 1 cup dry-roasted peanuts for the dried cherries in step 2, and ½ cup peanut butter chips for the semisweet chocolate chips in step 3.

Raspberry Streusel Bars

A great-tasting raspberry bar requires just the right balance of bright, tangy fruit filling and rich, buttery shortbread. Unfortunately, we've had our fair share of raspberry squares that were more crumb sandwich than bar cookie, landing on the floor rather than in the mouth. Worse than the loose crumbs was the meager layer of raspberry jam attempting to hold it all together—so overcooked that the fruit flavor was gone.

Many recipes use a single dough for both the top and bottom crusts, but we found this problematic. The same dough that gave us a firm and sturdy bottom layer also gave us a topping that was sandy and dry. Some recipes involve two separate mixtures for the top and bottom layers, but we were loath to make more work for ourselves. Our goal was to create a plain and simple shortbreadlike bottom crust, then somehow customize a portion of this dough to end up with a successful streusel topping.

For the bottom crust, we started with a basic shortbread recipe—a simple mixture of flour, sugar, salt, and a good dose of softened butter

(12 tablespoons for a batch that would fill a 13 by 9-inch pan). But this crust was a little dense. Apparently, we were a little conservative with the butter. Going up by 4 tablespoons helped, giving us a shortbread crust worth eating.

But even this butter-rich dough wasn't up to the task of forming a neat-crumbed topping for the jam. Streusel is generally on the loose side, but we wanted a more cohesive topping for these bars. We found that an extra 2 tablespoons of butter, which we rubbed into the reserved dough with our fingers, produced small hazelnut-size crumbs that melded in the oven yet remained light and crunchy. Light brown sugar lent a distinct sweetness, and a few oats and chopped nuts added interesting flavor and texture to our streusel.

We moved on to the filling. To live up to their potential, these bars would need a fresh-tasting fruity layer in the middle. Plain old raspberry jam was the filling of choice for most recipes. We tested jam, jelly, and preserves, and tasters liked the preserves the most. Yet even the good preserves (those that weren't overly sweet) lost significant flavor when cooked again in the raspberry bars. We tried baking the bars for less time (at a higher temperature to brown the topping), but this only made the jam wet and runny, with no flavor improvement.

Resigned to a more moderate cooking time and temperature, we added a dash of lemon juice to brighten the filling. This worked against the deadening heat of the oven, but it didn't fool a single taster into believing there were fresh berries anywhere near these bars. The logical solution? Use fresh berries to get fresh berry flavor. But berries alone produced a sodden, mouth-puckeringly tart raspberry bar. Clearly, there's a reason why all recipes for raspberry bars call for jam or preserves— their viscous, sweet nature is essential to the filling.

We found success with a combination of preserves and fresh berries (lightly mashed for easier spreading), which produced a well-rounded flavor and perfectly moist consistency.

RASPBERRY STREUSEL BARS

MAKES 24 BARS

Frozen raspberries can be substituted for fresh; be sure to defrost them before combining with the raspberry preserves. If your fresh raspberries are very tart, add only 1 or 2 teaspoons of lemon juice to the filling.

2½	cups all-purpose flour
⅔	cup granulated sugar
½	teaspoon salt
16	tablespoons (2 sticks) plus 2 tablespoons unsalted butter, cut into ½-inch pieces and softened
½	cup old-fashioned rolled oats
½	cup pecans, chopped fine
¼	cup packed light brown sugar
¾	cup raspberry preserves
¾	cup fresh raspberries (see note above)
1	tablespoon fresh lemon juice (see note above)

1. Adjust an oven rack to the middle position and heat the oven to 375 degrees. Following the photo on page 202, line a 13 by 9-inch baking pan with an aluminum foil sling and grease the foil.

2. Whisk the flour, granulated sugar, and salt together in a large bowl. Beat in 16 tablespoons of the butter with an electric mixer on low speed until the mixture resembles wet sand, 1 to 2 minutes. Reserve 1¼ cups of the flour mixture for the topping.

3. Sprinkle the remaining flour mixture into the prepared pan and, following the photo on page 210, press into an even layer with the bottom of a measuring cup. Bake the crust until fragrant and the edges begin to brown, 14 to 18 minutes.

4. Meanwhile, add the oats, nuts, and brown sugar to the reserved flour mixture and toss to combine. Add the remaining 2 tablespoons butter and pinch the mixture between your fingers into hazelnut-size clumps of streusel.

5. Combine the preserves, raspberries, and lemon juice in a small bowl. Following the photo, mash the mixture with a fork until just some of the berry pieces remain.

6. Spread the filling evenly over the hot crust and sprinkle the streusel topping evenly over the filling (do not press the streusel into the filling). Bake the bars until the topping is deep golden brown and the filling is bubbling, 22 to 25 minutes, rotating the pan halfway through baking. Transfer the pan to a wire rack and let the bars cool completely, about 2 hours. Remove the bars from the pan using the foil, cut into 24 squares, and serve.

MASHING FRUIT FOR STREUSEL BARS

Using a fork, mash the raspberries with the raspberry preserves and lemon juice for a berry filling with a thick consistency and rustic texture.

SHOPPING WITH THE TEST KITCHEN

Raspberry Preserves: On the hunt for the best possible preserves to use in our Raspberry Streusel Bars, we tested a variety of jams and preserves, looking for one with a flavor that spoke loudly of raspberry, without tartness or cloying sweetness. Smucker's Red Raspberry Preserves was the best of the bunch. Tasters praised its "classic, clean flavor" and noted that it had just the right amount of seeds.

Lemon Squares

With their thin smear of timidly flavored filling, most lemon squares seem designed to please people who like the shortbread crust more than the lemon filling. But we like our lemon squares to have a thick, creamy topping with a bold—though not mouth-puckering—lemon flavor.

Most recipes instruct you to mix lemon juice, sugar, and eggs, pour this mixture over a prebaked crust, and then continue baking until the filling has set. Unfortunately, we found that these easy recipes produce a lemon layer that's thin and rubbery. A better option is to cook the filling ingredients into a thick curd. Once poured onto the crust and popped into the oven, the curd bakes up creamy and rich.

A combination of yolks and whole eggs is necessary to give the curd its structure and creaminess, whole eggs providing the former and yolks the latter. For a curd that was solid enough to hold its shape but was plenty creamy as well, the winning combination was two whole eggs and seven egg yolks. For even more creaminess, we finished the curd with 4 tablespoons of butter and 3 tablespoons of heavy cream.

For serious lemon flavor, we learned that it's essential to use both juice and zest. Many recipes rely on juice alone, but its flavor fades in the oven. The zest has the stronger, brighter lemon flavor. Tasters weren't wild about the stringy bits of zest in their lemon squares, though, and we easily eliminated them by straining the cooked curd.

The shortbread crust is nothing more than flour, confectioners' sugar, salt, and butter. To support a thick layer of lemon curd, the crust has to be sturdier than most. A few extra tablespoons of butter ensured a firm crust that didn't crumble under the thick lemon topping.

LEMON SQUARES

MAKES 16 SQUARES

It is important that both the filling and the crust be warm when assembling the bars in step 4; this ensures that the lemon curd filling will cook through evenly. Be sure to zest the lemons before juicing them.

CRUST

1¼	cups all-purpose flour
½	cup confectioners' sugar
½	teaspoon salt
8	tablespoons (1 stick) unsalted butter, cut into 8 pieces and softened

FILLING

2	large eggs plus 7 large egg yolks
1	cup plus 2 tablespoons granulated sugar
¼	cup grated fresh lemon zest and ⅔ cup fresh lemon juice (4 lemons)
	Pinch salt
4	tablespoons (½ stick) unsalted butter, cut into 4 pieces
3	tablespoons heavy cream
	Confectioners' sugar, for dusting

MAKING LEMON CURD

1. Cook the lemon curd until it thickens and a finger dragged through the curd on the back of a spoon leaves an empty trail behind.

2. Press the curd through a fine-mesh strainer to remove the lemon zest before stirring in the cream and pouring the curd over the crust.

1. Adjust an oven rack to the middle position and heat the oven to 350 degrees. Following the photo on page 202, line an 8-inch baking pan with an aluminum foil sling and grease the foil.

2. FOR THE CRUST: Process the flour, confectioners' sugar, and salt together in a food processor to combine, about three pulses. Sprinkle the butter over the top and pulse the mixture until it resembles coarse sand, about eight pulses. Sprinkle the mixture into the prepared pan and, following the photo on page 210, press into an even layer with the bottom of a measuring cup. Bake the crust until fragrant and beginning to brown, about 20 minutes.

3. FOR THE FILLING: Meanwhile, whisk the eggs and egg yolks together in a medium saucepan. Whisk in the granulated sugar until combined, then whisk in the lemon zest, lemon juice, and salt. Add the butter and cook over medium heat, stirring

constantly, until the mixture thickens slightly and registers 170 degrees on an instant-read thermometer, about 5 minutes. Strain the mixture immediately into a bowl and stir in the cream.

4. Pour the filling over the warm crust. Bake the squares until the filling is shiny and opaque and the center jiggles slightly when gently shaken, 10 to 15 minutes, rotating the pan halfway through baking.

5. Transfer the pan to a wire rack and let the bars cool completely, about 2 hours. Remove the bars from the pan using the foil, cut into 16 squares, and dust with confectioners' sugar before serving.

SHOPPING WITH THE TEST KITCHEN

Measuring Spoons: Even though eyeballing small amounts of ingredients might pass when you're making dinner, this imprecise measuring method definitely won't cut it when it comes to baking. To find the best measuring spoons on the market, we tested five brands. We filled them, leveled them, and then weighed the contents. Every brand was sufficiently accurate, so preferences came down to design. We found that fat spoons, spoons with short handles, overly bulky spoons, and spoons with raised handles make leveling off the contents or holding the spoons difficult. When measuring out liquid ingredients, shallow spoons pose a higher risk of spillage than deep spoons. We ultimately found our winner in the Cuisipro Stainless Steel Oval Measuring Spoons ($13.95). These spoons feature an elongated, oval shape that proved optimal for scooping ingredients from narrow jars. In addition, the ends of the handles curl down, allowing a full measure to be set down on the counter with no tipping and no mess.

All-Season Peach Squares

A peach square should be packed with peach flavor and be sturdy enough that it can be eaten out of hand—just like the perfect summer peach. But judging from the half-dozen recipes we made at the outset of our research, both of those qualities are pretty rare in most peach squares. Some squares collapsed in our hands as we took a bite, and others were devoid of peach flavor. We had our work cut out for us.

The biggest discovery we made in our testing was frozen peaches. Not only were they more convenient than fresh (no peeling, pitting, and chopping), but their quality was more consistent. Chopping the peaches in the food processor before cooking them down in a skillet with peach jam gave us a rich, deeply flavored filling, and because excess liquid evaporated during cooking, the filling also had just the right texture: not wet but jammy, with bits of peach to bite into. We found that both lemon zest and lemon juice brightened the filling's fruit flavor.

With our filling down, we turned to the crust. Taking a cue from our Raspberry Streusel Bars (page 215), we created a simple crust that could then be reserved for the topping, too. Tasters found a crust made with brown sugar to be richer-flavored than one made with granulated sugar and a better match to our peach filling. Almonds are a natural flavor pairing with peaches, so we decided to add some to the crust; we also sprinkled a handful over the top of the bars before baking.

Once the bars were cooled, we cut into them, and tasters gave a thumbs-up to these summery bars that, with the help of frozen peaches, we could enjoy year-round.

ALL-SEASON PEACH SQUARES

MAKES 24 SQUARES

Lay the thawed peaches on a kitchen towel to rid them of excess moisture before using.

CRUST

1½	cups all-purpose flour
1¾	cups sliced almonds
⅓	cup granulated sugar
⅓	cup plus 1 tablespoon packed light brown sugar
½	teaspoon salt
12	tablespoons (1½ sticks) unsalted butter, cut into 12 pieces and softened

FILLING

1½	pounds (6 cups) frozen peaches, thawed and drained (see note above)
½	cup peach jam
½	teaspoon grated fresh lemon zest and 1 teaspoon fresh lemon juice
	Pinch salt

1. Adjust an oven rack to the middle position and heat the oven to 375 degrees. Following the photo on page 202, line a 13 by 9-inch baking pan with an aluminum foil sling and grease the foil.

2. FOR THE CRUST: Process the flour, 1¼ cups of the almonds, granulated sugar, ⅓ cup of the brown sugar, and salt together in a food processor until combined, about 5 seconds. Add the butter and pulse the mixture until it resembles coarse meal with a few pea-size pieces of butter, about 20 pulses. Reserve ½ cup of the flour mixture for the topping.

3. Sprinkle the remaining flour mixture into the prepared pan and, following the photo on page 210, press into an even layer with the bottom of a measuring cup. Bake the crust until fragrant and golden brown, about 15 minutes.

4. Meanwhile, add the remaining 1 tablespoon brown sugar to the reserved flour mixture and pinch the mixture between your fingers into hazelnut-size clumps of streusel.

5. FOR THE FILLING: Pulse the peaches and jam together in the food processor until the peaches are roughly ¼-inch chunks, five to seven pulses. Cook the peach mixture in a large nonstick skillet over high heat until it is thickened and jamlike, about 10 minutes. Off the heat, stir in the lemon zest, lemon juice, and salt.

6. Spread the cooked peach mixture evenly over the hot crust, then sprinkle with the streusel topping and remaining ½ cup almonds. Bake until the almonds are golden brown, about 20 minutes, rotating the pan halfway through baking.

7. Transfer the pan to a wire rack and let the bars cool completely, about 2 hours. Remove the bars from the pan using the foil, cut into 24 squares, and serve.

Variations

ALL-SEASON APRICOT SQUARES

Substitute 1 pound dried apricots for the frozen peaches and apricot jam for the peach jam. Add 1 cup water to the food processor with the apricots in step 5.

ALL-SEASON CHERRY SQUARES

Substitute frozen pitted cherries for the frozen peaches and cherry jam for the peach jam. Omit the lemon zest, reduce the amount of fresh lemon juice to ½ teaspoon, and add ¼ teaspoon vanilla extract in step 5.

HAZELNUT CHEWIES

CHAPTER SEVEN

Holiday Cookie Swap

Holiday Cookie Swap

The holidays aren't complete without a platter full of freshly baked cookies to share with family and friends. Every year, we invite the readers of *Cook's Country* magazine to submit their favorite holiday cookie recipes, the ones that they make every year for holiday parties and gift giving.

This collection represents the test kitchen's top picks and encompasses a wide variety of cookies, from a simple butter cookie dressed up with a minty pink swirl to coconut-flavored sandwich cookies filled with chocolate to brownies layered with a classic drugstore candy. Whether you're looking for something to pair with a cup of tea (look no further than Boozy Biscotti) or a super-nutty treat (Hazelnut Chewies made with Nutella and rolled in toasted nuts), you'll certainly find something you'll want to share during the holiday season.

CHERRY CHEESECAKE COOKIES

MAKES ABOUT 48 COOKIES

These cookies have a base similar to cheesecake filling, a graham cracker "crust," and a gooey cherry topping.

8	whole graham crackers, broken into rough pieces
3½	cups all-purpose flour
2	teaspoons baking powder
1	teaspoon salt
2	(8-ounce) packages cream cheese, softened
20	tablespoons (2½ sticks) unsalted butter, softened
1½	cups sugar
2	large eggs, room temperature
2	teaspoons vanilla extract
3	(20-ounce) cans cherry pie filling, drained

MAKING CHERRY CHEESECAKE COOKIES

1. Make an indentation in each cookie by gently pressing with a rounded tablespoon measure.

2. Place 3 cherries in each indentation and bake the cookies.

1. Process the graham cracker pieces in a food processor until finely ground, about 30 seconds. Transfer to a shallow baking dish or pie plate and set aside.

2. Combine the flour, baking powder, and salt in a medium bowl. With an electric mixer on medium-high speed, beat the cream cheese, butter, and sugar together until smooth and creamy, about 2 minutes. Add the eggs and vanilla and mix until incorporated. Reduce the mixer speed to low, add the flour mixture, and mix until just combined. Divide the dough in half, wrap each half tightly in plastic wrap, and refrigerate until firm, about 2 hours.

3. Adjust the oven racks to the upper-middle and lower-middle positions and heat the oven to 350 degrees. Line two large baking sheets with parchment paper. Working with 2 tablespoons of chilled dough at a time, roll the dough into 1½-inch balls. Roll the dough balls in the reserved graham cracker crumbs to coat. Lay the balls on the prepared baking sheets, spaced about 2 inches apart, eight dough balls per sheet. Following the photos on page 222, and using a rounded tablespoon measure, make an indentation in the center of each ball (if the measure sticks to the dough, dip it in graham cracker crumbs to coat before pressing). Place 3 cherries in each indentation.

4. Bake the cookies until they have cracked and are set, 12 to 14 minutes, switching and rotating the sheets halfway through baking. Let the cookies cool on the baking sheets for 10 minutes, then transfer to a wire rack and let cool completely before serving. Repeat with the remaining dough.

BOOZY BISCOTTI

MAKES ABOUT 24 COOKIES

These biscotti contain a surprising secret ingredient: instant grits. The grits lend an appealingly light, crunchy texture. Because these cookies are packed with cherries and nuts, be sure to cut the logs into slices gently so that the pieces don't fall apart. For an extra treat, dip the baked biscotti in melted chocolate.

1	cup dried cherries
¼	cup spiced rum
1¼	cups instant grits
1¼	cups all-purpose flour
1	teaspoon salt
½	teaspoon baking powder
8	tablespoons (1 stick) unsalted butter, softened
1	cup sugar
1	tablespoon grated fresh orange zest
2	large eggs, room temperature
1	cup macadamia nuts, chopped

1. Adjust an oven rack to the middle position and heat the oven to 350 degrees. Line a baking sheet with parchment paper. Microwave the cherries and rum together in a medium bowl, covered, until bubbling, about 1 minute. Let the cherries sit until they have plumped, about 5 minutes. Drain the cherries.

2. Combine the grits, flour, salt, and baking powder in a medium bowl. With an electric mixer on medium-high speed, beat the butter, sugar, and orange zest together in a large bowl until light and fluffy, 3 to 6 minutes. Add the eggs and mix until incorporated. Reduce the mixer speed to low and add the flour mixture, nuts, and drained cherries. Mix until just combined. Following the photo, divide the dough in half and shape each half into a 7 by 3-inch log on the prepared baking sheet. Bake the logs until light golden and just beginning to crack on top, 30 to 35 minutes, rotating the sheet halfway through baking (do not turn the oven off). Let the logs cool on the baking sheet for 30 minutes.

3. Transfer to a cutting board and, using a serrated knife, slice the logs crosswise into cookies about ½ inch thick. Place the cookies on a freshly lined

MAKING BISCOTTI

1. Shape the dough into two logs, each measuring 7 inches long and 3 inches across.

2. After the logs have baked and cooled, slice them crosswise into ½-inch slices, using a serrated knife, before baking them again.

baking sheet, cut side down, and bake until light golden, about 10 minutes, flipping each slice halfway through baking. Let the cookies cool on the sheet for 10 minutes, then transfer to a wire rack and let cool completely before serving.

SPUMONI BARS

MAKES ABOUT 48 COOKIES

Like the classic striped Italian ice cream, spumoni, this cookie boasts cherry, walnut, and chocolate layers. The cherry and chocolate doughs may be softer than the walnut dough and may require a little extra chilling time before being rolled into ropes; this will ensure neater-looking bars. If the ropes do not adhere well to each other, brush them lightly with water to get them to stick.

2	cups all-purpose flour
¼	teaspoon baking powder
⅛	teaspoon salt
12	tablespoons (1½ sticks) unsalted butter, softened
⅔	cup sugar
3	large egg yolks
1	teaspoon vanilla extract
¼	cup semisweet chocolate chips
12	maraschino cherries, drained, stemmed, and chopped fine
¼	cup walnuts, toasted (see page 130) and chopped fine

1. Combine the flour, baking powder, and salt in a medium bowl. With an electric mixer on medium-high speed, beat the butter and sugar together until light and fluffy, 3 to 6 minutes. Add the egg yolks and vanilla and mix until incorporated. Reduce the mixer speed to low, add the flour mixture, and mix until just combined. Divide the dough into thirds and transfer each third to a separate bowl.

ASSEMBLING SPUMONI BARS

1. After pressing the ropes together and chilling the dough, use a rolling pin to roll the dough into a 24 by 3-inch rectangle.

2. Then cut the rolled dough crosswise into 1-inch cookies.

2. Adjust the oven racks to the upper-middle and lower-middle positions and heat the oven to 375 degrees. Line two large baking sheets with parchment paper. Microwave the chocolate chips in a small bowl, stirring occasionally, until smooth, about 1 minute; let cool slightly.

3. Add the melted chocolate, cherries, and walnuts each to a separate bowl of dough and mix until incorporated. Refrigerate the doughs until slightly firm, about 15 minutes. Roll each dough into two 12-inch ropes on a lightly floured work surface. Place one rope of each color side by side, then gently press them together. Wrap the dough in plastic wrap and chill until firm, about 30 minutes.

4. Following the photos, working with one dough block at a time, roll the dough into a 24 by 3-inch rectangle on a lightly floured work surface. Cut the dough crosswise into 1-inch cookies. Lay the cookies on the prepared baking sheets,

spaced about ¾ inch apart, 12 cookies per sheet. Bake the cookies until just set, about 12 minutes, switching and rotating the sheets halfway through baking. Let the cookies cool on the baking sheets for 5 minutes, then transfer to a wire rack and let cool completely before serving. Repeat with the remaining dough.

CANDY CANE PINWHEELS

MAKES ABOUT 54 COOKIES

In this recipe the flavor of a candy cane is swirled into rich butter cookie dough for a pretty and peppy treat. Chilling the rolled dough until firm but pliable before rolling it into a log helps to get an even swirl throughout each cookie. You will need about 20 peppermint candies for this recipe; to grind them, use a food processor.

3	cups all-purpose flour
¾	teaspoon baking powder
¼	teaspoon salt
16	tablespoons (2 sticks) unsalted butter, softened
1	cup sugar
1	large egg, room temperature
1	teaspoon vanilla extract
½	cup finely ground peppermint candies (see note above)
1	teaspoon peppermint extract
6	drops red food coloring

1. Whisk the flour, baking powder, and salt together in a medium bowl. With an electric mixer on medium-high speed, beat the butter and sugar together in a large bowl until light and fluffy, 3 to 6 minutes. Beat in the egg and vanilla until incorporated. Reduce the mixer speed to low, add the flour mixture, and mix until a dough forms.

MAKING CANDY CANE PINWHEELS

1. After layering the peppermint dough over the plain dough, roll the layers together into a tight log.

2. After chilling the dough, trim the ends and neatly cut the dough into ¼-inch cookies.

Remove and reserve half of the dough. Add the peppermint candies, peppermint extract, and food coloring to the remaining dough and mix until combined.

2. Between two sheets of parchment paper, roll the peppermint dough into a 14 by 8-inch rectangle. With the dough still between the sheets of parchment, chill until firm but pliable, about 15 minutes. Repeat rolling and chilling with the plain dough.

3. Remove the top sheet of parchment from each chilled dough, then flip the peppermint dough on top of the plain dough. Following the photo, with the long side facing you, roll the layered dough into a log. Wrap the dough tightly in plastic wrap and refrigerate until firm, about 2 hours.

4. Adjust the oven racks to the upper-middle and lower-middle positions and heat the oven to 375 degrees. Line two large baking sheets with parchment paper. Trim the ends of the dough, then cut the dough into ¼-inch cookies. Lay the cookies on the prepared baking sheets, spaced about 1 inch apart, eight cookies per sheet. Bake until the edges are just golden, 12 to 14 minutes, switching and rotating the sheets halfway through baking. Let the cookies cool on the baking sheets for 10 minutes, then transfer to a wire rack and let cool completely before serving. Repeat with the remaining dough.

PEPPERMINT BROWNIE BITES

MAKES 36 SMALL BROWNIES

Peppermint Patties are sandwiched in the batter to create a smooth, minty layer in these brownies. Instead of cutting the brownies into squares, you can use cookie cutters to cut other shapes, such as stars and crescents. Because inserting a toothpick isn't a good indicator for when these brownies are done (because of the candy layer), be sure the center is set.

¾	cup all-purpose flour
½	teaspoon baking powder
¼	teaspoon salt
8	tablespoons (1 stick) unsalted butter, cut into 8 pieces
2	ounces unsweetened chocolate, chopped coarse
2	large eggs
1	cup sugar
1	teaspoon vanilla extract
16	(1½-inch) York Peppermint Patties, unwrapped

1. Adjust an oven rack to the middle position and heat the oven to 350 degrees. Following the photo on page 202, line an 8-inch square baking pan with an aluminum foil sling and grease the foil. Combine the flour, baking powder, and salt in a bowl. Microwave the butter and chocolate together in a bowl, stirring occasionally, until smooth, 1 to 2 minutes. Set aside to cool slightly.

2. Whisk the eggs and sugar together in a large bowl. Add the cooled chocolate mixture and vanilla and mix until combined. Add the flour mixture and stir until just incorporated. Scrape all but 1 cup of the batter into the prepared pan. Arrange the Peppermint Patties on top of the batter, spaced about ½ inch apart. Scrape the remaining batter on top of the candy and gently spread into an even layer.

3. Bake until the brownies are just set in the center, 30 to 35 minutes, rotating the pan halfway through baking. Transfer the pan to a wire rack and let the brownies cool completely, about 2 hours. Remove the brownies from the pan using the foil, cut into 36 squares, and serve.

MAKING PEPPERMINT BROWNIE BITES

1. Place the Peppermint Patties over the bottom layer of brownie batter, leaving about ½ inch of space between the candies so they have room to melt together.

2. Gently spread the remaining batter over the candies, covering them with an even layer of batter.

MINTY MERINGUE KISSES

MAKES ABOUT 72 COOKIES

These cookies combine crushed peppermint candies and mini chocolate chips in a meringue base. For a festive look, the baked meringues are dipped in chocolate, which is mixed with vegetable oil to help it spread smoothly. Try to work as quickly as possible when shaping the kisses; they will deflate if left too long before baking. You will need about 8 peppermint candies for this recipe.

2	large egg whites
⅛	teaspoon cream of tartar
⅛	teaspoon salt
⅔	cup sugar
½	teaspoon vanilla extract
2	cups mini semisweet chocolate chips
3	tablespoons crushed peppermint candies (see note above)
2	teaspoons vegetable oil

1. Adjust the oven racks to the upper-middle and lower-middle positions and heat the oven to 275 degrees. Line two large baking sheets with parchment paper.

2. With an electric mixer on medium-high speed, whip the egg whites in a large bowl until foamy, about 1 minute. Whip in the cream of tartar and salt until the egg whites are shiny and soft peaks form (see page 5), 2 to 3 minutes. Whip in the sugar, 1 tablespoon at a time, and vanilla and continue to whip until the mixture is glossy and stiff, about 2 minutes. With a rubber spatula, fold in 1 cup of the chocolate chips and peppermint candies.

3. Using a pastry bag fitted with a ½-inch tip or a teaspoon, pipe or dollop teaspoon-size dots of batter, about 1 inch high, onto the prepared baking

sheets, spaced about 1 inch apart. Bake the cookies until they begin to crack and are light golden, 25 to 30 minutes, switching and rotating the sheets halfway through baking. Let the cookies cool completely on the baking sheets.

4. Microwave the remaining 1 cup chocolate chips in a small bowl, stirring occasionally, until smooth, about 1 minute. Stir in the oil. Dip the bottoms of the cookies in the melted chocolate, scrape off the excess, and place the cookies on a parchment-lined baking sheet until the chocolate sets, about 1 hour.

COCONUT SNOWDROPS

MAKES ABOUT 72 COOKIES

These small, delicate sandwich cookies combine the tropical flavor of coconut with rich bittersweet chocolate. Finely chopped almonds and a touch of light brown sugar add both texture and flavor to the dough.

16	tablespoons (2 sticks) plus 3 tablespoons unsalted butter, softened
1	cup granulated sugar
¼	cup packed light brown sugar
1	large egg plus 1 large egg yolk
1	teaspoon vanilla extract
1	teaspoon coconut extract
2	cups all-purpose flour
2	cups sweetened shredded coconut
½	cup blanched almonds, chopped fine
¾	cup semisweet chocolate chips

1. With an electric mixer on medium-high speed, beat 16 tablespoons of the butter, granulated sugar, and brown sugar together in a large bowl until light and fluffy, 3 to 6 minutes. Beat in the egg, egg yolk, vanilla, and coconut extract until

SHAPING COCONUT SNOWDROPS

To make quick work of shaping the cookies, cut one of the chilled squares into smaller ½-inch squares, then roll into ¾-inch balls. Repeat with the remaining square of dough.

incorporated. Reduce the mixer speed to low, add the flour, coconut, and almonds and mix until just combined. Divide the dough in half, shape each half into a square disk about 1 inch thick, and wrap tightly in plastic wrap. Refrigerate until firm, about 1 hour.

2. Adjust the oven racks to the upper-middle and lower-middle positions and heat the oven to 350 degrees. Line two large baking sheets with parchment paper. Following the photo, and working with one square at a time, cut the dough into ½-inch squares and roll into ¾-inch balls. Lay the balls on the prepared baking sheets, spaced about 1 inch apart, 12 dough balls per sheet. Bake until the edges are just golden, 12 to 14 minutes, switching and rotating the sheets halfway through baking. Let the cookies cool on the baking sheets for 10 minutes, then transfer to a wire rack and let cool completely. Repeat with the remaining dough.

3. Microwave the chocolate chips and remaining 3 tablespoons butter in a small bowl until melted, stirring frequently, 1 to 2 minutes. Spread ½ teaspoon of the chocolate mixture over the bottom of half of the cookies, then top with the remaining cookies. Serve.

RASPBERRY-ALMOND SANDWICH COOKIES

MAKES ABOUT 24 COOKIES

This sandwich cookie boasts the same rich flavors as those found in a linzertorte, but the method is much easier. The dough scraps may be gathered and rerolled, but they may need to be wrapped in plastic wrap and chilled if the dough has become too soft to work with. Filling the cookies with jam and coating them with sugar while they are still warm helps them stick together and the sugar adhere. Any brand of raspberry jam will work here, but the test kitchen's preferred brand is Smucker's Red Raspberry Preserves. Blanched, sliced almonds can be substituted for the slivered almonds.

1	cup sugar
2	cups all-purpose flour
1¼	cups slivered almonds (see note above)
16	tablespoons (2 sticks) unsalted butter, cut into ½-inch pieces and chilled
1	teaspoon vanilla extract
½	cup raspberry jam (see note above)

1. Adjust the oven racks to the upper-middle and lower-middle positions and heat the oven to 350 degrees. Line two large baking sheets with parchment paper. Place ½ cup of the sugar in a shallow baking dish or pie plate and set aside. Process 1 cup of the flour and almonds together in a food processor until finely ground, about 1 minute. Add the remaining 1 cup flour and remaining ½ cup sugar and process until combined. Add the butter and vanilla and pulse until a dough forms.

2. On a lightly floured work surface, roll the dough to a ¼-inch thickness. Using a 2-inch round cookie cutter, cut out cookies and lay them on the prepared baking sheets, spaced about 2 inches apart, gathering and rerolling the dough as necessary,

MAKING SANDWICH COOKIES

1. Spread the bottom of half of the cookies with 1 teaspoon raspberry jam. Top with the remaining cookies.

2. Then gently roll the sandwiches in sugar to coat.

eight cookies per sheet. Bake the cookies until the edges are light brown, about 15 minutes, switching and rotating the sheets halfway through baking. Let the cookies cool on the baking sheets for 5 minutes, then transfer to a wire rack.

3. Following the photos, quickly spread 1 teaspoon of the jam on the bottom of half of the warm cookies, then top with the remaining cookies, pressing gently to form sandwiches. Gently roll the cookies in the reserved sugar to coat. Let the cookies cool completely on a wire rack before serving. Repeat with the remaining dough.

HAZELNUT CHEWIES

MAKES ABOUT 84 COOKIES

Nutella, a rich chocolate-hazelnut spread, brings sweetness and richness to these cookies; instant espresso powder lends a note of bitterness and heightens the chocolate flavor. You will need one 13-ounce jar of Nutella for this recipe.

3	cups all-purpose flour
2	teaspoons baking powder
½	teaspoon salt
1¼	cups Nutella spread (see note above)
4	tablespoons (½ stick) unsalted butter, softened
1⅓	cups granulated sugar
2	large eggs
1	teaspoon vanilla extract
1	teaspoon instant espresso powder
⅓	cup milk
2	cups hazelnuts, toasted (see page 130) and chopped fine
1	cup confectioners' sugar

1. Combine the flour, baking powder, and salt in a medium bowl. With an electric mixer on medium-high speed, beat the Nutella, butter, and granulated sugar together in a large bowl until light and fluffy, 3 to 6 minutes. Add the eggs, vanilla, and espresso powder and mix until incorporated. Reduce the mixer speed to low and add half of the flour mixture, followed by half of the milk, mixing until just combined after each addition. Repeat with the remaining flour mixture and remaining milk. Fold in ½ cup of the hazelnuts. Divide the dough in half and wrap tightly in plastic wrap. Refrigerate the dough until firm, about 2 hours.

2. Adjust the oven racks to the upper-middle and lower-middle positions and heat the oven to 375 degrees. Line two large baking sheets with parchment paper. Place the remaining hazelnuts and confectioners' sugar in separate bowls. Working with one dough half at a time, roll the dough into 1-inch balls, roll the balls in the hazelnuts, then in the confectioners' sugar. Lay the balls on the prepared baking sheets, spaced about 2 inches apart, eight dough balls per sheet.

3. Bake the cookies until set, 8 to 10 minutes, switching and rotating the sheets halfway through baking. Let the cookies cool on the baking sheets for 5 minutes, then transfer to a wire rack and let cool completely before serving. Repeat with the remaining dough.

CRANBERRY-PISTACHIO COCONUT TRIANGLES

MAKES 18 COOKIES

This moist, chewy bar cookie is packed with dried cranberries, shredded coconut, and chopped pistachios and dipped in melted white chocolate. We prefer white bar chocolate over white chocolate chips for a smooth texture when melted.

1	cup plus 2 tablespoons all-purpose flour
1	cup plus 2 tablespoons packed light brown sugar
5	tablespoons unsalted butter, cut into 5 pieces and chilled
1	cup pistachios, toasted (see page 130) and chopped
1	cup dried cranberries
¾	cup sweetened shredded coconut
1	large egg
2	tablespoons maple syrup
¾	teaspoon vanilla extract
½	teaspoon almond extract
½	teaspoon salt
4	ounces white chocolate, chopped (see note above)

1. Adjust an oven rack to the middle position and heat the oven to 375 degrees. Following the photo on page 202, line an 8-inch square baking pan with an aluminum foil sling and grease the foil. Pulse 1 cup of the flour, 2 tablespoons of the sugar, and butter in a food processor until the

mixture resembles wet sand. Sprinkle the mixture into the prepared pan and, following the photo on page 210, press into an even layer with the bottom of a measuring cup. Bake until light golden, about 15 minutes. Let the crust cool completely.

2. Toss the pistachios, cranberries, and coconut together in a bowl, breaking up any clumps. Whisk the remaining 1 cup sugar, remaining 2 tablespoons flour, egg, maple syrup, vanilla, almond extract, and salt together in a large bowl. Fold in the pistachio-cranberry mixture, then spread the filling evenly over the cooled crust. Bake until deep golden brown and set, 20 to 25 minutes, rotating the pan halfway through baking. Transfer the pan to a wire rack and let the bars cool completely, about 2 hours.

3. Line a baking sheet with parchment paper. Remove the bars from the pan using the foil. Following the photos, cut the bars into nine squares and cut each square diagonally into two triangles. Microwave the white chocolate in a medium bowl,

MAKING COCONUT TRIANGLES

1. After cutting the cooled bars into nine even squares, cut each square diagonally to form two triangles.

2. Dip one corner of each triangle into the melted white chocolate, then refrigerate until set.

stirring occasionally, until melted, 30 to 60 seconds. Dip one corner of each triangle in the melted chocolate and place on the prepared baking sheet. Refrigerate the triangles until set, about 30 minutes. Serve.

CHOCOLATE TURTLE COOKIES

MAKES ABOUT 30 COOKIES

In this spin on the traditional jam-filled thumbprint cookie, the jam is replaced with a simple caramel filling and the cookies are flavored with chocolate. When melting the caramel and cream in the microwave, be sure to stir the mixture occasionally to prevent it from bubbling over or scorching.

1	cup all-purpose flour
⅓	cup Dutch-processed cocoa powder
¼	teaspoon salt
8	tablespoons (1 stick) unsalted butter, softened
⅔	cup sugar
1	large egg, separated, plus 1 large egg white
2	tablespoons milk
1	teaspoon vanilla extract
1¼	cups pecans, chopped fine
14	soft caramel candies
3	tablespoons heavy cream

1. Combine the flour, cocoa, and salt in a medium bowl. With an electric mixer on medium-high speed, beat the butter and sugar together in a medium bowl until light and fluffy, 3 to 6 minutes. Add the egg yolk, milk, and vanilla and mix until incorporated. Reduce the mixer speed to low and add the flour mixture until just combined. Wrap the dough tightly in plastic wrap and refrigerate until firm, about 1 hour.

FILLING TURTLE COOKIES

1. To make room for the caramel filling, make an indentation in each cookie by gently pressing with a rounded ½-teaspoon measure.

2. After baking the cookies, gently repress the indentations and fill each with ½ teaspoon of the caramel filling.

2. Adjust the oven racks to the upper-middle and lower-middle positions and heat the oven to 350 degrees. Line two large baking sheets with parchment paper. Beat the egg whites in a medium bowl until frothy. Place the pecans in a second bowl. Roll the dough into 1-inch balls, dip in the egg whites, then roll in the pecans. Lay the balls on the prepared baking sheets, spaced about 2 inches apart. Following the photos, using a rounded ½-teaspoon measure, make an indentation in the center of each ball. Bake the cookies until set, about 12 minutes, switching and rotating the sheets halfway through baking.

3. Microwave the caramels and cream together in a medium bowl, stirring occasionally, until smooth, 1 to 2 minutes. When the cookies are removed from the oven, gently repress the existing indentations. Fill each with ½ teaspoon of the caramel mixture. Let the cookies cool on the baking sheets for 10 minutes, then transfer to a wire rack and let cool completely before serving.

CONVERSIONS AND EQUIVALENCIES

Some say cooking is a science and an art. We would say that geography has a hand in it, too. Flour milled in the United Kingdom and elsewhere will feel and taste different from flour milled in the United States. So we cannot promise that the loaf of bread you bake in Canada or England will taste the same as a loaf baked in the States, but we can offer guidelines for converting weights and measures. We also recommend that you rely on your instincts when making our recipes. Refer to the visual cues provided. If the bread dough hasn't "come together in a ball," as described, you may need to add more flour—even if the recipe doesn't tell you to. You be the judge.

The recipes in this book were developed using standard U.S. measures following U.S. government guidelines. The charts below offer equivalents for U.S., metric, and Imperial (U.K.) measures. All conversions are approximate and have been rounded up or down to the nearest whole number.

EXAMPLE:

| 1 teaspoon | = | 5 milliliters (rounded up from 4.9292 milliliters) |
| 1 ounce | = | 28 grams (rounded down from 28.3495 grams) |

VOLUME CONVERSIONS

U.S.	METRIC
1 teaspoon	5 milliliters
2 teaspoons	10 milliliters
1 tablespoon	15 milliliters
2 tablespoons	30 milliliters
¼ cup	59 milliliters
⅓ cup	79 milliliters
½ cup	118 milliliters
¾ cup	177 milliliters
1 cup	237 milliliters
1¼ cups	296 milliliters
1½ cups	355 milliliters
2 cups (1 pint)	473 milliliters
2½ cups	592 milliliters
3 cups	710 milliliters
4 cups (1 quart)	0.946 liter
1.06 quarts	1 liter
4 quarts (1 gallon)	3.8 liters

WEIGHT CONVERSIONS

OUNCES	GRAMS
½	14
¾	21
1	28
1½	43
2	57
2½	71
3	85
3½	99
4	113
4½	128
5	142
6	170
7	198
8	227
9	255
10	283
12	340
16 (1 pound)	454

CONVERSIONS FOR INGREDIENTS COMMONLY USED IN BAKING

Baking is an exacting science. Because measuring by weight is far more accurate than measuring by volume, and thus more likely to achieve reliable results, in our recipes we provide ounce measures in addition to cup measures for many ingredients. Refer to the chart below to convert these measures into grams.

INGREDIENT	OUNCES	GRAMS
Flour		
1 cup all-purpose flour*	5	142
1 cup cake flour	4	113
1 cup whole wheat flour	5½	156
Sugar		
1 cup granulated (white) sugar	7	198
1 cup packed brown sugar (light or dark)	7	198
1 cup confectioners' sugar	4	113
Cocoa Powder		
1 cup cocoa powder	3	85
Butter†		
4 tablespoons (½ stick, or ¼ cup)	2	57
8 tablespoons (1 stick, or ½ cup)	4	113
16 tablespoons (2 sticks, or 1 cup)	8	227

* U.S. all-purpose flour, the most frequently used flour in this book, does not contain leaveners, as some European flours do. These leavened flours are called self-rising or self-raising. If you are using self-rising flour, take this into consideration before adding leavening to a recipe.

† In the United States, butter is sold both salted and unsalted. We generally recommend unsalted butter. If you are using salted butter, take this into consideration before adding salt to a recipe.

OVEN TEMPERATURES

FAHRENHEIT	CELSIUS	GAS MARK (IMPERIAL)
225	105	¼
250	120	½
275	130	1
300	150	2
325	165	3
350	180	4
375	190	5
400	200	6
425	220	7
450	230	8
475	245	9

CONVERTING TEMPERATURES FROM AN INSTANT-READ THERMOMETER

We include doneness temperatures in many of the recipes in this book. We recommend an instant-read thermometer for the job. Refer to the above table to convert Fahrenheit degrees to Celsius. Or, for temperatures not represented in the chart, use this simple formula:

Subtract 32 degrees from the Fahrenheit reading, then divide the result by 1.8 to find the Celsius reading.

INDEX

Note: Page numbers in *italics* refer to photographs.

C

Frostings
   applying, tip for, 86
   Easy Chocolate, 160
   Easy Coffee, 161
   Easy Peppermint, 161
   Easy Vanilla, 160
Fruit. *See* Berry(ies); Fruit desserts; *specific fruits*
Fruit desserts
   Baked Apple Dumplings, 59–62, *60*
   Blueberry Grunt, 54–56
   Brown Sugar Berry Shortcakes, 52–54, *53*
   Cranberry-Apple Crisp, *50,* 62–63
   Peach Brown Betty, 56–58
Furr's Cafeteria, 35

G

Gingerbread Cake, Bold and Spicy, 110–11
Graham crackers
   Cherry Cheesecake Cookies, 222–23
   Coconut Cream Pie, 37–38
   Icebox Key Lime Pie, 43–45
   Mixed-Berry Streusel Pie, 21–22
   Seven-Layer Bars, 210–12, *211*
Grits
   Boozy Biscotti, 223–24
Grunt, Blueberry, 54–56

H

Hazelnut Chewies, *220,* 231–32
Hermits, 193–94
Hermits, history of, 193
Hershey's Kisses, history of, 182
Holiday cookie swap
   Boozy Biscotti, 223–24
   Candy Cane Pinwheels, 226–27
   Cherry Cheesecake Cookies, 222–23
   Chocolate Turtle Cookies, 233
   Coconut Snowdrops, 228–30, *229*
   Cranberry-Pistachio Coconut Triangles, 232–33
   Hazelnut Chewies, *220,* 231–32
   Minty Meringue Kisses, 228
   Peppermint Brownie Bites, 227
   Raspberry-Almond Sandwich Cookies, 230–31
   Spumoni Bars, 224–26, *225*
Honey, measuring, 3

I

Icebox Key Lime Pie, 43–45
Icebox Lemon Cheesecake, 121–24, *122*
Icebox Oreo Cheesecake, 124–25
Icebox Strawberry Pie, 45–47, *46*
Ingredients
   dry, measuring, 3
   high-quality, for recipes, 2
   liquid, measuring, 3
   sticky, measuring, 3
   substituting, note about, 2
Ingredients, tastings of
   dark chocolate chips, 178
   lemon curd, 124
   raspberry preserves, 216
   store-bought pie crusts, 20

J

Jefferson Davis Pie, 33–34

K

Key Lime Pie, Icebox, 43–45
Key lime pie, origins of, 43
Kringle, Pecan, 137–40, *139*

L

Lady Baltimore Cake, 85–90, *87*
Lemon(s)
   Buttermilk Sheet Cake, 101–2
   Cheesecake, Icebox, 121–24, *122*
   Chess Pie, 22–25, *24*
   curd, taste tests on, 124
   Meringue Pie, Mile-High, 25–27
   –Poppy Seed Angel Food Cake, 120
   Pound Cake, Classic, 111–14, *113*
   7UP Pound Cake, 115–17
   Squares, 216–18
Lime(s)
   Key, Pie, Icebox, 43–45
   Key, pie, origins of, 43
   7UP Pound Cake, 115–17

S